SIMULATION AND GAMING

Edited by **Dragan Cvetković**

Simulation and Gaming
http://dx.doi.org/10.5772/intechopen.69391
Edited by Dragan Cvetković

Contributors

Tien Nguyen, Andy Guillen, Sumner Matsunaga, Hien Tran, Tung Bui, Juin-Ling Tseng, Chia-Wei Chu, Ivan Zelinka, Martin Němec, Roman Senkerik, Hugo Luz Dos Santos, Anis Zarrad, Ahmed Hadi Shubber, Amirmudin Bin Udin, Asnul Bin Minghat, Pablo Garaizar, Andoni Eguíluz, Mariluz Guenaga, Ebru Yılmaz İnce, Kara Krinks, Douglas Clark, Heather Johnson, Deanne Adams, Satyugjit Virk, Paul Medlock-Walton, Raúl Boquín, Eric Klopfer

Published by InTech

Janeza Trdine 9, 51000 Rijeka, Croatia

Publishing Process Manager Teo Kos
Technical Editor SPi Global
Cover InTech Design team

First published February, 2018
Printed in Croatia
Legal deposit, Croatia: National and University Library in Zagreb

Additional hard copies can be obtained from orders@intechopen.com

Simulation and Gaming, Edited by Dragan Cvetković
p. cm.
Print ISBN 978-953-51-3803-7
Online ISBN 978-953-51-3800-6

For EU product safety concerns:
IN TECH d.o.o., Prolaz Marije Krucifikse Kozulić 3, 51000 Rijeka, Croatia,
info@intechopen.com or visit our website at intechopen.com.

Meet the editor

Dragan Cvetković graduated in Aeronautics from the Faculty of Mechanical Engineering, University of Belgrade, in 1988. In the Aeronautical Department, he defended his doctoral dissertation in December 1997. So far, he has published 62 books, scripts, and practicums about computers and computer programs, aviation weapons, and flight mechanics. He has published many scientific papers in the country and abroad.
Since March 20, 2007, he has been working at the Singidunum University in Belgrade as an assistant professor. Since October 1, 2013, he has been working as the Dean of the Faculty of Informatics and Computing at the Singidunum University, Belgrade. He became a full professor in the field of Informatics and Computing in March 2014.

Contents

Preface

The development of simulation and gaming as a specific area of scientific and practical research has started at the beginning of twentieth century. Computer simulations and gaming have become a useful part of mathematical modeling of many natural systems in physics, quantum mechanics, chemistry, and biology and then in economic systems, psychology, and social sciences, as well as in the engineering processes of new technologies, in order to gain a better insight into their way of working and behaving. Recently, social sciences have become even more engaged in the study of various video materials and computer games as a way of expression of new media cultures. Game theory and specific modeling of various parameters have gained pretty good position in the economy. Business simulations and games, in general covering the management field, have been already integrated into many programs of business schools.

Computer simulations differ from computer programs in time required to finish running, programs run a few minutes, while the simulation can be run for hours or if it is a demanding simulation, it can last even for days. It can be said that the simulations have surpassed the efficiency of methods that use pencil and paper to problem-solve.

Nowadays, computer simulations are used to solve problems in all spheres of life. Meteorological forecasts, such as the calculation of rainfall, water flows in rivers, underground water flow, and oil exploitation, are just some of the tasks that cannot be accomplished without the use of computers. One of the most interesting computer applications is the simulation of processes in the human body. Modern software solutions enable the calculation of muscle fatigue in certain activities, the deposition of fat in the blood vessels, the risk of cancer, and so on. In the future, these programs will be able to allow the realization of virtual surgeries and to predict the effects of surgery before they are performed in reality.

When it comes to gaming, attention should be paid to the meaning of word game and what is considered by that word, what knowledge is required for designing the game, what kind of knowledge is included in the process of playing games, and so on. Answers to these questions put the word gaming in proper category, determine the difference between declarative and procedural knowledge, and define the nature and scope of necessary knowledge in order to create the desired product. Obviously, gaming is an interdisciplinary and a multidisciplinary field, and those who want to participate in the process of creating a simulation in a game must deal with the fact that natural, technical, technological, social sciences, and humanities should be linked and intertwined. Creating simulations in a game is not a simple task and requires a lot of knowledge and effort.

The book "Simulation and Gaming" discusses the following topics and research areas:

- Game-based methods of problem solution and data processing, analysis, and information mining. Attention is mainly focused on swarm algorithm and principles applied to the task of complex problem solving by using computer games.

- Educational games and game features such as game characteristics, story, mechanics, and methodology. The studies about educational computer games in higher education are included as well and analyzed in the light of a deep literature review. At the end of this chapter, a new educational game named Computer Hardware Game (CHG) is explained.

- The development of integrated games whose task is, through formal presentation, to help students interpret, translate, and manipulate the field of kinematics. Attention is paid to the way a game looks such as in the context of classroom with special accent on what is required of students in order to progress through the game and to deepen their conceptual knowledge.

- A research study regarding the possibility of research integration through real and practical examples and games as well, in the field of physics.

- The rapid development of hardware and system platforms, providing a favorable foundation for game development, including game engines.

- Virtual reality, the use of computer simulation to produce a virtual world, providing users with a variety of sensory simulation, which enables the feeling as though one is in the virtual world. System interaction is mainly done through specific interactive devices for system control, such as the popular Arduino technology.

- Analysis, development, design, implementation, and evaluation of the simulation model engineering and metallurgy subject, according to ADDIE model. Due to the business needs and growing importance of technology in society in the last few years, the concept of computational thinking has emerged putting an accent on its inclusion in compulsory education as a relevant complement to traditional subjects.

- The development of various interactive digital tools, designed in order to encourage students to think through a series of activities such as games.

- An overview of the current prominence of artificial intelligence (AI) or AI simulation based in the gaming leisure industry, mainly for research purposes in the context of problem gambling and forecasting of online casino patron's churn behavior.

- An innovative modeling and simulation approach is described using newly proposed advanced game-based mathematical framework, unified game-based acquisition framework, and a set of war-gaming engines to address the challenges for acquisition of future space systems.

- The modification of simulation of a complex system and a physics model using a block-based programming language. It was done by students, and the creation of these simulations required combinations and modifications of the Gameblox and StarLogo platforms.

I would like to express my sincere gratitude to all the authors and coauthors for their contributions. The successful completion of the book "Simulation and Gaming" has been the result of the cooperation of many people. I would especially like to thank the Publishing Process Manager, Mr. Teo Kos, for his support during the publishing process.

Dragan Cvetković
Singidunum University
Faculty of Informatics and Computing
Belgrade, Republic of Serbia

Section 1

Educational Games

Chapter 1

Gamesourcing: Perspectives and Implementations

Ivan Zelinka, Martin Němec and Roman Šenkeřík

Additional information is available at the end of the chapter

http://dx.doi.org/10.5772/intechopen.71703

Abstract

This chapter discusses game-based methods of problem solution and data processing, analysis, and information mining. Attention is mainly focused on swarm algorithm and principles used in the task of complex problem solving using computer games. We intensively discuss the interdisciplinary intersection between swarm systems dynamics and computer science, including a variety of data sources and examples. Possibilities of the new approach based on swarm algorithm used in a game or using principles of swarm algorithms to solve the problem are demonstrated here. More precisely, this chapter discusses modern methods of calculation and crowd use, so-called gamesourcing, i.e., game-driven crowdsourcing, from various points of view such as history, motivation, or paradigm and presents several examples of contemporary projects of this kind. Ideas, results, and methodologies reported and mentioned here are based on our previous results and experiments that are fully reported here for detailed study in the case of reader's interest. Therefore, this chapter is an overview survey of our research.

Keywords: swarm algorithm, swarm intelligence, dynamics, data, analysis, gamesourcing, game

1. Crowdsourcing and gamesourcing: a brief overview

Gamesourcing is a new term created by combining a pair of English word games and crowdsourcing. The game is a game, but the explanation of crowdsourcing is somewhat more extensive. It is a method where a job (often very difficult for a computer but relatively easy for a person) is divided among a large number of people and depending on the nature of the assignment, either by common forces or by each one of them. In the first case, all participants will cooperate, with only the best of the other being selected. By joining with the game, we offer a means of making crowdsourcing on a slightly different basis. That is, players do not even *need to know that they are doing any crowdsourcing at all*. While they still enjoy it.

The history and development of crowdsourcing over time and the gradual emergence of gamesourcing are quite new and young discipline. In the past decade, the new phenomenon—crowdsourcing—or the use of a large group of people to engage in some creative activity—is beginning to spread through the Internet, e.g., drawing ideas, ideas, content, or contributions, whether financial or professional. Usage can be virtually any: education (Wikipedia), research, health, transport (accident reporting), marketing and advertising, donation, volunteering, etc. However, even in the political sphere, the wisdom of the crowd has already found its application. After 2008, when Iceland was bankrupt due to the economic crisis, the creation of a new constitution took place, and its proposal was made available online for a wide-ranging discussion. By debating and commenting through social networks, Icelandic citizens could influence and correct the final form and text of the constitutional charter [1, 2].

The term crowdsourcing was first used in 2006 [3], which could lead (due to the Internet boom) to the erroneous assumption that it is exclusively an online affair. However, the process of using the masses to cooperate on a task has been working since time immemorial, starting with prehistory [4]. It was then only the adoption of advice and recommendations by the Chieftain from his subordinates, but in some way, it was some collective involvement in achieving the goal (e.g., how to survive the winter). So, a certain form of crowdsourcing existed for tens of thousands of years before the emergence of the all-knowing medium, so basically it is not a new thing.

Crowdsourcing has been used for some time already in architecture. In 1955, Prime Minister of the State of New South Wales, Joseph Cahill, announced a £ 5000 competition to design an opera house on the Gulf Coast in Sydney. A total of 233 proposals were sent from 32 different countries. The winning design of the Danish architect Jør Utzon was the beginning of one of the most innovative and innovative buildings of the present era. This type of architectural competitions continues to be widely used [5].

In 2006, Jeff Howe first used the term "crowdsourcing" [6] in his article and had since become more and more popular. The first purely crowdsourcing projects such as DesignCrowd (crowdsourcing of graphic designs, logos, websites, etc.) or Digg (crowdsourcing aggregator of news) were launched. Also, crowdfunding has begun to develop, contributing more individuals with smaller amounts to the target amount to fund an interesting project or product.

With the growing trend in the gaming industry, its potential for crowdsourcing has been properly estimated. The author professor Luis von Ahn (Carnegie Mellon University) launched it [7] under the auspices of Google. It was about describing images in a fun and catchy form.

The number of similar acts has been slowly rising since then, and awareness of the gameplay has begun to be gained among the wider public. For example, in 2016 the Sea Hero Quest [8] was also commercialized on domestic TV stations. It is a mobile device-based game to aid in the study of dementia. There has not been a year since the release, and the authors have been honored with excellent results.

Crowdsourcing is so slowly becoming a part of everyone's life slowly, without being aware of it. Its special forms are called gamesourcing, where the means of collective cooperation is playing games. It seems that gamesourcing is on the rise. It has already proved to be an excellent tool in several cases. However, its potential has not been fully utilized by far.

2. Swarm intelligence in computation

Swarm algorithms (called also swarm intelligence) have been very popular lately due to the features that are characteristic of this class. However, before we begin to discuss their application, it is appropriate to mention selected algorithms in this area, which are (or can be) further elaborated in research reported in this chapter. They are:

- Ant colony optimization (ACO) [9],
- Artificial immune system [10],
- Self-organizing migrating algorithm (SOMA) [11],
- Memetic algorithms [12],
- Grey wolf [13],
- Particle swarm [14],
- Artificial bee colony [15], and
- Fire fly [16],

among the others. These algorithms can be used to solve very different problems. Many more versions and strategies than it is mentioned above exist there. Given that their description would go beyond the scope of this text, it is only necessary to refer the applicant to the relevant literature. The SOMA [11] and ACO [9] have been used for our experiments, reported further.

Firstly discussed is the intro to crowdsourcing and gamesourcing. Then we use SOMA as a swarm intelligence in two computer games as a prelude to real gamesourcing that is represented by our experiments in the game called Labyrinth. This game has compared ACO against the human player crowd in the maze, which is equivalent to traveling salesman problem (TSP). At the end, we introduce a new version of Labyrinth for 3D that is dedicated to the new experiments of this kind.

3. Case studies

Here, in a few examples, our income on the field of swarm intelligence principles in computer games and gamesourcing is mentioned. Some of them were already published in conference and journals; so for more details, it is recommended to follow the references in the text.

First of all, we will discuss the use of swarm algorithm SOMA in Tic-Tac-Toe game [17], which is released on Google Play store [7], and anyone can easily download and play this game. Swarm intelligence is a counter player against human one in this game.

The second one is utilizing SOMA algorithm in the famous game StarCraft: Brood War. Swarm intelligence was controlling a combat unit strategy of movement in extraterrestrials wars, as explained in [17, 18].

The real gamesourcing is in the next section, where a human crowd plays a game Labyrinth, that is equivalent to a traveling salesman problem (TSP) problem [19, 20]. The results are then compared with ACO algorithm applied on the same problem. At the end is introduced our new platform for gamesourcing Labyrinth 3D for more extensive experiments.

3.1. SOMA Tic-Tac-Toe

This application is focused on swarm intelligence techniques and their practical use in a computer game. The aim is to show how a game player (based on swarm algorithms, in this case, SOMA) can replace a man in computer games. This provides an opportunity for effective, coordinated movement in the game fitness landscape. The implementation of our experiments uses classic techniques of artificial intelligence environments, as well as unconventional techniques, such as swarm intelligence. Research reported here has shown the potential benefit of evolutionary computation in the field of strategy games.

SOMA is a stochastic optimization algorithm that is modeled based on the social behavior of competitive-cooperating individuals [11]. It was chosen because it has been proved that this algorithm can converge usually toward the global optimum of the given problem [11]. SOMA works on a population that consists of the possible candidate solutions in iterations. They are called migration loops. The population is initialized, as usual for this kind of algorithms, by uniform random distribution, i.e., over the search space at the beginning of the evolutionary search process. In each migration loop, the population is evaluated, and the individual with the lowest cost value (the best fitness) becomes the leader. Apart from the leader, in one migration loop, all individuals will traverse the space of possible solutions in the direction of the leader. Mutation, the random perturbation of individuals, is an important operation for SOMA. It ensures diversity among all the individuals, and it also provides a means to restore lost information in a population. The mutation process is different in SOMA as compared with other evolutionary algorithms. A parameter, called PRT, is used to achieve mutations and perturbations. This parameter has in SOMA the same effect as mutation for other EAs. The PRT vector defines the final movement of an active individual in the search space. It is a randomly generated binary perturbation vector, which controls the allowed dimensions for an active individual. If an element of the perturbation vector is set to zero, then the individual is not allowed to change its position in the corresponding dimension. An individual will travel over a certain distance (PathLength) toward the leader in finite steps on PathLength. If the PathLength is chosen to be greater than one, then the individual overshoot the leader. This path is perturbed randomly. The main principle of SOMA, i.e., traveling of an individual over space of possible solutions, is depicted in **Figure 1**. The initial parameter sets of SOMA for our experiments can be set in the Android program, as demonstrated in **Figures 2** and **3**. For more details about SOMA, see [11]. SOMA can be considered as a member of swarm intelligence class algorithms.

It is true that all experiments are influenced by the player itself and algorithm setting. The screenshot from one game is depicted in **Figures 4** and **5**. If SOMA parameters would be set differently in a nonoptimal way, then, of course, the performance would be different. Thus, the performance of the SOMA depends on two factors: human skills and SOMA setting. For more details and game description, it is recommended to refer [17] and game on Google Play store [7].

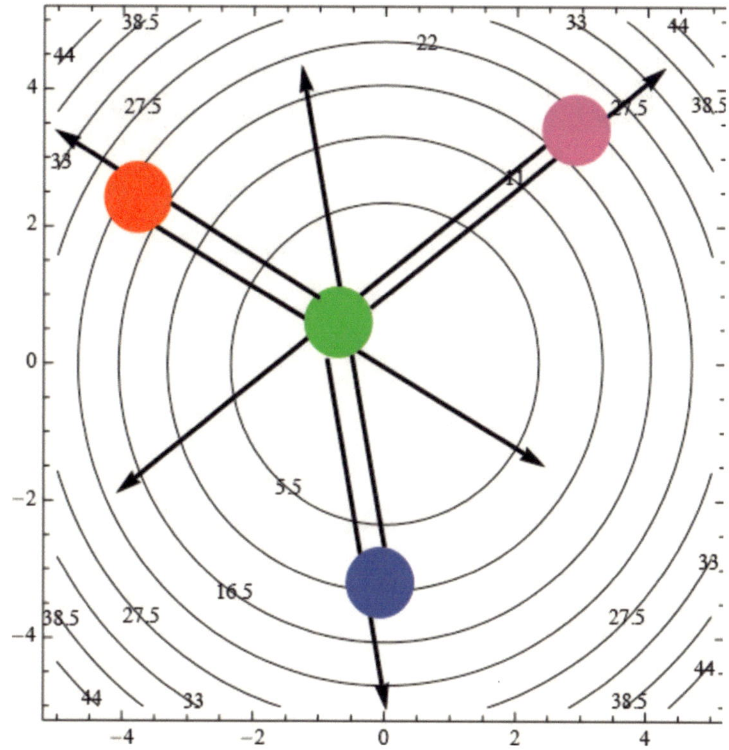

Figure 1. The SOMA principle.

3.2. SOMA StarCraft: Brood War

StarCraft: Brood War is a well-known real-time strategy game in which swarm intelligence was used again. In [17, 18], SOMA implementation is focused on applications and practical utilization in combat units control. The goal of the war (and its results are partially reported here) is to implement computer player replacing a human in a real-time strategy StarCraft: Brood War. The computer player behavior is provided by the decision-making tree together with SOMA and is used to remote movement of combat units. A particular implementation of SOMA algorithm provides an opportunity for efficient, coordinated movement of combat units over the map. The work and its results reported in [17, 18] has shown great benefit of evolutionary techniques in the field of real-time strategy games.

Similar to other strategic games, it is also crucial to provide acceptable amount of resource materials for creating an army to win. Materials are located on several places as well as at the starting position. The game allows a choice of three races: the **Protoss** are strong extraterrestrial beings with an expensive units. The **Zergs** seems to be primitive and overgrown kind of insects. Their units have a low price and are weaker than Protoss units. The last race is **Terrans**, a race of human-like being, a compromise between mentioned races that have balanced prices and efficiency of theirs combat units. For the use of the SOMA swarm intelligence, a *Zergs race has been chosen*. The techniques such as decision-making tree or unconventional techniques in the

Figure 2. SOMA setting in Tic-Tac-Toe.

form of evolutionary algorithms (SOMA algorithm) have been used. The algorithm controlled a movement of the combat units on the landscape. The game also further do not allow random placement of a population on the landscape. Starting positions of the units are on purpose near the structures used for production of the units.

In the case of the incorrect objective function, we would be challenging problems with the speed of finding the enemy. The contact with the enemy would stabilize the process of searching so that searching units would be attracted to this place. It can be solved by the right setting of the parameters of SOMA algorithm and modified implementation of the objective function. Other problems could not be solved this way. Parameter PathLength [11] was set to a value 1 for the units to stay on the position of the leader. Experiments have shown that various numerical settings of the parameter Step were not so beneficial, and small numerical

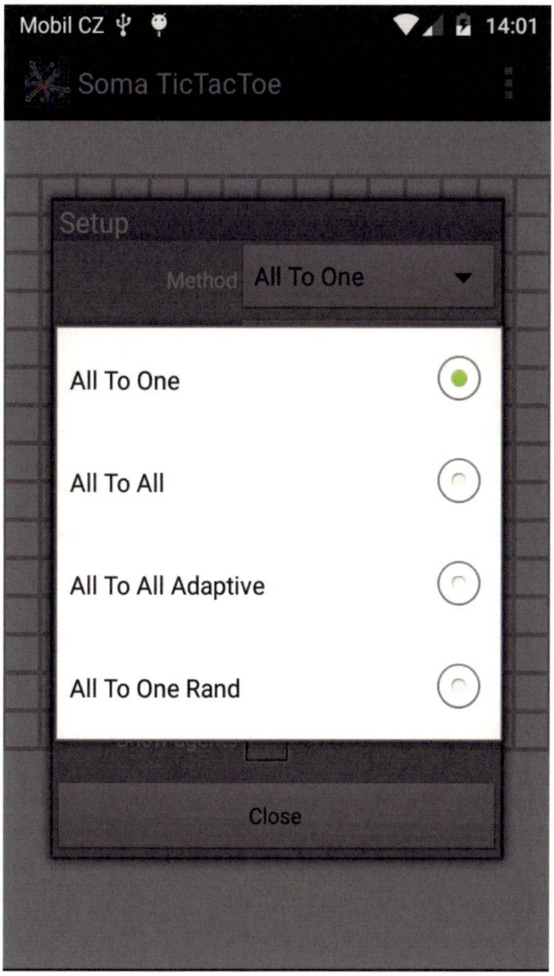

Figure 3. SOMA setting in Tic-Tac-Toe—strategy setting.

values had no significant impact on the combat unit performance. The unit was particularly searching by Step long as its own; it was set to Step = 0.5. Parameter PRT was selected near 1 so that the units would not deviate from each other so much, and at least some random searching came to pass. PRT was set to value 0.8. Dimension was set to 2 since we were searching in two-dimensional map given by coordinates x and y. PopSize is an adjustable parameter. Each combat unit was added to the population until its death. All the SOMA stop criterion, i.e., Migrations & MinDiv were ignored—SOMA was working through whole game until any unit was present. The positions of the enemy units were a part of the fitness function as well as important locations on the map. SOMA algorithm thus works on the dynamic function in order to maximize success of combat units to win.

The largest value was associated with the enemy units. The biggest fitness, the more enemies are present there. The closer position of the individual to enemy position guarantee the bigger fitness. Starting position itself was set to 0. The significant problem in this implementation was

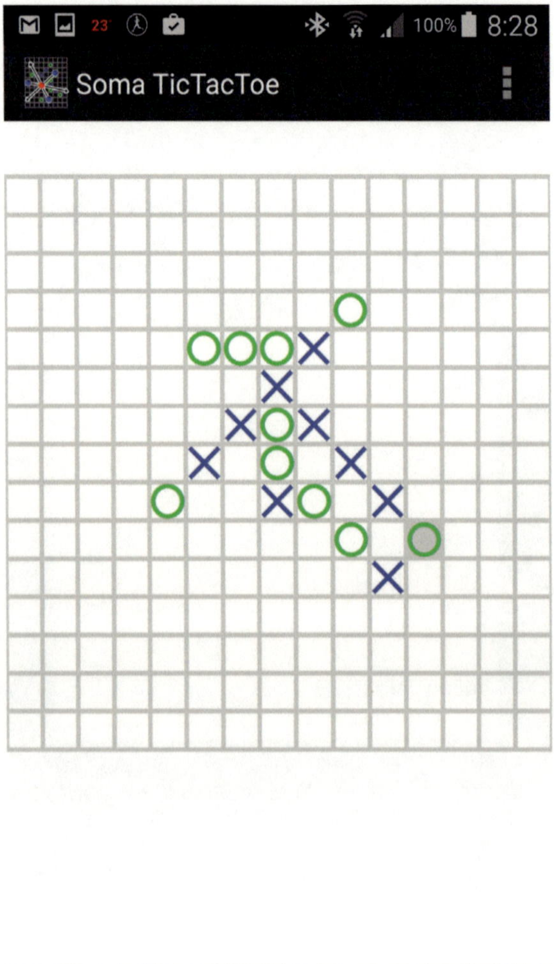

Figure 4. Tic-Tac-Toe screenshot. The game in the process: blue cross—human player, green circles—SOMA.

a nonrandom placement of the population as well as the inefficiency of the random search on the landscape. The position of the headquarters of the enemy was known. It is one of the starting positions. These problems were solved by the division of the population into two subpopulations: static and dynamic. A dynamic subpopulation consists of a classical individual who yields to recombination and mutation. It is migrating individual in the terminology of SOMA algorithm. Static individuals, on the other hand, are not migrating. They are located in the important positions on the map like locations with materials and starting positions. They can also be placed on the position of each existing structure. Their role is important because the static individual, at the starting position of the enemy, is calculated the biggest fitness. Moreover, they attract all of the units albeit from only one position. If they encounter the enemy on their route, this kind of individual is chosen as a leader [11] (regarding the highest value of the enemy's hit points). If any of our structures are attacked by the enemy, this structure is activated to be a leader (there is a static

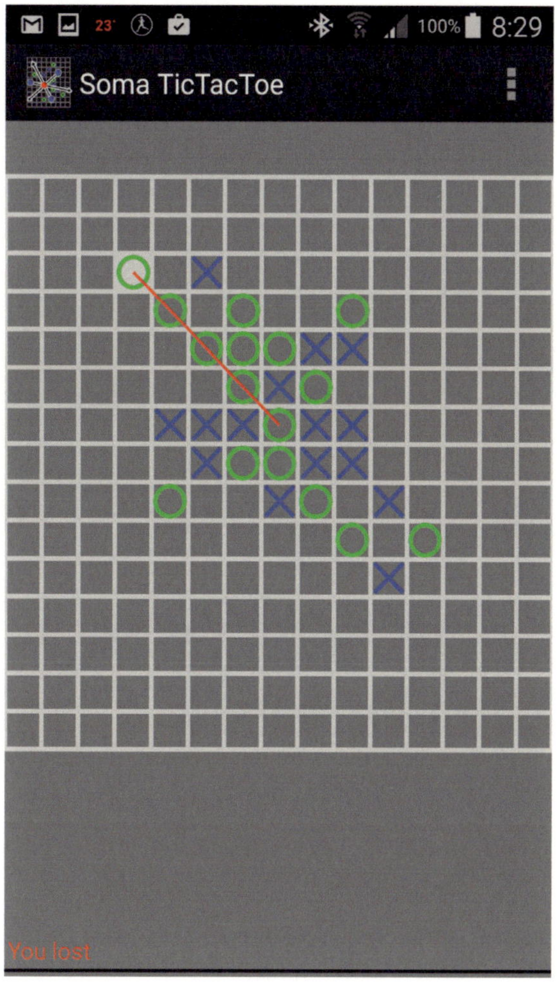

Figure 5. Game over.

individual). In this case, the leader will attract friendly combat units. These individuals also create a kind of alarm system. The screenshot from many battle situations is shown in **Figure 6**, and the results of the fights are reported in [18]. All experiments were done with one human player against four SOMA strategies (AllToOne, AllToOnenRand, AllToAll, and AllToAllAdaptive) in 100 experiments in total (i.e., 25 experiments per strategy).

3.3. Traveling salesman, gamesourcing versus swarm intelligence

In this experiment, real gamesourcing experiment with real human players in the game Labyrinth that is equivalent of TSP is reported. Labyrinth is a web game embedded in an existing game portal environment [21]. The problem of a traveling salesman is transformed into a maze, and players, by collectively crafting, mimic the behavior of the ant algorithm [9]—the swarm technique that is currently, widely, and successfully applied to this problem. The aim is

Figure 6. Zerg units are driven by SOMA in combat action in [18].

to collect data about players' moves, from which it will then be possible to read their strategies and tactics that could lead to the improvement of ant algorithms.

For gamesourcing, it is crucial to be able to combine the problem we want to address with the game. There must be very close ties between them. It is necessary for the game by its execution to lead the player exactly to what we want to achieve, i.e., to solve the problem, so that they will not be able to understand the problem.

In this case, we have decided to solve the problem of a traveling salesman and get inspired by ant colony optimization (ACO) algorithms. Individual ants are represented by humans. This could help to find new variants and adjustments to these algorithms, thus making them more efficient.

Traveling salesman problem, used in a game, is a simple idea. The salesman needed to make a trip to certain cities (each to visit only once) and to go back home. For high efficiency, the trip has to be planned to be as short as possible. This is a NP-heavy problem [19]. That is, all NP problems are convertible to it in polynomial time, and it is not in the NP itself.

If we describe this role as a graph, then its vertices (nodes) represent the starting point and the places that traveling salesman has to visit. Each of the two vertices is linked to the graph by an edge, which is evaluated by the distance that is needed to offset the trader from the place represented by the first node to the point representing the second node. This is a nonoriented complete graph. The aim is then to find the shortest Hamiltonian circle (cycle).

All the possible Hamiltonian circles in the graph (at the starting point does not matter) depends on the number of cities, so the number of possibilities needed for exploration is growing very (exponentially) fast. There are several exact algorithms (Brute-force, Branch & Bound, Cutting Plane) that can solve the TSP but only in 40–80 cities [22] in a reasonable time. For this reason, heuristic algorithms have found abundant use, which does not guarantee the correctness of the result, but in most cases, the solution found is of sufficient quality and is achieved in an acceptable time. One of those algorithms is the ant colony optimization.

Optimization using ant colonies is a group of algorithms inspired by the real behavior of ants in nature. Every ant leaves pheromones in their path, which then attract others. The stronger the pheromone trace is, the more ants follow it. The heavily used paths keep constantly high levels of pheromones, while the pheromones finally evaporate from the unused ones.

Thus, in general, there is an iteration of the ACO algorithm. Various versions of ant algorithms then have different ways of making decision rules and different rules for pheromones.

3.3.1. Proposal

Due to the mission and focus of the experiment, its appearance is obvious. For the sake of easy access and the ability to play as many players as possible, it must essentially be playable on the Internet. At the same time, it is quite intuitive that the best illustration of a TSP is a maze. The graph nodes will be represented as rooms (or city in TSP) and edges as corridors. The weight of each edge can then be specified as some form of obstacle. The Labyrinth crawling is also popular since time immemorial, and according to the game developer's focus, these games continue to thrill our heads.

3.3.2. Used platform

There are plenty of games that try to make the most of the human brain's potential to achieve something useful. People still surpass computers in many tasks, such as recognizing objects such as galaxies (Galaxy Zoo). Meanwhile, none of these projects have even reached popularity, say, Minecraft, which has already published 107.86 million copies since its release (2009), and this has grown by another 53,000 [23] each day. With such a huge shot, gamesourcing would be interesting things, but unfortunately, such a popular crowdsourcing game did not make it so popular.

So, to design the experiment, it was approached in this way: do not try to think of a game that would solve a problem and then try to make it as fun and popular as possible, instead try to take a game that has already gained and edited its popularity, so that our problem can be solved.

Just imagine—could a combination of all those players who play shooters like Call of Duty or strategic games like StarCraft help in curing cancer? Could a "farm" of gold, which is so crucial in World of Warcraft or Farmville-type social games, to do something useful? Many developers would say that not playing is fun because it is not a job. However, there are elements in these games that are computerized, but easy for a computer? If scientists have been able to answer this question, they should have a powerful tool to solve great problems. It should be noted that even regarding financial profit, it would certainly be an interesting thing.

For example, such elements are already-mentioned in the game Minecraft. The player is pumping materials for the construction of tools and buildings so that he have where to spend nights full of dangerous creatures. It is a simple concept, but there are countless variants and modes. Everything is made from cubes, which directly calls for easy creation, just like mazes. I can imagine the mode where it would be necessary to build Foldit-style proteins or build a rocket and then fly it through an asteroid-like universe as in Genes in Space. The potential regarding gamesourcing is enormous and, in our opinion, it is only a matter of time, when someone sees this idea. So far, only attempts have been made to use it for educational purposes [24].

For our purposes, online browser game Immortal Fighters has been used. This is a portal available at http://www.immortalfighters.net/, which allows you to play game Dragon Lair online. Dragon's Lair is a legendary Czech hero game inspired by the Dungeons & Dragons system. The game is led by the Lord or the Lady of the Cave (abbreviated **PJ**). This adventure narrator knows the rules of the game and in his imagination, he creates the world in which other players play through his fanciful characters. The game is usually run by PJ describing what is going on, and the players will tell how their character responds. PJ is governed by the mechanisms described in the rules, and even when he has the main word in the game, he often throws dice and uses data (strength, dexterity, intelligence, charisma, etc.). Each character has different depending on race (man, Dwarf, etc.) and vocations (warrior, sorcerer, border guard, etc.).

Dragon's Lair is a role-playing game (RPG): a hero game. Role-play means that a player lives in a fanciful character and plays for her as if he were alive. Players often play the characters in their characters, but it is important to realize that the player is not a character and that it is necessary to separate them. While playing for his character, he has to act not only with his attributes (especially intelligence and charisma) but also to separate his knowledge from his character's knowledge (for example, he cannot know that someone is a thief).

The best players are not those whose characters kill the most monsters, but those who play the best RP (role-playing). While the classic Dragon Lane requires players and PJ to come together physically and tell the story aloud, the online version is based on writing. Offline personal contact and game are missing from the offline version.

The algorithm behind our modification of the Labyrinth is called human ant system (HAS) for obvious reason. Each player represents one ant. The main differences from the above-mentioned alternative algorithms are:

1. A person decides about the transfer of an ant. This is the biggest and most fundamental difference. In the game, players are provided statistical information about the available edges, but the final decision depends on and only on the player. The reasons for player's decision can be very complex and are not limited to comparing the calculated probability with a randomly generated number from 0 to 1, as is the case with the classical ACO.

2. Pheromones. Pheromones as such are not present in the game. Each player can, however, look at any route of any player and arrange it accordingly. It is to be assumed that mainly the better routes will be observed; on the contrary, the worst will not be interested in almost anyone. This simulates the addition and evaporation of pheromones. However, if a player decides not to do so at all, nobody will be against it.

3. Starting point. The choice of the starting point depends on the player's consideration. This does not have to be a purely random matter, as with other algorithms.

4. Does not engage in the local extreme. With game mechanics, when duplicate paths are not rewarded, players are constantly trying to find new variants of Labyrinth passages and want to avoid going the same way as anyone before them. This way, the algorithm can never get stuck in local extrema and obey.

5. Parallelism. Ants (players) move in this form of the algorithm unbounded. They do not have to wait for each other. Moreover, it may well happen that one already goes through the chart 10 times while the other only once. This makes it impossible to talk about iterations throughout the colony. Every human-ant has a free will. He can only go through the graph after others have "provided" the right way. However, waiting at the same time, he risks being overtaken by someone. This brings to the last point.

6. Motivation. Unlike the artificial ants, the human drives the desire to win. It is a feature that each of us have to a varying degree. Trying to overcome others and become the best—it cannot replicate exactly with your computer.

3.3.3. Results and comparison

The HAS performance has been compared with the classical ACO algorithms, which were used in all cases with 10 ants (the SW limitation), and in the beginning, in all cases, a $1/n$ pheromone was placed on all edges, where n is the number of nodes in the graph. The number of iterations was 10,000 or until the right solution was found. Each variant of the algorithm run five times. With the average of the results of each variation, the comparison with HAS was done. Since the Labyrinth with HAS does not work synchronously (the players can play when they want), the comparison was carried out according to the number of ant moves (AM). For cases where an algorithm has been converted to the local minimum, the quality of the solution means the ratio of the ideal distance to the best found. HAS and ACO were tested on a TSP test problems and information on how the algorithm has dealt with them is listed here.

1. Burma14. It is a map of 14 cities in Burma. The shortest possible distance for TSP is 3323 km. In total, 37 people were involved in playing the Labyrinth and solved the TSP on this map in 64 hours, 2 minutes, and 52 seconds.

2. Ulysses16. Map of the Odysseus path that leads through 16 places. The ideal circular route is 6859 km long. Here, the game was played by eight players for only 7 hours, 3 minutes, and 52 seconds.

3. Gr17. Problem with 17 cities from Groetschel. The requested distance is 2085 km. At the time of writing this chapter, this problem has not yet been resolved by the Labyrinth. A total of 28 people were involved in the solution, and in 11 days, they made a total of 1035 ant movements. It can be assumed that for 100,000 AM (10,000 iterations with 10 ants) that other algorithms have available in this case, players will find the ideal path to find, and again much faster.

From the choice of ACO algorithms, only the classic and elitist variants have always managed to find the right solution for up to 10,000 iterations. Ranked, best-worst, and min-max alternatives quickly converged, and in 28 cases out of 45, they landed at the local minimum (best-worst tackled every time). The ant colony system did not show convergence, but in 12 of 15 attempts, it failed to reach the right solution in 10,000 iterations. It is possible, however, that it would be achieved in subsequent iterations. The human ant system on 14 and 16 peaks far outperformed all the others, and on a graph of the Gr17 problem, it managed to find a very satisfactory solution with a much lower number of ant movements than the competitors did. Results are visually summarized in **Figure 7**.

At this point, it cannot be explained what makes the HAS so successful. The answer lies in the data that were taken during the game. Each player's movement was recorded along with the time stamp and current distance at that time. However, analyzing these data is not easy, and it is not finished yet. Likely human intelligence, intuition, and total freedom in decision-making have played a crucial role in those results. Certain similarities in watching the course of play at each maze have been noticed. Once someone who has found a way to a much better score than the best ones has come up, it has begun a massive improvement of all the following results, and the ideal solution has quickly been reached. This is probably the consequence of our human property to want to be the best. Moreover, this is probably the most important driving force of the entire Labyrinth.

3.4. LabyrinTS: a new platform for experimentation

The previous version of the Labyrinth was sufficient for initial experiments, but it had its limitations, for example, graphics (the game was mainly based on the imagination and imagination of the player) or the number of players. To enhance the game, increasing its attractiveness and enhancing its graphical interface, a new and separate version is created.

Currently, we are working on an experimental multiplayer maze application (unlimited number of players and no PJ presented), **Figures 8** and **9**, where users aim to collect as many items as possible in the maze. The goal of the game is to investigate the behavior of people who can see the

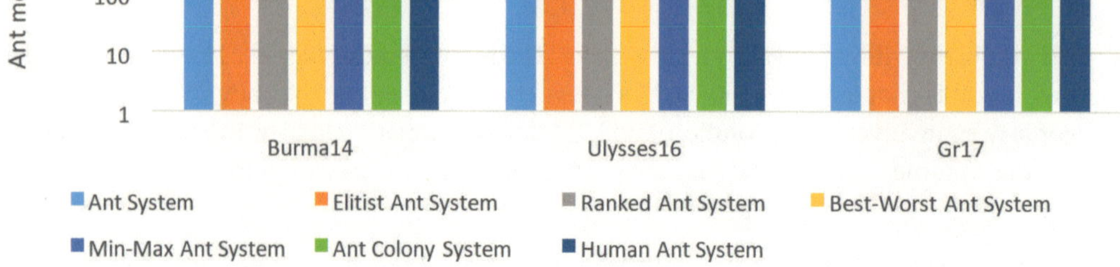

Figure 7. Comparison of ACO algorithms regarding required number of ant moves (logarithmic vertical axis).

Figure 8. Screenshot of our prototype 3D maze application.

Figure 9. An example of a static maze created in blender.

score and position of other players. This is the same principle as in the previous version. All this can be modified. The whole application is designed so that players start randomly on the outer edge of the maze and start the maze and begin searching for and collecting items inside the maze.

Within each application, each player is represented by his avatar, through which the current 3D maze runs. The player follows the character of his avatar from a third person perspective (**Figure 8**), so that he can watch what his avatar has before him and where he can move.

The primary objective of the player is to collect as many items as possible in the scene for which points are awarded. As a result, the player with the highest number of points wins. After the game is started, players will accidentally appear on the margins (perimeter) of the maze, from where players can step in and start browsing the maze and collecting items.

In the current version, the maze is created for static experiments in different sizes (**Figure 10**). In the future, the maze should be generated randomly and automatically, according to the specified parameters. It would also be possible to create a 3D maze and move between levels through stairs or teleports.

To collect objects, two basic objects, a gold ring and a diamond can be found in the scene (**Figure 10**). The gold ring is rated one credit, and the diamond is rated ten credits. Regarding deployment, golden rings are randomly placed within the scene when creating a game, while diamonds are generated only in the narrow neighborhood in the center of the maze. The presence of diamonds in the center of the maze motivates players to try to get to the center of the maze as quickly as possible. In the future, it is possible either to expand the range of subjects or to modify the possibilities of occurrence of objects with different credit ratings and to test how these changes affect the behavior of the players.

In addition to collecting items, users can throw bombs, which are important when two players meet inside a maze, which happens in experimental applications, especially when players try to get diamonds in the middle of a maze. Each player has a 100% of his life at the beginning,

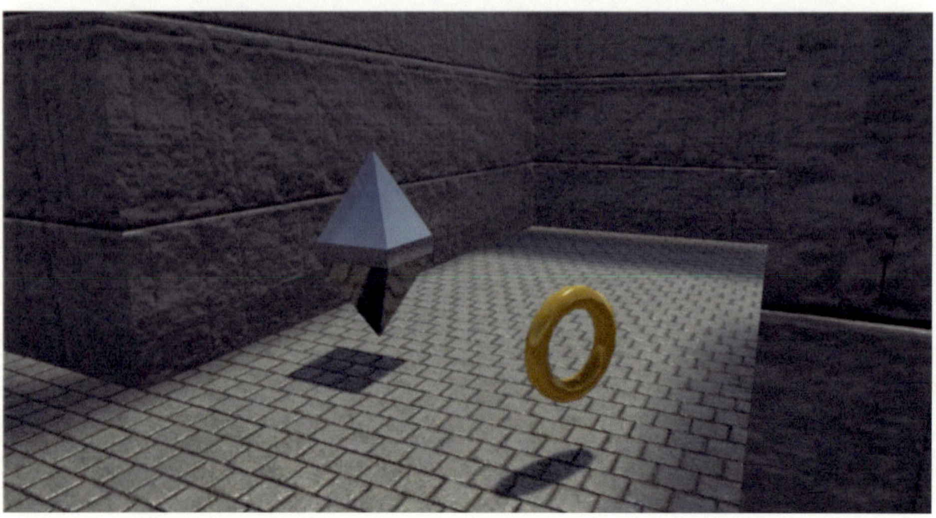

Figure 10. A sample of objects that users search inside a maze.

and his opponent can use a bomb against him. When the bomb explodes, the life is reduced. If his life drops below zero, the user will be relocated to a randomly generated location on the maze, where he can re-enter and continue collecting items.

The movement of all players during a maze crawl is automatically logged into the log file. These resulting log files of all players allow us to perform subsequent analysis of individual games. This allows us to look for different patterns of individual player's behavior.

- 10:10:46 | 5.8.2017;-2891.54;-1536.56;418.151;23;not picked;25;Alive;NotThrown
- 10:10:46 | 5.8.2017;-2891.54;-1536.56;418.151;23;not picked;25;Alive;NotThrown
- 10:10:46 | 5.8.2017;-2891.54;-1536.56;418.151;23;not picked;25;Alive;NotThrown
- 10:10:46 | 5.8.2017;-2891.54;-1536.56;418.151;23;not picked;25;Alive;NotThrown
- 10:10:46 | 5.8.2017;-2891.54;-1536.56;418.151;23;Coin Picked;25;Alive;NotThrown
- …

The entire application is developed in Unreal Engine 4 [25], one of the best 3D game and visualization designer tools. Using Unreal Engine enables us to use state-of-the-art algorithms and rendering techniques for real-time 3D games and applications. The static mazes themselves were created using the Blender modeling tool [26] and subsequently imported into the UE4. The application source code was created in C++ or using the blueprint (**Figure 11**), which is a visual scripting system in Unreal Engine.

This game is going to be an updated version of Labyrinth, described in the previous section. The game allows us to record movements of all players and consequent visualizations and analysis. As an example of possible outputs can serve **Figures 12–16. Figure 12** visualize a 2D trajectory in the Labyrinth (**Figure 9**), **Figure 13** shows all trajectories of all eight simultaneously playing players and **Figure 14** shows trajectories of first and sixth players in 2D coordinates. Those trajectories are less more similar and shows that there was a mutual influence of movements between players, as can be better observed from **Figure 16**, which captures the same moves but only for *x* coordinate. **Figure 15** shows trajectories of all eight players for *x* coordinate. It is clear that massive statistical analysis is needed to capture relevant information about swarm behavior of the players. This is the open research on which our group is working now. The entire application is currently under development and experimental testing.

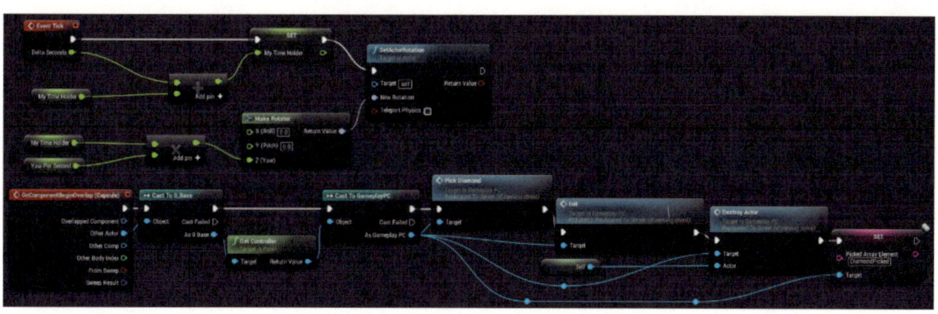

Figure 11. An example of creating an application for blueprint editor in UE4.

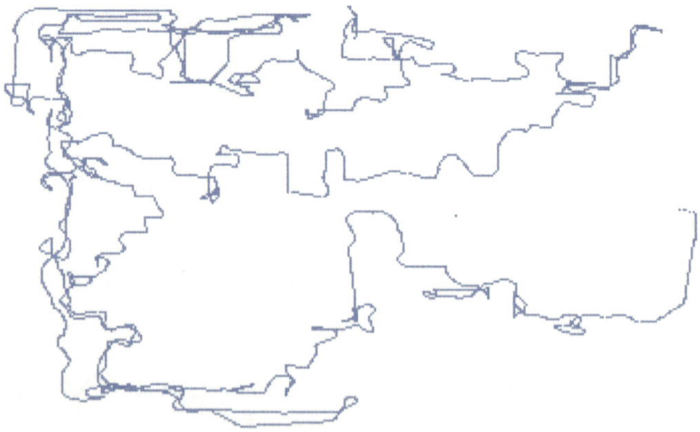

Figure 12. The 2D trajectory in the LabyrinTS.

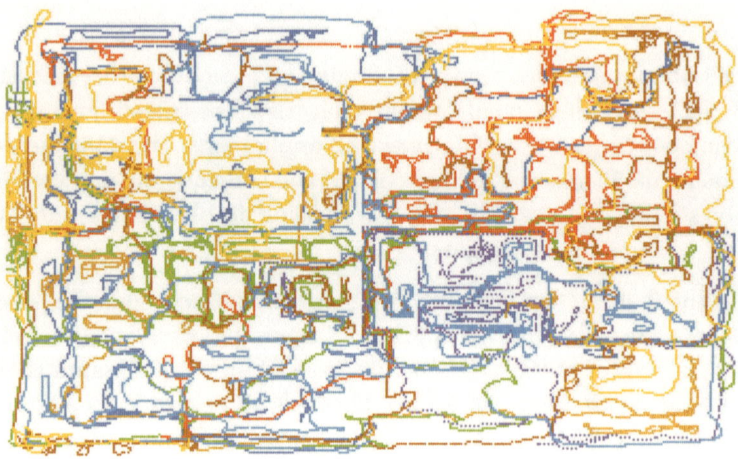

Figure 13. All eight players' 2D trajectories in the LabyrinTS.

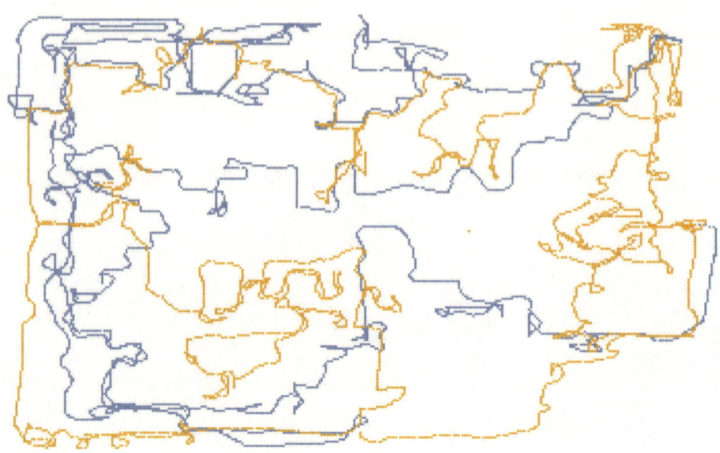

Figure 14. The second and sixth player trajectories in 2D.

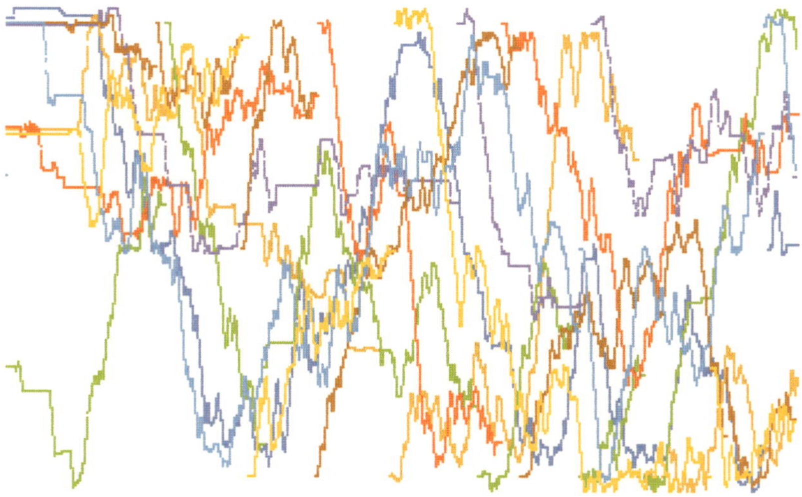

Figure 15. All eight players' x coordinate-based trajectories in the LabyrinTS.

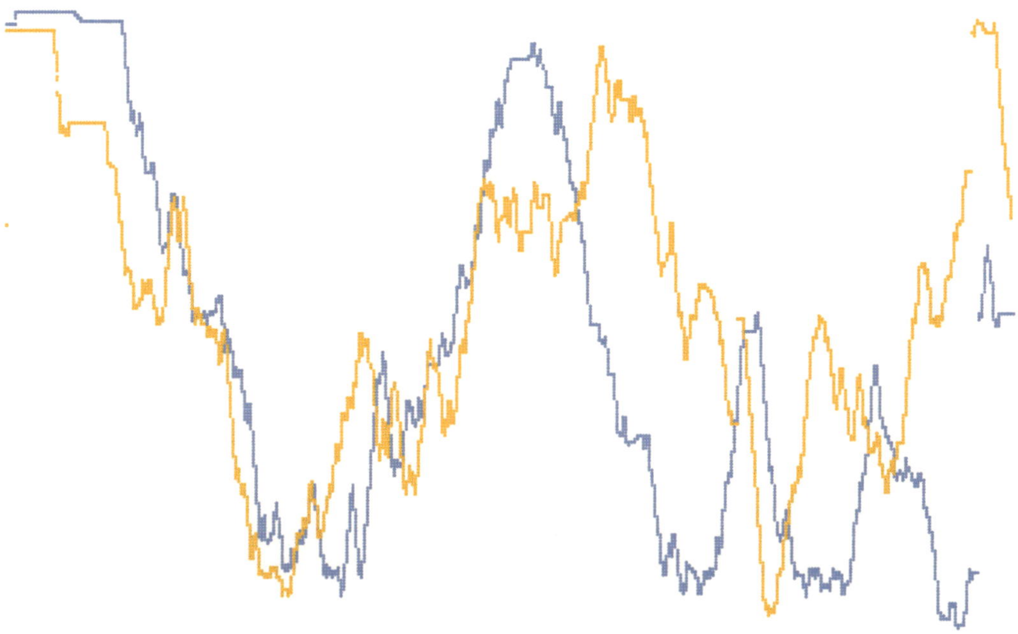

Figure 16. The second and sixth players' x coordinate-based trajectories in the LabyrinTS.

4. Conclusion

In this paper, we have demonstrated the use of swarm class algorithm in hybridization with computer games in three applications. The first two demonstrate the use of swarm algorithms as the human player counterpart in the game. The last one is the most important. It shows how can a crowd of human players be used to solve the problem via computer game environment. This is a real application of gamesourcing.

The first application refers to SOMA [11] used on Tic-Tac-Toe [17] game and the second to our previous application on strategic game StarCraft: Brood War [18]. Concerning to SOMA use, comparing to our previous results from [11], where SOMA dynamics have been modifying for game purpose and used to control movement of the combat units in order to win battle, here Tic-Tac-Toe was used and all experiments were done with one human player against four SOMA strategies in 100 experiments in total (i.e., 25 experiments per strategy). Our implementation and obtained results have shown (remember this is not a mathematical proof but a numerical demonstration) that EAs and swarm algorithms (in this case, SOMA) are applicable for such class of games with acceptable success ratio.

The most important experiment, the third one, was focused on real gamesourcing. In this work, a game that allows solving the symmetric variation of the optimization problem of a TSP has been created and tested; i.e., the shortest Hamiltonian circle in an undirected graph in the form of a collective walk through the maze was done. It was necessary to define the game to include barriers and principles that force players to less more indirectly cooperate.

The performance of experiment with different ACO variants on three TSP instances has been evaluated. The use of HAS in Labyrinth has exhibited a much lower number of steps that AM needed to resolve the problem. The reason is certainly the very human component HAS in connection with the structure of the algorithm that the players performed through the game. Also, very important point is that HAS consisted of intelligent agents (players) with free will, intuition, and intelligent thinking, while ACO does not. This is different from standard ACO [9].

When playing the Labyrinth, data about players' actions were logged. In their correct analysis lies the key to revealing patterns of behavior that would provide understanding crowd behavior when the problem is solved. This can be regarded as the scope extension of this work. To process those data will not be a trivial task. It is clear that also classical disciplines outside of traditional computer science such as psychology or neurology will be needed.

The work [22] contains a complete description of the entire development process of this game-based application, which is called the Labyrinth, including all implementation details. The Labyrinth [21] has been warmly welcomed by the community, and according to the number of players playing, who are still on the same level, it can be concluded that the concept is good and the game is also fun for players.

It is clear that computer games are promising field for unconventional solution of the given problem and its design on this "purpose" [27] becomes to be more important.

Acknowledgements

The following grants are acknowledged for the financial support provided for this research: SGS SP2017/61 grant agency of the Czech Republic—GACR P103/15/06700S, grant of No. SGS

2017/134, VSB-Technical University of Ostrava. The Ministry of Education, Youth and Sports from the National Programme of Sustainability (NPU II) project "IT4Innovations excellence in science -- LQ1602"; further by NPU I No. MSMT-7778/2014 by the Ministry of Education of the Czech Republic and by the European Regional Development Fund under the project CEBIA-Tech no. CZ.1.05/2.1.00/03.0089, and COST Action CA15140.

Author details

Ivan Zelinka[1]*, Martin Němec[1] and Roman Šenkeřík[2]

*Address all correspondence to: ivan.zelinka@vsb.cz

1 Department of Computer Science, Faculty of Electrical Engineering and Computer Science VŠB-TUO, Ostrava-Poruba, Czech Republic

2 Department of Informatics and Artificial Intelligence, Faculty of Applied Informatics, Tomas Bata University in Zlín, Zlín, Czech Republic

References

[1] Kuipers S. Citizen Crowds Can Make a Big Impact on Elections. Daily Crowdsource [Internet]. Available from: http://dailycrowdsource.com/content/open-innovation/1286-crowd-leader-shelley-kuipers-citizencrowds-can-make-a-big-impact-on-elections

[2] Fish LP. Island Create a New Constitution, Czech ed. Aktuálně.cz [Internet]. 14 July 2011. Available from: http://zpravy.aktualne.cz/ekonomika/technika/island-tvori-novou-ustavu-on-line/r~i:article:703969/

[3] Marie F. Crowdsourcing. Wikisofia [Internet]. 10 January 2015. Available from: https://wikisofia.cz/index.php/Crowdsourcing

[4] Handl Jan .Crowdsourcing is not new, Czech ed. Lupa.cz [Internet]. 14 August 2010. Available from: http://www.lupa.cz/clanky/crowdsourcing-neni-novinka/

[5] Crowdsourcing Is Not New—The History of Crowdsourcing (1714 to 2010). DesignCrowd [Internet]. 28 October 2010. Available from: http://blog.designcrowd.com/article/202/crowdsourcing-is-not-new--the-history-ofcrowdsourcing-1714-to-2010

[6] Jeff H. The Rise of Crowdsourcing. Wired [Internet]. June 2006. Available from: https://www.wired.com/2006/06/crowds/

[7] Google Play. SOMA TicTacToe [Internet]. Available from: https://play.google.com/store/apps/details?id=cz.bukacek.soma_tictactoe [Accessed: 22 August 2016]

[8] Sea Hero Quest [Internet]. Available from: http://www.seaheroquest.com/cs/faq [Accessed: 6 February 2017]

[9] Marco D, Birattari M, Stutzle T. Ant colony optimization. IEEE computational intelligence magazine. 2016;**1**(4):28-39

[10] DasGupta D. An overview of artificial immune systems and their applications. In: Artificial Immune Systems And Their Applications. Berlin Heidelberg: Springer; 1993. pp. 3-21

[11] Davendra D, Zelinka I, editors. Self-Organizing Migrating Algorithm, New Optimization Techniques in Engineering. 1st ed. Heidelberg: Springer; 2016

[12] Moscato P, Cotta C, Mendes A. Memetic algorithms. In New optimization techniques in engineering. Berlin Heidelberg: Springer; 2004. pp. 53-85

[13] Mirjalili S, Mirjalili SM, Lewis A. Grey wolf optimizer. Advances in Engineering Software. 2014;**69**:46-61

[14] Kennedy J. Particle swarm optimization. In: Encyclopedia of Machine Learning. US: Springer; 2011. pp. 760-766

[15] Karaboga D, Basturk B. A powerful and efficient algorithm for numerical function optimization: Artificial bee colony (ABC) algorithm. Journal of Global Optimization. 2007;**39**(3): 459-471

[16] Yang XS. Firefly algorithm, stochastic test functions and design optimisation. International Journal of Bio-Inspired Computation. 2010;**2**(2):78-84

[17] Zelinka I, Bukacek M. SOMA swarm algorithm in computer games. In: International Conference on Artificial Intelligence and Soft Computing. Vol. June 2016. Zakopane, Poland: Springer; 2016

[18] Zelinka I, Sikora L. StarCraft: Brood War—Strategy powered by the SOMA swarm algorithm. IEEE Conference on Computational Intelligence and Games (CIG), August 2015. pp. 511-516

[19] Puget Jean Francois. No, The TSP Isn't NP Complete [Internet]. 29 December 2013. Available from: https://www.ibm.com/developerworks/community/blogs/jfp/entry/no_the_tsp_isn_t_np_complete?lang=en

[20] Solving the Travelling Salesman Problem Using the Ant Colony Optimization [Internet]. 23 September 2011. Available from: http://www.ef.uns.ac.rs/mis/archive-pdf/2011%20%20No4/MIS2011_4_2.pdf

[21] Immortal Fighters—Online Web Game [Internet]. Available from: http://www.immortalfighters.net/

[22] Jiri A. Computer games, gamesourcing and swarm intelligence in problem solution [Master thesis]. Ostrava: VSB-TU; 2017

[23] Chloi R. Minecraft Sales Surpass 100 Million Copies. IGN [Internet]. 2 June 2016. Available from: http://www.ign.com/articles/2016/06/02/minecraft-sales-surpass-100-million-copies

[24] The Minecraft Phenomenon Will also Find Work in Schools, Czech ed. Novinky.cz [Internet]. 2 November 2016. Available from: https://www.novinky.cz/internet-a-pc/hry-a-herni-systemy/419424-fenomen-minecraft-najdeuplatneni-i-ve-skolach.html

[25] Epic Games Inc.: Unreal Engine 4 [Internet]. Available from: https://www.unrealengine.com

[26] Blender Foundation: Blender [Internet]. Available from: https://www.blender.org

[27] Von Ahn L, Dabbish L. Designing Games With A Purpose. Carnegie Mellon University [Internet]. June 2008. Available from: http://www.cs.cmu.edu/~biglou/GWAP_CACM.pdf

Chapter 2

Educational Games in Higher Education

Ebru Yilmaz İnce

Additional information is available at the end of the chapter

http://dx.doi.org/10.5772/intechopen.71017

Abstract

Technological innovations change the learning environments and transform the traditional methods. Educational computer game is one of the most popular emerging educational technologies. In this chapter, documentation method is used to analyze studies about educational games in higher education, in light of a deep literature review. A case study design based on the qualitative research paradigm is employed for organizing the literature review data around categories. An educational game is designed about learning computer hardware, named Computer Hardware Game (CHG). CHG is a game aiming convenience and permanence of learning with providing a close-up view of the computer hardware in three dimensions. The CHG was used in the computer hardware course of the Department of Computer Technologies at Suleyman Demirel University.

Keywords: educational computer games, higher education, digital natives, motivation, serious games

1. Introduction

Technological innovations change the learning environments and transform the traditional methods. Hence, the development of Internet Communication Technologies skills usage of technologies in teaching has become inevitable [1]. Educational computer game is one of the most popular emerging educational technologies. Important student learning principles involved by an educational simulation game [2]. Video games give problem-solving experience to students [3] and provide situated experience in which students are involved in complex problem-solving tasks. Strategic thinking is developed within games that have active, nonlinear and immersive environments because games necessitate the use of logic, memory, problem-solving, and thinking skills [4]. Moreover, educational games brought a new dimension to education by increasing student motivation, providing students the option to learn while having fun, and supporting student-centered education [5]. In addition, educational games are suitable for digital natives.

Employing educational computer games in teaching and learning gained popularity at all educational levels, and has become the subject of scientific research. In this research, in light of literature review, educational computer games in higher education were conducted and analyzed in higher education. In addition, a tutorial was offered on the development of educational game in the field of computer engineering.

This chapter informs about educational games and its features such as game characteristics, story, and mechanics. The second section describes the methodology. In the third section, the studies about educational computer games in higher education are analyzed in light of a deep literature review. In the fourth section, a created educational game named Computer Hardware Game (CHG) is explained. The conclusion covers the consideration and suggestions for future research.

2. Educational games

Computer games are classified as educational that contain educational items that are created for educational aim. An educational game can be used as an educational material in a course. Educator can use an already available educational game or develop a new game appropriate to the course content if it has technical information such as programming. In addition to technical knowledge, developer must know game features such as game characteristic, story, and mechanics.

2.1. Game characteristics

Garris et al. [6] concluded that game characteristics can be described in six categories based on a review of the literature. Game characteristic categories are described as follows:

- fantasy: imaginary or fantasy context, themes, or characters
- rules/goals: clear rules, goals, and feedback on progress toward goals
- sensory stimuli: dramatic or novel visual and auditory stimuli
- challenge: optimal level of difficulty and uncertain goal attainment
- mystery: optimal level of informational complexity
- control: active learner control

The structural characteristics of video games include sound, graphics, background and setting, duration of game, rate of play, advancement rate, use of humor, control options, game dynamics, winning and losing features, character development, brand assurance, and multiplayer features [7]. Players' reasons to play the game when examined according to multi-motivation theory and significant effect of characteristics of the game were found [8].

2.2. Game story

Game story informs us about the game subject. There is a time difference between the narrator and the things told in book story, but game story processes interactively by player. Being interactive, game story causes the formation of concepts such as sequencing, timing, progressive stories, and repeatability [9]. According to the research [10], game interactivity is the most important feature that influences the motivation of the user against the game, and limitations in game storytelling cause restriction of player's freedom and reduce the game's satisfaction.

2.3. Game mechanics

Game mechanics include game rules that exist during a game. Also, it is a system that includes game control, interactivity between players, storytelling, player experience, game hardware, and player feelings [11]. "Game mechanics are an important type of player-game interactions" [12]. As a pedagogical approach to explain the game mechanics, it can also be named as game procedure, and defined as "events that occur within the rules, behaviours and methods." It is stated that the game mechanics guide the player's behavior [13].

3. Method

In this study, documentation method is used to analyze the studies about educational games in higher education, in light of a deep literature review. Google Scholar is used as an electronic database; the reviewed papers are identified through keywords; and the term game with higher education is used as a keyword employing the Boolean operator AND. The papers are considered, which have content about educational game design and implementation for teaching. Then, a case study design based on the qualitative research paradigm is employed for organizing the literature review data around categories. The papers are sorted by date and categorized as research, department, technology, developer, and year.

In this chapter, an educational game developed about computer hardware course is discussed. The game development steps are demonstrated and game characteristic, game story, and game mechanics are explained in detail. The game was used in a hardware course at the department of computer technologies, and interview results were provided.

4. Educational games in higher education

Educational games have a massive potential in science and engineering education [14]. Five reasons for its use in education are described as scale, anytime, compelling, brain chemistry, and better than a lecture to explain contribution to higher education:

- Scale: video games appeal to very large numbers of people (may be graduated people from higher-education system in science and engineering);

- Anytime: students can play game in their spare time;
- Compelling: video games are unintentionally being designed according to effective learning paradigms;
- Brain chemistry: video games stimulate chemical changes in the brain that promote learning; and
- Better than a lecture: initial studies comparing video game teaching effectiveness to the classic lecture show positive improvements, typically 30% or more.

In this section, taking into account the fact as the games' contribution to higher education, the reviewed papers that are researched are presented considering having content with respect to an educational game design and implementation for teaching.

Critical mass is a game, which is used in data structures course, and developed based on competitive programming. In a tournament environment, students can improve their codes and compete their code with other students or instructor code in the critical mass game. According to this research, student-coding performance is increased by the game, being a motivator and competition [15].

The online game Internal Force Master (IFM) was designed for civil engineering and was used during structural concrete course at masters level [16]. IFM was programmed with Macromedia Flash to assist students learning the process by using visualizations and animations. It is found that students like learning with enjoyable and incidental learning materials as educational games.

Recursive algorithm game had used Algorithms with C course in the Department of Applied Informatics, which was created based on snakes and ladders using Savie's online Educational Games Central [17]. According to the research results, the game can be used as a guide for learning algorithms, and helped them realize the misunderstandings and misconceptions on algorithm concepts.

EMERGO project contains a methodology and a toolkit to develop scenario-based serious games, even applicable for higher education. The developer can create complex scenario-based games, on the account of having essential objects and interaction modes for scenario-based game play in the project. EMERGO uses the J2EE/Java development platform. EMERGO aims to:

- study together at a distance;
- actively acquire complex skills;
- within the context of a multimedia and realistic practice;
- through gaming, simulation and pedagogical elements; and
- by using a mixture of both embedded and real-life guidance, including peer feedback.

EMERGO methodology and toolkit can be used to support serious game developers in delivering more efficient scenario-based serious games [18].

The SIMPLE game is designed for three courses (production and operation management, supply-chain management, and introduction to industrial engineering) in the Department of Industrial Engineering and Management [19]. The SIMPLE game is an effective learning environment, and can be used for peer interaction, learning motivation, and course-directed learning interest.

Cheops is a game aiming to help students understand some of the basic concepts of modern computer networks. The game is designed with Macromedia Flash program. According to researchers' perceptions, online serious games can be effective and useful elements in higher education [20].

In a general chemistry course for engineering students, an educational game about molecular geometry, polarity, and intermolecular forces was designed. The results showed that the board game is effective in reconstructing students' knowledge [21].

For programming courses in higher education, a game was designed using action script codes in flash. The game is useful for students' self-learning in introductory programming with the help of using virtual but realistic programming jobs in the game [22].

Uro-Island is created using an open source Wintermute game engine and played by medical students. According to the research results, Uro-Island has a high positive motivational impact on learning and used as an effective teaching method for self-instruction [23].

Students use programming knowledge to solve contextualized problems in Train B&P educational game. The game constitutes an effective approach to assisting novice programmers to learn computational problem-solving skills. Also, the game motivated students toward programming [24].

Pharmacy Challenge is a multiplayer game, designed for pharmacy students and used by Kingston University. According to students' perceptions, the game is interesting, stimulating, and helpful. The game can be added to pharmacy curriculum, as being a motivator [25].

Skills-O-Mat is a game designed for training rhythmic and period motor skills in dental education. The game requires only a training video and motion data as input, and is designed as a reusable component. The game is a valuable instrument for teaching and developing practical skills [26].

Digital games in 3D simulations are used to develop self-management and teamwork. OpenSim multiuser virtual environment is used to develop the game and training activity. Students had a positive perception to use the simulation environment for the development of transferable skills [27].

Ztech de Object-Oriented is a game that aims to learn Object-Oriented programming in an easy and relaxing environment. Most of the computer science and software engineering students enjoyed playing the game. Students can concentrate on the learning topic with the game [28].

DesigMPS is a game which is designed in java platform for software engineering. A software process can be modeled with this serious game by students. Playing the DesigMPS can have a positive learning effect [29].

To train emergency care skills, an educational game named abcdeSIM is designed. Medical students play the game and it has a positive effect on development of students' cognitive skills and motivation [30].

According to literature review of this research, there are examples of the serious games designed for higher education that are used in different departments. Brief information about these researches is given in this section. In **Table 1**, these papers are categorized as research, department, technology, developer, and year.

Research	Department	Technology	Developers	Year
Teaching data structures using competitive games	Computer Science	MySQL, PHP, Java, HTML	Lawrence R	2004
Successful implementation of user-centered game-based learning in higher education: an example from civil engineering	Civil engineering	Macromedia Flash	Ebner M, Holzinger A	2005
Educational games in higher education: a case study in teaching recursive algorithms	Applied Informatics	Savie's online Educational Games Central	Rossiou E, Papadakis S	2007
EMERGO:a methodology and toolkit for developing serious games in higher education	All departments	J2EE/Java development platform	Nadolski RJ, Hummel HG, Van Den Brink HJ, Hoefakker RE, Slootmaker A, Kurvers HJ, Storm J	2008
Serious games for use in a higher education environment.	Computer Science	Macromedia Flash	Liarokapis F, Anderson EF, Oikonomou A	2010
Examining the effects of learning motivation and of course design in an instructional simulation game	Industrial Engineering and Management	Web based	Chang YC, Peng HY, Chao HC	2010
Educational games for self-learning in introductory programming courses-a straightforward design approach with progression mechanisms	Computer and System Sciences	Flash	Ljungkvist P, Mozelius P	2012
Design and implementation of an educational game for teaching chemistry in higher education	Engineering students in a general chemistry course	Game board	Antunes M, Pacheco MAR, Giovanela M	2012
A constructionism framework for designing game-like learning systems: Its effect on different learners	Computer Science	Physics engine	Li ZZ, Cheng YB, Liu CC	2013
Game-based E-learning is more effective than a conventional instructional method: a randomized controlled trial with third-year medical students.	Medical	Wintermute game engine	Boeker M, Andel P, Vach W, Frankenschmidt A	2013

Research	Department	Technology	Developers	Year
Skills-O-Mat: computer supported interactive motion-and game-based training in mixing alginate in dental education	Dental	Flash	Hannig A, Lemos M, Spreckelsen C, Ohnesorge-Radtke U, Rafai N	2013
The design and evaluation of a multiplayer serious game for pharmacy students	Pharmacy	Web application	Dudzinski M, Greenhill D, Kayyali R, Nabhani S, Philip N, Caton H, Ishtiaq S, Gatsinzi F	2013
Developing self-management and teamwork using digital games in 3D simulations	Marketing	OpenSim	Cela-Ranilla JM, Esteve-Mon FM, Esteve-González V, Gisbert-Cervera M	2014.
Computer game as learning and teaching tool for object oriented programming in higher education institution	Computer Science and Software Engineering	2D tile based design game engine	Seng WY, Yatim MHM	2014
Experimental evaluation of a serious game for teaching software process modeling	Information system and Computer Science	Java	Chaves RO, von Wangenheim CG, Furtado JCC, Oliveira SRB, Santos A, Favero EL	2015
An experimental study on the effects of a simulation game on students' clinical cognitive skills and motivation	Medical	Web site	Dankbaar MEW, Alsma J, Jansen EEH, van Merrienboer JJG, van Saase JLCM, Schuit SCE	2016

Table 1. Serious games designed for higher education.

Educational games increase motivation to do the course, and can be an effective way to enhance learning. Considering these contributions of the serious computer games to education, new educational games must be designed and implemented in education with recent technological advances.

5. Educational games in higher education

In this section, an educational game, designed for learning computer hardware, named Computer Hardware Game (CHG) is discussed. CHG is a game aiming convenience and permanence of learning with providing a close-up view of the computer hardware in three dimensions (**Figure 1**). The CHG was used in computer hardware course in the Department of Computer Technologies at Suleyman Demirel University.

Figure 1. Computer hardware game view.

In CHG, a teen room was designed considering digital natives preferences (**Figure 2**). A worktable and course books were added in the CHG room. In the computer hardware book, computer technical parts such as mainboard, processor, hard disk, RAM, video card, DVD-ROM, and

Figure 2. Teen room view.

Ethernet card were modeled in three dimension. The CHG was designed with 3D Studio Max, animations were programmed to the objects by adding anchor link and using touch and sensor.

In the introduction part of the CHG, "Welcome to your virtual room, you can go around and find the special file in your bookcase, have a good time!" was written to attract student's attention to the game. With the opening of the bookcase door, a link is activated (**Figure 3**). Then students could open the special file that contained 3D computer hardware parts. In **Figure 4**, 3D view of mainboard from CHG is shown. Students can study with the 3D mainboard view as it is in the computer hardware laboratory. Also, technical information about mainboard is given to users. After getting information, questions about mainboard are asked to users such as "how many ports are there on the main board?" and user must answer the question in a limited time. User score could be higher, and getting a high score depends on how fast they answer questions. If correct answers are given to the questions and users have enough points, users were able to see another part of computer hardware in 3D as the next level of the game. Also, user must solve puzzles about course content to win the game with the highest score.

The students' perceptions about CHG is analyzed with semistructured interview method. According to the interview data, playing game is funny even if it is being about course content according to students, and students also mentioned that they liked 3D content and the game. According to instructors' perceptions, the game increased students' motivation as being the students are in the race with the game to gain the highest score. As a proposal for a new version of CHG given from students is multi-player version of the game can be developed.

Figure 3. Opened bookcase door view for getting special file view.

Figure 4. Mainboard view.

6. Conclusion

So many developed educational games are aiming to motivate the students to the course. According to the research [31], if a game is designed for learning, it should support the learning context perceived by the students as the best way to learn that game being the right type of game. The right games provide active and experiential learning, and are highly engaging. For this reason, new educational games must be developed as a training material. In this chapter, a new game is designed.

In this research, a well-done categorized educational game studies literature review is exhibited. This literature review helps to see all instances about educational game for digital natives in higher education. The studies were categorized as research, department, technology, developer, year, and titles. Research titles are presented to have information about educational games. Departments are provided to determine the usage of educational games. Technology is used for programs or coding languages to help researchers who want to develop a new educational game. In addition, developer and year of publication of the paper information is also given. According to the brief information of the paper, in conclusion, educational games increase motivation to do the course and can be an effective way to enhance learning.

In addition, an educational game development, that acts as an example of educational games in higher education, is demonstrated. Game characteristic, story, and mechanic themes are explained to help people who have developed a great interest in developing educational games. The CHG game is developed for the hardware course, aiming to teach computer hardware to students. The game has 3D views of the computer hardware part, so students can practice and learn about the course subject. The CHG provides information about computer hardware and then asks questions to students about the subject. As being a game, a limited time and score cause challenge when answering questions and solving puzzles in the game. According to instructors' perceptions, the game increased students' motivation. Students found the game funny, and they liked the game.

Author details

Ebru Yilmaz İnce

Address all correspondence to: ebruince@sdu.edu.tr

Süleyman Demirel University, Isparta, Turkey

References

[1] Psycharis S, Chalatzoglidis G, Kalogiannakis M. Moodle as a learning environment in promoting conceptual understanding for secondary school students. Eurasia Journal of Mathematics, Science and Technology Education. 2013;**9**(1):11-21

[2] Gee JP. What video games have to teach us about learning and literacy. Computers in Entertainment (CIE). 2003;**1**(1):20-20

[3] Squire K. Game-Based Learning: Present and Future State of the Field. Madison, WI: University of Wisconsin-Madison Press; 2005

[4] Pivec M, Koubek A, Dondi C. Guidelines for game-based learning. Lengerich, Germany: Pabst Science Publishers, 2004

[5] Cankaya S, Karamete A. The effects of educational computer games on students' attitudes towards mathematics course and educational computer games. Procedia Social and Behavioral Sciences. 2009;**1**:145-149

[6] Garris R, Ahlers R, Driskell JE. Games, motivation, and learning: A research and practice model. Simulation & Gaming. 2002;**33**(4):441-467

[7] Wood RTA, Griffiths MD, Chappell D, Davies MNO. The structural characteristics of video games: A psycho-structural analysis. Cyberpsychology & Behavior. 2004;**7**(1):1-10

[8] Tüzün H, Özdinç F. Öğretmen Adaylarının Bilgisayar Oyunu Oynama Alışkanlıkları ve Tercihlerine Yönelik Bir Durum Çalışması. In: Uluslararası Öğretmen Yetiştirme Politikaları ve Sorunları Sempozyumu II, 16-18 May 2010 , Hacettepe Üniversitesi, Beytepe-ANKARA. 2010

[9] Juul J. A Clash Between Game and Narrative: Interactive Fiction. (Why Computer Games do not Tell Good Stories and Why This is Not a Problem). Paper presented at Digital Arts and Culture 1998. http://cmc.uib.no/dac98/papers/juul.html

[10] Jenkins H. Game design as narrative architecture. In: Wardrip-Fruin N, Harrigan P, editors. First Person: New Media as Story, Performance, Game. Cambridge: MIT Press; 2004

[11] Lundgren S, Björk S. Game mechanics: Describing computer-augmented games in terms of interaction. Paper presented at the 2003. Technologies for Interactive Digital Storytelling and Entertainment conference. March, Darmstadt, Germany

[12] Cook M, Colton S, Raad A, Gow J. Mechanic miner: Reflection-driven game mechanic discovery and level design. In: European Conference on the Applications of Evolutionary Computation. Berlin, Heidelberg: Springer; 2013, April. p. 284-293

[13] Fullerton T, Swain C, Hoffman S. Game Design Workshop. Designing, Prototyping and Playtesting Games. San Francisco: CMP Books; 2004

[14] Mayo MJ. Games for science and engineering education. Communications of the ACM. 2007;**50**(7):30-35

[15] Lawrence R. Teaching data structures using competitive games. IEEE Transactions on Education. 2004;**47**(4):459-466

[16] Ebner M, Holzinger A. Successful implementation of user-centered game based learning in higher education: An example from civil engineering. Computers & Education. 2007;**49**(3):873-890

[17] Rossiou E, Papadaki S. Educational games in higher education: A case study in teaching recursive algorithms. In: Proceedings of the Fourth International Conference on Education in a Changing Environment. Vol. 149157. Salford, United Kingdom: University of Salford, Informing Science Press; 2007

[18] Nadolski RJ, Hummel HG, Van Den Brink HJ, Hoefakker RE, Slootmaker A, Kurvers HJ, Storm J. EMERGO: A methodology and toolkit for developing serious games in higher education. Simulation & Gaming. 2008;**39**(3):338-352

[19] Chang YC, Peng HY, Chao HC. Examining the effects of learning motivation and of course design in an instructional simulation game. Interactive Learning Environments. 2010;**18**(4):319-339

[20] Liarokapis F, Anderson EF, Oikonomou A. Serious games for use in a higher education environment. In Proceedings of the Emerging Games Platforms, Technologies

and Applications Workshop (EGPTA'10), 15th Int"l Computer Games Conference: AI, Interactive Multimedia, Virtual Worlds and Serious Games Louisville, Kentucky, 2010, USA (pp. 28-31)

[21] Antunes M, Pacheco MAR, Giovanela M. Design and implementation of an educational game for teaching chemistry in higher education. Journal of Chemical Education. 2012;**89**(4):517-521

[22] Ljungkvist P, Mozelius P. Educational games for self learning in introductory programming courses-a straightforward design approach with progression mechanisms. In: Proceedings of the 6th European Conference on Games Based Learning, ECGBL. 2012. p. 285-293

[23] Boeker M, Andel P, Vach W, Frankenschmidt A. Game-based E-learning is more effective than a conventional instructional method: A randomized controlled trial with third-year medical students. PLoS One. 2013;**8**(12):e82328. DOI: 10.1371/journal.pone.0082328

[24] Li ZZ, Cheng YB, Liu CC. A constructionism framework for designing game-like learning systems: Its effect on different learners. British Journal of Educational Technology. 2013;**44**(2):208-224

[25] Dudzinski M, Greenhill D, Kayyali R, Nabhani-Gebara S, Philip N, Caton H, Ishtiaq S, Gatsinzi F. The design and evaluation of a multiplayer serious game for pharmacy students. The 7th European Conference on Games Based Learning; 2013; Porto, Portugal. 2013. Oct, pp. 3-4

[26] Hannig A, Lemos M, Spreckelsen C, Ohnesorge-Radtke U, Rafai N. Skills-o-mat: Computer supported interactive motion-and game-based training in mixing alginate in dental education. Journal of Educational Computing Research. 2013;**48**(3):315-343

[27] Cela-Ranilla JM, Esteve-Mon FM, Esteve-González V, Gisbert-Cervera M. Developing self-management and teamwork using digital games in 3D simulations. Australasian Journal of Educational Technology. 2014;**30**(6):634-651

[28] Seng WY, Yatim MHM. Computer game as learning and teaching tool for object oriented programming in higher education institution. Procedia-Social and Behavioral Sciences. 2014;**123**:215-224

[29] Chaves RO, von Wangenheim CG, Furtado JCC, Oliveira SRB, Santos A, Favero EL. Experimental evaluation of a serious game for teaching software process modeling. IEEE Transactions on Education. 2015;**58**(4):289-296

[30] Dankbaar MEW, Alsma J, Jansen EEH, van Merrienboer JJG, van Saase JLCM, Schuit SCE An experimental study on the effects of a simulation game on students' clinical cognitive skills and motivation. Advances in Health Sciences Education. 2016;**21**(3):505-521

[31] Whitton NJ. An investigation into the potential of collaborative computer game-based learning in higher education. [PhD thesis]. Edinburgh Napier University. 2007

Chapter 3

Digital Games in the Science Classroom: Leveraging Internal and External Scaffolds during Game Play

Kara Krinks, Heather Johnson and Douglas B. Clark

Additional information is available at the end of the chapter

http://dx.doi.org/10.5772/intechopen.72071

Abstract

We have developed a disciplinarily integrated game (DIG) to support students in interpreting, translating, and manipulating across formal representations in the domain of Newtonian kinematics. In this study, we seek to understand what game play looks like in a classroom context with particular attention given to how students leverage internal and external scaffolds to progress through the game and deepen their conceptual knowledge. We investigate the following questions: (1) In what ways do students interact with the game, with each other, and with their teacher when they play *SURGE Symbolic* in a classroom environment? (2) How do game scaffolds, both within and outside of the game, support or impede student learning and game play? (3) What are the implications of these observations for teachers and game designers? We found that although most students used internal scaffolds in some way to assist their game play, many found that these scaffolds were insufficient to get through challenges. They quickly sought help from external resources available to them outside the game to help them advance in the game. The source of information they needed to make progress came from various people or resources outside the game, what we are calling "knowers."

Keywords: game-based learning, disciplinarily integrated games, science education, game design, scaffolds

1. Introduction

Interpreting, translating, and manipulating across formal representations is central to scientific practice and modeling [1–3]. We have developed a disciplinarily integrated game (DIG) such that players' actions in the game focus on iteratively developing and manipulating formal representations as the core game mechanics [4, 5]. These formal representations are computational and mathematized representations of focal science phenomena. Through playing a DIG, students investigate key conceptual relationships in the domain while also developing facility with the representations and inscriptions themselves [6]. Supporting students in manipulating and transforming across representations, however, is challenging in terms of having students build connections between the formal representations and patterns of events that they represent [7–10]. This study extends work from our previous pilot study [11] and used a DIG in the context of Newtonian kinematics. This DIG is designed to engage students in the manipulation of both formal representations and events (in this case, patterns of motion) to control one another in order to develop a deeper conceptual understanding of physics concepts. In this study, we seek to understand what game play looks like in a classroom context with particular attention given to how students leverage internal and external scaffolds to progress through the game and deepen their conceptual knowledge.

2. Background

2.1. Internal and external scaffolds

The notion of scaffolding was originally conceived as a process by which teachers, other adults, or peers provide assistance to help learners with tasks that are normally beyond their reach [12]. Scaffolds can be directly embedded into an activity in order to provide learners with "just in time" resources that help students overcome a challenge at the moment they encounter the challenge. In games for learning, these internal scaffolds can take the form of hints, questions, terminology, character dialogs, feedback screens, etc. Researchers have found that internal scaffolds can support students in developing science content and skills [13]. It is important that internal scaffolds go beyond helping students simply progress to the next level in the game but also engage them in learning from their efforts on a level so that they can then apply that newfound knowledge to the subsequent game levels [14]. In the context of this paper, internal scaffolds are supports that are embedded within the game that are designed to foster students' conceptual understanding of Newtonian kinematics and intended to help students make connections between the informal context of the game and the formal physics vocabulary and representations used to describe motion of objects. These scaffolds include help screens and hints when a student fails to solve a level, as well as tutorials that provide new information (e.g., explanations of formal physics representations like graphs and dot traces) for future levels.

In addition to internal scaffolds embedded within the game environment, external scaffolds can also be used to enhance students' learning [15]. In the context of games, external scaffolds may come from a teacher or peers in the form of scientific explanations of concepts in the game or advice on when to perform certain actions in a game. Additionally, providing collaboration opportunities between peers during game play can serve as a productive external scaffold that allows students to leverage discourse in order to negotiate meaning of concepts and actions within games, construct ideas, resolve conflicts, etc. [16, 17]. In the context of the current study, although most students used internal scaffolds in some way to assist their game play, many also found that these scaffolds were not enough to get through challenges. They quickly sought help from external resources available to them *outside* the game to help them advance *in* the game. The source of information they needed to make progress came from various people or resources outside the game, what we are calling "knowers." Students chose to seek help from the teacher, each other, and even other tools and materials to reason through the math and science needed to pass a level.

Despite the well-known affordances of digital games for students' conceptual development, these games have not been widely adopted in secondary science classrooms [15]. A primary goal of this project was to explore what real game play with DIGs looks like in the classroom context to improve our understanding of how students engage with the game and the science concepts embedded within the game. In addition to exploring the impact of the new world-view levels, we were also particularly interested in exploring how students overcome challenges in the game when they have access to a classroom of peers and a teacher. Honey and Hilton [15] call for research to "investigate how best to integrate games into formal learning contexts…this should include how *internal scaffolds* in the game and *external scaffolds* provided by a teacher, mentor, peers, or other instructional resources support science learning" (p. 124). It was of interest to us to explore when, who, and how students solicit support to succeed with their personal game play goals. This exploratory study addresses this research need by investigating the following questions: (1) In what ways do students interact with the game, with each other, and with their teacher when they play *SURGE Symbolic* in a classroom environment? (2) How do game scaffolds, both within and outside of the game, support or impede student learning and game play? (3) What are the implications of these observations for teachers and game designers?

2.2. Disciplinarily integrated games

SURGE Symbolic (**Figures 1** and **2**) is the prototypical DIG template that we used in this study, and is the result of evolution of design, research, and thinking chronicled in Clark et al. [4, 5]. Whereas earlier versions of *SURGE* supported reflection on the results of game play through formal representations as a means to support strategy refinement, the formal representations were not the medium through which players planned, implemented, and manipulated their game strategies. Earlier versions of *SURGE* provided vector representations, for example, to help students understand what was happening and how they might adjust their control strategy, but these formal representations only communicated information that a player might or might not use. The challenges and opportunities in a given game level, however, were communicated through the layout of elements in the game world, not in the formal representations. Similarly, the player's controls for executing a strategy were also independent of the formal representations. Thus, while attending to the formal representations might help a player succeed in a level, earlier *SURGE* games did not use formal representations as the medium through which challenges and opportunities were communicated to the player, nor did earlier *SURGE* games use diagrammatic formal representations as the medium of control. In *SURGE Symbolic*, we made Cartesian graphs of position and velocity over time the medium through which the player controlled their avatar in the game, and we also made those same types of Cartesian graphs the medium through which the game communicated goals and challenges to the players.

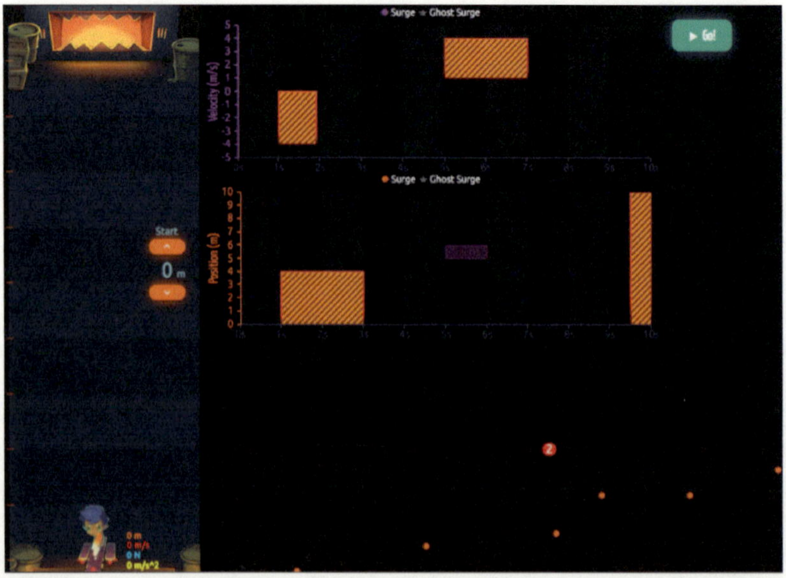

Figure 1. Anatomy of an introductory block level.

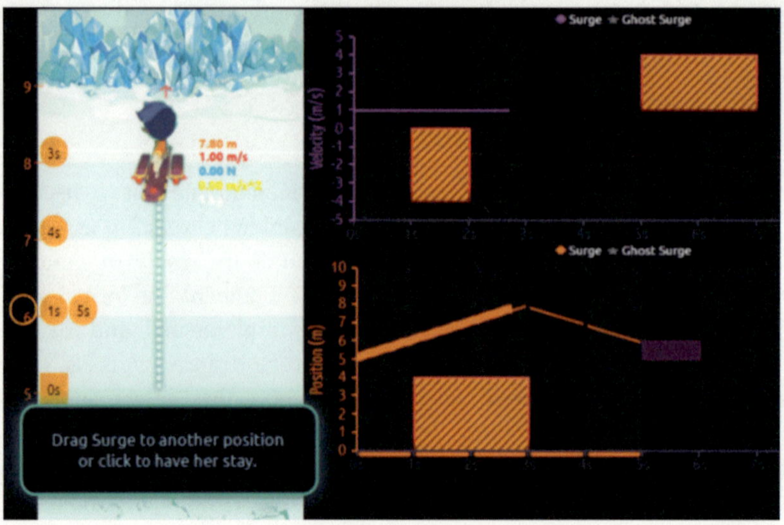

Figure 2. Anatomy of an introductory worldview level.

Students in *SURGE Symbolic* play from the perspective of the space navigator, Surge. Game play is divided into levels, each focused on a specific navigational challenge or Newtonian concept. Students must move Surge forward or backward on her space board to find the appropriate position or velocity to navigate Surge to the exit portals, represented by a purple box, while avoiding electricity zones, represented as orange boxes (see **Figure 1**). Surge's path is traced onto a graph representing the magnitude of position and velocity over time. Students use an interface to set up their strategies by dragging blocks that contain segments of a graph to create a graph to specify position or velocity versus time. When students have finished designing their path, they must click the "Run" button to launch their plan. As the plan is launched, the players can watch as the plan unfolds in terms of the game character's motion on the map as well as in the formal representations.

In this study, we used two different versions of *SURGE Symbolic*. These two versions provided different types of internal scaffolds to students. The purpose of this study is not so much to compare which version of the game "worked better," but rather the purpose was to explore how students made use of these various internal scaffolds as well as external scaffolds in the classroom, such as the teacher and the other students. The two versions of the game were very similar and differed only in the way that students controlled the game character and generated the graphs to design their path on a subset of the levels. In each level, students attempted to create a path for Surge to avoid the electricity zones and make it the exit portal. In one version, called block level (BL), students first used a toggle button to set Surge's initial position (**Figure 1**). Students then constructed position or velocity graphs to control Surge with "blocks" representing segments of the graph. Students could organize the blocks in any order to create a graph, and students could swap blocks in and out of the graph. In the second version, called worldview (WV), players used the block interface on most levels, but used a different control interface on a subset of levels. In the worldview subset of levels, players clicked and dragged Surge to create a sequence of positions to which Surge would move over the course of the level (**Figure 2**). Thus, the player specified where Surge should be at each second during the level. In both versions, the level goals and parameters (starting position, exit portal position, required velocities) were identical for each level so that students playing each version had to pass the same challenges in order to progress in the game. While the BL version exclusively had students drag blocks to create a path, the WV version used both block levels and worldview levels. Whereas the block interface focuses on connections between graphs, the WV interface was designed to help students develop understandings of the connections between the graphs and the motion of the avatar, Surge, herself. Through designing the worldview interface, we, therefore, hoped to help students develop a more intuitive understanding of the nature of motion communicated by the various relationships communicated in the Cartesian graphs.

3. Methods

3.1. Setting and participants

The study was conducted in a suburban school with 98 students in six sections of an STEM class spanning seventh grade (N_7 = 51) and eighth grade (N_8 = 47). The teacher of the class, Mrs. L, was a veteran teacher and had worked with the research team in previous years to pilot earlier versions of the game in her classroom. During the study, she walked around the classroom to assist students as needed with questions about the game or science concepts. The research team addressed only technical difficulties that students encountered during game play and recorded field notes of student game play and discourse. They intentionally did not provide assistance to students regarding conceptual questions or hints on how to solve levels.

The study lasted for six consecutive school days. Students took a pretest on the first day to assess prior understanding of concepts such as position and velocity, as well as interpretation of position-time and velocity-time graphs of an object's motion. They played the game for the next three and a half days. At the end of game play on the fifth day, students took a posttest that was identical to the pretest. On day 6, students talked with the research team about their perceptions of and struggles with the game and questions on the posttest.

Before the study began, Mrs. L's classroom was arranged in traditional rows of desks all facing the front of the classroom. For this study, Mrs. L chose to rearrange the desks into groups of four that were facing each other. As students entered the classroom on the first day of the study, students were allowed to self-select into groups. Approximately half of the groups were assigned to play the BL version, and the other half of the groups were assigned to play the WV version. Students in each group were encouraged to talk to each other for help, but groups were not allowed to talk to other groups since they were playing different versions of the game. **Table 1** shows the number of students and groups in each class period.

3.2. Data collection

Data collected for this study included pre-post scores and detailed daily field notes. Due to school district rules, video data collection was not allowed, so the researchers circulated around the room during game play taking copious notes of student game play, including student talk, teacher talk, observations of silent game play, and level completion for each student at the end of each class period. One researcher primarily focused on interactions between the teacher and students, while the second researcher focused on student talk among the groups. The researchers compared notes at the end of each day, discussed any observed patterns, and subsequently adjusted the focus of observations for the following day. On day 3, one of the researchers talked with each group in five of the six classes about how they worked through the struggles encountered in the game and how they worked together as a group. No group interview data were collected in period 6 because students in this class discovered a previously unknown bug in the game that allowed them to "complete" levels without actually solving them. Several students in this class used the bug to make progress in the game instead

Class period	Grade	Number of students in each class	Number of students playing BL version	Number of students playing WV version
Second	7	15	$N_{2BL} = 7$ (2 groups)	$N_{2WV} = 8$ (2 groups)
Third	8	14	$N_{3BL} = 7$ (2 groups)	$N_{3WV} = 7$ (2 groups)
Fourth	7	17	$N_{4BL} = 7$ (2 groups)	$N_{4WV} = 10$ (3 groups)
Fifth	7	19	$N_{5BL} = 9$ (3 groups)	$N_{5WV} = 10$ (3 groups)
Sixth	8	13	$N_{6BL} = 5$ (2 groups)	$N_{6WV} = 8$ (3 groups)
Seventh	8	20	$N_{7BL} = 13$ (4 groups)	$N_{7WV} = 7$ (2 groups)
Total		*98*	$N_{BL} = 48$ *(15 groups)*	$N_{WV} = 50$ *(15 groups)*

Table 1. Number of students and groups playing each version of *SURGE Symbolic*.

of soliciting help to work through challenges. Because this shortcut prevented them from working together in the same way as other classes, no group interview data were collected in this class period.

3.3. Data analysis

Data analysis included quantitative comparison of pre-post scores using paired t-tests and qualitative analysis of the field notes using inductive thematic analysis [18, 19]. Qualitative data analysis began by reviewing all field notes in order to become familiar with the data. We first coded the data to identify all instances of student talk and teacher talk recorded in the data. Since we were particularly interested in how students interacted with each other during game play and how they were making sense of the game and embedded physics concepts using the designed scaffolds, we made a second pass to identify instances when students were observed using or talking about the internal scaffolds or science concepts embedded in the game and when students were interacting with each other during game play. We also closely analyzed student responses to the researcher's question about types of help they used in the game and how the groups interacted with each other.

In order to identify themes in the data, we developed an initial open coding scheme for the data using the constant comparative method [20] and iteratively applied these codes to data, revising codes and grouping codes together as needed. Specific codes included such things as use of the level map, use of help screens, student talk about mechanics of the game (i.e., how do you reset the level?), student talk about the help within the game (i.e., what does that map show?), student talk about concepts in the game (i.e., the farther apart the dots, the faster Surge goes), teacher talk about concepts or game mechanics, attempts to seek help from a peer, and attempts to seek help from the teacher. Once the codes were applied to the data through an iterative process, we searched for themes among codes. Themes that emerged from this analysis centered on the use of both internal and external scaffolds to make sense of the game and progress to higher levels. These themes are examined in greater detail in the following section.

4. Analysis and findings

To provide a backdrop for our analysis of how students made use of internal and external scaffolds during game play, we first analyze the pre-post scores. We then proceed to the focal analyses of how students made use of the internal and external scaffolds.

Analysis of pretest and posttest scores showed that students made gains in conceptual understanding of formal representations after playing the game. Paired t-tests compared pretest scores ($M = 47.0$, $SD = 19.9$) to posttest scores for all students ($M = 53.5$, $SD = 21.7$). These results showed that students made significant, albeit modest, gains in the posttest scores ($t(97) = 3.79$, $p < 0.001$) with an effect size of 0.31 and suggest that the game did indeed help students develop a better understanding of the target physics concepts in the game. Independent t-tests were also conducted to compare changes in pre-post scores for the BL group ($M = 6.1$, $SD = 17.0$) and the

WV group (M = 6.8, SD = 17.0), as well as changes in pre-post scores for seventh graders (M = 5.9, SD = 14.2) and eighth graders (M = 7.1, SD = 19.6), but no significant differences were found between either of the two groups ($t(96) = -0.19$, $p = 0.85$ for BL and WV groups; $t(96) = -0.36$, $p = 0.72$ for seventh and eighth grade groups). These results suggest that while the game did indeed help students develop a better understanding of the target physics concepts in the game, the differences in interface and representational design between the BL and WV groups did not significantly affect pre-post scores. Additionally, both seventh and eighth graders experienced similar amounts of growth in the pre-post scores. **Table 2** shows the mean scores for each subgroup.

Against this quantitative backdrop, we now shift the analysis to students' use of internal and external scaffolds during game play. We will illustrate the themes that emerged through this analysis by focusing on one group of four eighth grade boys in period 2. This group was chosen because the four members all interacted with the game in different ways, seeking help from different sources, yet very actively interacting with each other. All of the group members were also very verbal and articulated their group interactions in great detail, thus allowing for robust data collection in the field notes. We will use this group to provide examples of how they differentially leveraged internal and external scaffolds to help them progress through the game, and we will also include data from other groups to provide examples of additional instantiations of these themes.

The members of our focus group were Dylan, Connor, Preston, and Grant (pseudonyms). The four boys approached their game play in different ways. **Table 3** shows the performance of each group member on the pre and posttest, as well as the levels completed on each day as a way to show the different rates of progression through the game. Dylan was the first group

	Pretest mean score (%)	Posttest mean score (%)	Change in mean score (%)
Total (N = 98)	47.0	53.5	+6.5
Seventh ($N_7 = 51$)	43.5	49.4	+5.9
Eighth ($N_8 = 47$)	50.9	58.0	+7.1
WV ($N_{WV} = 50$)	45.5	52.3	+6.8
BL ($N_{BL} = 48$)	48.6	54.8	+6.2

Table 2. Mean average scores for pretest and posttest.

	Level at end of day 1	Level at end of day 2	Level at end of day 3	Level at end of day 4	Level at end of day 5	Pretest score (% correct)	Posttest score (% correct)
Dylan	20	57	66	Finished	Finished	95	100
Connor	14	41	60	66	Finished	65	80
Grant	11	38	51	61	64	30	35
Preston	10	34	44	50	50	75	35

Table 3. Levels completed at the end of each day of game play and pre-post performance for focus group.

http://dx.doi.org/10.5772/intechopen.72071

member (and the first person in all six class periods) to successfully complete all 66 levels in the game, and Connor finished all the levels shortly after he did. Both Dylan and Connor had participated in a research study the previous year with the same teacher that involved playing a different but related game, so their quick progression through the levels could be attributed, in part, to their prior exposure to a conceptually integrated game involving graphing and physics concepts. However, the design of the game for this study was significantly different from the game they played last year and presented conceptual challenges for them to navigate, as evidenced by their use of internal and external scaffolds during game play. Grant and Preston had no prior experience with games similar to this one.

Figure 3 shows a diagram of the seating positions of this group. All fours desks were facing toward each other to facilitate group conversation. While Dylan interacted with the group on multiple occasions, he was largely quiet as he intensely focused on solving his own levels as quickly as possible. In contrast, Grant, Preston, and Connor were consistently talking during game play, sharing ideas with each other, asking each other questions, and making general comments about their impressions of the game.

4.1. Internal scaffolds

In the context of this paper, internal scaffolds are supports that are embedded within the game that are designed to foster students' conceptual understanding of Newtonian kinematics and intended to help students make connections between the informal context of the game and the formal physics vocabulary and representations used to describe motion of objects. These scaffolds include help screens and hints (**Figure 4**) when a student fails to solve a level, as well as tutorials that provide new information (e.g., explanations of formal physics representations like graphs and dot traces) for future levels. Students had the option of using these supports at any time during game play, and we observed numerous students utilizing these in-game scaffolds when seeking help to pass levels, as evidenced by numerous observations of students reading help screens before starting levels, clicking on hints after failing a level, or making comments about the help screens. Some students continued to use these internal scaffolds exclusively as their help source throughout their game play. However, many students found these internal scaffolds to be insufficient when the game grew more complex.

One internal scaffold that many students appeared to use productively was the level map, which could be toggled on and off by students (**Figure 5**). This map showed Surge's required

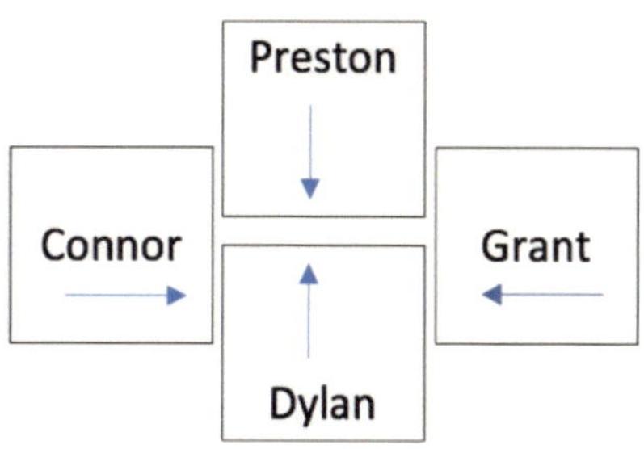

Figure 3. Group seating positions of focus group students, including direction desks are facing.

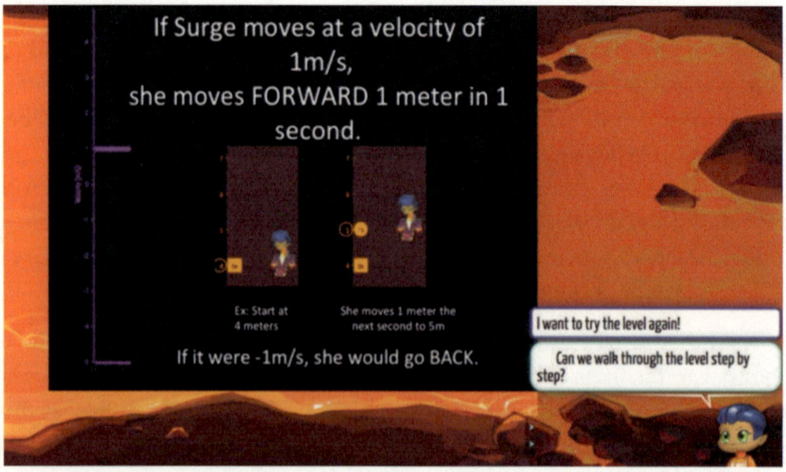

Figure 4. Sample help screen after student fails a level.

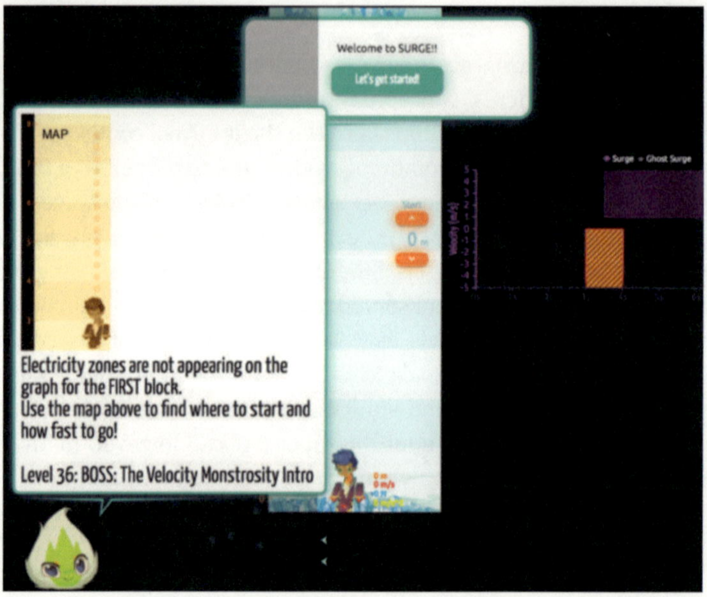

Figure 5. Level map showing starting position and dot trace.

initial starting position, as well as a dot trace to determine the necessary initial velocity for Surge to avoid a deadly electric field. Observation of student game play showed that students quickly learned how to determine the initial starting position from the map. However, many had difficulty interpreting the distance between dots as an indicator of Surge's speed and translating that speed to a meaningful slope on the graph. Field notes indicated that students who only used the level map to obtain starting position and did not use the dot traces to determine velocity often adopted an unproductive "guess and check" strategy to solve the level. For example, one student in period 2 was observed attempting level 19 numerous times. The student was seen viewing the level map and then moving Surge to the correct starting position, thus indicating a correct interpretation of required starting position from the map. However, he then appeared to guess as to which initial speed he needed to start, trying various speed blocks and failing the level several times before finally discovering the correct block to use through trial and error. While this student successfully determined the starting position using the map, he failed to notice or interpret any information about the required starting speed from the same map. Another student commented in the debrief session after game play that "the [map] wasn't very helpful. It told you the start position, but didn't say how fast it should be going each time," indicating that the student failed to understand that the dot traces could be used to determine the correct starting speed. Yet another student was overheard commenting on the map saying, "It says to notice the dots in the map. There are no dots on the map!" Apparently, this student never even noticed the dots on the map, much less made a connection between the dots and velocity.

Others who used the map for both starting position and initial velocity appeared to solve levels more quickly and demonstrated a stronger understanding of the targeted concepts in the game. An example of this usage can be seen in our focus group where Grant attempted to solve Level 19. He skipped through the explanation screens at the beginning of the level, looked at the map, and correctly moved Surge to a starting position of 8 m. However, he chose an incorrect initial velocity block, causing Surge to crash and fail the level. Reading the hint block, Grant exclaimed, "Too slow! What?!?!" He then enlisted the help of another member of his group, Connor, to figure out how to solve the level. Connor came over to Grant's chair to look at his screen and asked, "Where does the dot trail start?" Grant answered, "8." Then, Connor replied, "Good. How are the dots spread out?" In this exchange, Connor tried to get Grant to notice the dot traces and use the spacing between the dots to determine if he needed to start at a slow speed or a faster speed. In another example, Connor used the dot traces to calculate the initial velocity he needed for a level. While looking at the level map showing dots spaced far apart and thinking aloud, he said, "That [spacing] is like big. 4 per second-ish." He then chose the 4 m/s block and successfully solved the level. Connor demonstrated his understanding of how to use the spacing between the dots to determine his initial velocity, seemingly understanding that the farther apart the dots are, the faster the speed.

Dylan also demonstrated using the map for information on both starting position and velocity. In one instance, he noticed Grant struggling to solve a level. Dylan looked at Grant's level map and told him to start at 4. Then Dylan said, "the dots are close together. 4 s. You need to make her go forward in 4 s." In this exchange, Dylan demonstrated that he was using the map for information on both starting position and velocity. Not only did Dylan and Connor finish all the game levels before anyone else in the class, they also scored high on the posttest at the end, demonstrating strong conceptual understanding through their game play performance and scores on the posttest. While Dylan started with a high pretest score, Connor had one of the larger gains across all the classes, possibly suggesting that his interaction with the game helped him make sense of the science embedded within the game. His gains could also possibly be attributed to his close proximity and access to Dylan, a student in his group who had a more sophisticated conceptual understanding of the science and math ideas in the game, as evidenced by his high pretest score.

Unlike other members in the class, Connor had the opportunity to tap into Dylan's expertise and use him as an external scaffold during game play.

4.2. External scaffolds

Although most students used internal scaffolds in some way to assist their game play, many also found that these scaffolds were not enough to get through challenges. They quickly sought help from external resources available to them outside the game to help them advance in the game. The source of information they needed to make progress came from various people or resources outside the game, what we are calling "knowers." Students chose to seek help from the teacher, each other, and even other tools and materials to reason through the math and science needed to pass a level.

We noticed that the type of *knower* students sought out and the nature of the questions they asked varied by student. Students who primarily wanted to pass levels but did not care as much about the reasoning behind their success or failure tended to solicit assistance that would help them advance in the moment on a particular level. Students who were motivated by this type of help possessed what we termed a "game play orientation." Students who wanted to make sense of the rules and strategies behind Surge's movements often sought help to reason through the math and physics in the game. We refer to this as a "sense-making orientation." We have observed related patterns in studies with other games (e.g., [17]).

An example of these orientations can be seen in the focus group. Preston's game-play orientation was evident from the beginning when he approached the game from the perspective of a kid playing a video game in an informal setting. He quickly jumped into the storyline of the game and was primarily concerned about saving "fuzzies" and unlocking new settings (i.e., "Oh, there's SNOW!!"). At some point in his game play, however, he got somewhat frustrated that he could not do more with the rescued fuzzies. He made the least progress in his group and actually showed losses in his posttest score. He never tried to make sense of the math or science behind the game level, admitting in the whole class debrief at the end of the study, "I'm going to be honest. After taking the post-test, I didn't feel I learned anything. I was focused on beating the game." Dylan, however, demonstrated a sense-making orientation, as illustrated on day 2 when he worked through a level and failed. We observed him reading the feedback, presumably to reanalyze his approach. After he thought about it, he said to the computer, "Oh, OK," and succeeded on his next attempt. Dylan's repeated attempts to integrate the feedback indicate that he was trying to make sense of Surge's movements and using the game feedback to inform his next strategy.

With either orientation, students identified different *knowers* in the learning environment when they wanted help to make progress toward their goal. We conjecture that an individual student's orientation toward the game influenced the nature of questions asked and the type of *knower* they sought for help. In this study, we surveyed each student that was present on day 3 of game play and asked how they typically got help when they encountered a sticking point in the game. All students first responded that they started with internal scaffolds within the game. When the game did not provide the help they needed, some of them identified four categories of external scaffolds, what we are calling in this case *knowers*, that they turned to for

Type of knower	Second Period	Third period	Fourth period	Fifth period	Seventh period	*Total*
Game as knower	2	3	2	4	4	15
Self as knower	2	4	1	2	2	11
Peer as knower	9	7	10	7	14	47
Teacher as knower	2	0	3	1	1	7
Total	15	14	16	14	21	80

Table 4. Type of knowers used by number of students per period.

further help. While some students explained that they had a chain of knowers they could go to next if one failed, **Table 4** identifies the *first knower* each student would seek when the Surge's internal scaffolds no longer provided the help they needed.

4.2.1. Game as knower

Students who identified the "game as knower" were students who showed little or no use of external scaffolds. They leaned on the internal scaffolds to help them figure out what to do: they would revisit earlier levels of the game to help with later levels, repeatedly consult help screens or hints, or write down notes from the help screens. There was little audible or visible evidence of the use of this scaffold, but students self-reported these behaviors when speaking with researchers. In the focus group, both Dylan and Preston were classified into this category as they rarely, if ever, sought help from an external scaffold and relied on the game to help them progress through levels. However, since Dylan possessed a sense-making orientation, while Preston demonstrated a game-play orientation, their interactions with the internal scaffolds looked different, as described previously. Students in other groups showed their reliance on the game as knower in a couple of different ways. One boy said that when he gets stuck, he generally, "tries a couple of levels before" his current level to review any instructions that he might have gone through too quickly or to see if the earlier levels could provide some guidance that he did not pay enough attention to earlier. Another student described how he would copy and paste the help tips into an internet browser so he could flip back to see them when he got stuck. For some students, these strategies suggest they are applying knowledge of games outside the classroom to be successful with this game. For example, students who are familiar with games may expect help features within the game to provide all the assistance that is necessary to succeed with game play. One boy had such high expectations that the game was going to help him advance that he "sat a full period on one level trying to use the game to help get through the level." He thought it should have been easy and was "too embarrassed" to ask for any external help to get through the level. He kept reading the help in the game but did not understand what it was telling him to do. No students in his group nor Mrs. L knew that he was stuck for a full class period.

4.2.2. Self as knower

The "game as knower" strategy is closely connected to the "self as knower" strategy and is sometimes impossible to tease apart. There were a few students who showed visible evidence beyond the screen that they were doing something more in the game than just getting through levels. Students who fell in this category often used the feedback and help from the game to then integrate their prior knowledge of math and physics before deciding on their next strategy. These students worked through the challenge on their own, often succeeding with just the help suggestions within the game. Yet, there were times they tapped into external tools or representational resources, such as paper and pencil to extend graph lines, to help them with their sensemaking. Thus, the students who fell into the "self as knower" category and made their math and science thinking visible were students who had a sensemaking orientation. For example, while a level was running, one student moved her arms in gestures that mirrored the graph lines that were being generated in the game. When Surge crashed, she froze her arms, and reacted, "Oh…The down is not right. I've got to keep going down, down, down. Gosh!" She reshaped her arms while talking this through to imagine what move she needed to try next. A few students used paper to do some inscriptional work with mathematical notations that were not in the game or modified representations in the game by using extra paper to stretch graph lines to better obtain data. For example, Connor used an index card to mark a dot on one card that he held up to a graph, and then he moved that card up to the graph above it, demonstrating his strategy of coordinating information across graphs to inform his next move. While it is difficult to identify students who rely on their "self as knower" versus the "game as knower," we did notice that the students who did extend their reasoning beyond the game often advanced to higher levels in the game more quickly and had either greater gains or higher posttest scores.

4.2.3. Peer as knower

Students who used a "peer as knower" identified someone in their group to ask for help to solve levels. It was not always any member of the group who could serve as the knower, however. Students had multiple reasons for selecting different peers. Sometimes, the same student would call on different peer knowers for different reasons. For example, Grant positioned Connor and Dylan as his knowers at different times. Initially, when he asked for help, he adopted a game play orientation to help him get through a level. He asked Dylan how to get through a level and was happy with a response to "start at 4." Yet, when that did not work moving forward and he realized that he was still getting stuck in the same part of each level, he took on more of a sense-making orientation when he asked Dylan, "How do you know where to start *in general*?" Here, he was trying to uncover the strategy behind getting started with each level, not just the number where he needed to start in order to pass that particular level. Later, when Grant realized that Dylan was so far ahead and working with the game in his own way, he called on Connor when he needed help making sense of the dot trace map. This was interesting because Preston and Dylan were the peers closest in proximity (see **Figure 3**), but Grant recognized that the two of them had their own game play strategies that would be interrupted if he asked a question. He knew Connor was ahead of him, but closer to his own level than Dylan, so he asked Connor to physically walk around to his computer and help him. Here, we see an example where the group member that was the farthest along in the game (Dylan in this case) was not always positioned as the knower in the group. Many students responded that they preferred to get help from a group member that was just slightly ahead of them in the game instead of the student who was several levels ahead.

In this group, Grant selected his peer knower based on what he needed—a quick response to get through a level, or someone who could spend more time with him to make sense of the level. Other students had different reasons for calling on different peers. Some students identified a *partner as knower*. Early on in game play, there were some groups where two or more members explicitly decided to work through each level together. They often repositioned their desks so they could more easily see each other's screens, or they engaged in more talk-alouds while they were making decisions on how to proceed in a level. These groups tended to move relatively slowly through game play, making sure that each member in the partnership was progressing. For example, there were times when one member had a lucky guess that allowed him to pass the level, but he struggled to get his partners through the same level because he did not have sound reasoning. But, he would not move on to the next level until his other partners were with him. In general, students that worked in partnerships would hang back with the slowest member to work together to identify the inputs that would yield successful outputs.

Other groups just said "*anyone in the group*" would serve as their knower. In these groups, each individual worked independently. If one student got stuck, he or she said something like, "Did anyone get through level 21? How did you do it?" Any member of the group could respond at any time. Sometimes it was an individual who recently completed the level. Other times, it was a student who was willing to take the time to work through a level with someone else.

Finally, some groups had one student who would serve as the knower for anyone in the group. In one group, when the students were asked who they go to for help, they all identified the same *individual in the group*. He also identified himself as the group knower. When pressed on playing this role, he responded, "it is just what I do." Apparently, in this class and others, he is perceived as a "knower" by his peers, and he is comfortable with this role.

We also observed what we termed "*reluctant peer knowers*" in a group, which is someone that a group member calls on for help, but is reluctant to help because he/she would rather play his/her own game. Reluctant knowers often gave short tips like, "Start at 4," with no reasoning, as Dylan did for Grant in an earlier example. They would provide some assistance, but it was often terse and more of a cheat. Reluctant knowers sometimes took a group member's computer and did the level for them, or simply turned their computer around to show a level solution to help the other member. If their help did not work, they most often did not spend any more time trying to help the student who asked for assistance.

Whether reluctant or not, the peer as knower group was the external help that most students turned to when they got stuck in the game. It seems that working in groups, or just having the ability to talk to peers when needed, is an external scaffold to game play that students are comfortable using for assistance. Students respond well to the peer feedback, and this keeps them engaged in game play by helping them work through obstacles collaboratively.

4.2.4. *Teacher as knower*

A final category included students who identified their "teacher as knower" and repeatedly asked Mrs. L for help. This group included students who first tried to work with the internal scaffolds of the game, still got stuck on a level, and immediately turned to Mrs. L to help them work through the challenge. These students rarely consulted with their group members, preferring instead to work exclusively with Mrs. L. Students in this category indicated that they went to Mrs. L because she could "explain it better" than anyone else or that they liked to problem-solve with her. In our focus group, no one solicited help from Mrs. L. but we did see a few examples of this from other groups, particularly in earlier levels of game play. It was clear early on that Mrs. L. did not have the quick answers to help students get through levels, but she was willing to pull up a chair and work alongside students to beat a level. One girl happened to be in a group where the other members all missed a day and she ended up being many levels ahead of her peers. Thus, because she did not feel she had a peer in her group who could help her with the game, she instead went straight to Mrs. L. for help.

Mrs. L. knew enough about the game to get through the early levels easily. Still, when students asked for help on these early levels, she did not give them a direct answer to their questions. Instead, she pressed their reasoning and encouraged them to try different options. Whether their attempts failed or succeeded, she then encouraged them to reflect on what they did to make sense of the failure or success. She spent a lot of time with students when they requested help in the early levels. As the levels got more complex, she tended to hover over a student and watch their game play decisions, but she asked fewer questions and interacted on the whole much less frequently with students. This could be one reason why more students did not call on her for additional help and instead chose another strategy—either within the game or asking a peer for help.

5. Discussion

While digital games for learning have been shown to support students' conceptual development in science, they have not been widely adopted in classrooms. This paper explores how students used the internal scaffolds in the game and external scaffolds provided by other knowers in the classroom to successfully play a game for learning physics. A key finding, while not surprising, was that not all students engage in game play in the same manner. Some students approached the game from a game-play orientation where they were simply focused on solving levels, while others approached the game from a sense-making orientation where they sought to truly understand the target concepts and formal representations.

In this study, most students started within the game to find the help they needed to advance in levels. When they ran into a need for help, their game-play orientation influenced who they turned to and for what reason. Whether they turned to their own ability to make sense of the game, requested help from a peer, or solicited Mrs. L's help, this classroom game play experience provided students with opportunities to locate the help they needed when they needed it. External resources, from paper to peers, were accessible by all students. Even the desk arrangement, from traditional rows in their typical class sessions to groupings of four for the game sessions, seemed to be an invitation for students to work together. Communication among peers was clearly encouraged.

These findings have important implications for how teachers design a game play learning environment in their classroom. Physically, different arrangements of furniture, particularly when computers are used, imply different kinds of participant structures. Teachers should consider what kind of access they want their students to have to external scaffolds, including their peers, during game play. Teachers also need to be aware of different orientations that students may adopt during game play and how their stance may influence how they are attending to the conceptual underpinnings of the game. This could mean that teachers take an active role during game play to facilitate connections between the game and science learning either through intentional discourse with groups or in whole-class instruction interspersed throughout the game play period. This kind of discourse can be invaluable to foster the necessary science thinking during game play. Research has shown that students can get very distracted while *doing* a particular activity and forget to attend to what they are supposed to be *understanding* [21]. In a game play, this same stance can happen, particularly for students who have a game play orientation like Preston and who are very concerned with beating the game, but not learning along the way. Teachers can play a role to facilitate the game-to-science content connection for students. Allowing students to work in groups, even if they are playing the game individually, encourages students to talk, which allows their thinking to become visible [22]. Teachers can use this talk as a formative assessment opportunity to identify ideas that need to be addressed and questions that can be asked to deepen student thinking [23]. Leveraging effective teaching practices with the affordances of digital games for learning can potentially lead to rich, meaningful student engagement with scientific ideas.

We believe this paper also has implications for the designers of future games for learning. In our study, we noted the crucial role that external scaffolds played in most students' game play experience. While some students relied exclusively on internal scaffolds and their own prior knowledge and resources, many students preferred to seek help from a peer or Mrs. L. We think game designers should consider the social capital present in most classrooms and leverage the discourse that will likely emerge when games are played in a traditional K-12 classroom. This could take the form of online discussion forums or embedded videos that serve as a virtual teacher and explain challenging concepts within the game.

This study has provided an examination of what DIG game play looked like in real classrooms. While much needs to be learned, this study showed that the DIG itself provided a goal (whether that goal was just to beat a level or a deeper goal of making sense of the character's motions and learning more about math and science in order to pass a level). Progress toward the goal was interrupted by challenges, also presented by the game. When these challenges proved too difficult to overcome, students sought help, and this is where the game extended its reach into the classroom context. Understanding more about when students are reaching for help, who they are turning to, and what kind of help they are seeking can help game designers and teachers learn how to design effective learning environments that support game play in secondary science classrooms. Essentially, while much research on the design of scaffolding in games for learning has focused on internal scaffolds, future research on external scaffolds may prove much more productive, with the added bonus of potentially even greater generalizability.

Acknowledgements

This material is based upon work supported by the National Science Foundation under Grant No. 1119290. Any opinions, findings, and conclusions or recommendations expressed in this material are those of the author(s) and do not necessarily reflect the views of the National Science Foundation.

Author details

Kara Krinks[1]*, Heather Johnson[2] and Douglas B. Clark[3]

*Address all correspondence to: kara.krinks@lipscomb.edu

1 Lipscomb University, Nashville, TN, USA

2 Vanderbilt University, Nashville, TN, USA

3 University of Calgary, Calgary, AB, Canada

References

[1] Pickering A, Papineau D. The mangle of practice: Time, agency and science. Nature. 1995;**377**(6549):491-491

[2] Lehrer R, Schauble L. Cultivating model-based reasoning in science education. In: Sawyer RK, editor. The Cambridge Handbook of the Learning Sciences. Cambridge, England: Cambridge University Press; 2006. pp. 371-388

[3] Duschl RA, Schweingruber HA, Shouse AW, editors. Taking Science to School: Learning and Teaching Science in Grades K-8. National Research Council Board on Science Education, Center for Education, Division of Behavioral and Social Sciences and Education. Washington, DC: The National Academies Press; 2007

[4] Clark DB, Sengupta P, Brady C, Martinez-Garza M, Killingsworth S. Disciplinary integration in digital games for science learning. International STEM Education Journal. 2015;**2**(2):1-21. DOI: 10.1186/s40594-014-0014-4. Available from: http://www.stemeducationjournal.com/content/pdf/s40594-014-0014-4.pdf

[5] Clark DB, Virk SS, Sengupta P, Brady C, Martinez-Garza M, Krinks K, Killingsworth S, Kinnebrew J, Biswas G, Barnes J, Minstrell J, Nelson B, Slack K, D'Angelo CM. SURGE's evolution deeper into formal representations: The siren's call of popular game-play mechanics. International Journal of Designs for Learning. 2016;**7**(1):107-146. https://scholarworks.iu.edu/journals/index.php/ijdl/article/view/19359

[6] Clark DB, Sengupta P, Virk SS. Disciplinarily-integrated games: Generalizing across domains and model types. In: Russell D, Laffey J, editors. Handbook of Research on

Gaming Trends in P-12 Education. Hershey, PA: IGI Global; 2016. pp. 178-194. DOI: 10.4018/978-1-4666-9629-7

[7] Ainsworth SE. DeFT: A conceptual framework for considering learning with multiple representations. Learning and Instruction. 2006;**16**(3):183-198

[8] Ainsworth S. The multiple representation principle in multimedia learning. In: Mayer R, editor. The Cambridge Handbook of Multimedia Learning. 2nd ed. New York, NY: Cambridge University Press; 2014. pp. 464-486

[9] De Koning B, Tabbers H, Rikers R, Paas F. Attention cueing as a means to enhance learning from an animation. Applied Cognitive Psychology. 2007;**21**(6):731-746

[10] Hegarty M, Kriz S, Cate C. The roles of mental animations and external animations in understanding mechanical systems. Cognition and Instruction. 2003;**21**(4):209-249

[11] Virk SS, Clark DB. Signaling in disciplinarily-integrated games: Challenges in integrating proven cognitive scaffolds within game mechanics to promote representational competence. In: Rud AG, Adesope O, editors. Contemporary Technologies in Education: Maximizing Student Engagement, Motivation, and Learning. Palgrave Macmillan; in press

[12] Wood D, Bruner JS, Ross G. The role of tutoring in problem solving. Journal of Child Psychology and Psychiatry. 1976;**17**(2):89-100

[13] Anderson J. Games and the development of students' civic engagement and ecological stewardship. In: Design and Implication of Educational Games: Theoretical and Practical Perspectives. New York: IGI Global; 2010. pp. 189-205

[14] Reiser BJ. Scaffolding complex learning: The mechanisms of structuring and problematizing student work. The Journal of the Learning Sciences. 2004;**13**(3):273-304

[15] Honey MA, Hilton M. Learning Science through Computer Games and Simulations. Washington DC: National Academies Press; 2011

[16] Chen CH, Law V. Scaffolding individual and collaborative game-based learning in learning performance and intrinsic motivation. Computers in Human Behavior. 2016;**55**:1201-1212

[17] Van Eaton G, Clark DB, Smith BE. Patterns of physics reasoning in face-to-face and online forum collaboration around a digital game. International Journal of Education in Mathematics, Science and Technology. 2015;**3**(1):1-13. Available from: http://ijemst.com/issues/3.1.1.Van_Eaton_Clark_Smith.pdf

[18] Braun V, Clarke V. Using thematic analysis in psychology. Qualitative Research in Psychology. 2006;**3**(2):77-101

[19] Miles MB, Huberman AM. Qualitative Data Analysis: An Expanded Sourcebook. Thousand Oaks, CA: Sage; 1994

[20] Glaser BG. The constant comparative method of qualitative analysis. Social Problems. 1965;**12**(4):436-445

[21] Kanter DE. Doing the project and learning the content: Designing project-based science curricula for meaningful understanding. Science Education. 2010;**94**(3):525-551

[22] Ambitious Science Teaching (AST). Discourse Primer. 2015. Available from: http://ambitiousscienceteaching.org/

[23] Furtak EM. The Feedback Loop: Using Formative Assessment Data for Science Teaching and Learning. In: CU Authors Book Gallery. 2016. https://scholar.colorado.edu/books/57/

Chapter 4

Worked Examples in Physics Games: Challenges in Integrating Proven Cognitive Scaffolds into Game Mechanics

Deanne Adams, Douglas B. Clark and Satyugjit Virk

Additional information is available at the end of the chapter

http://dx.doi.org/10.5772/intechopen.72152

Abstract

The current study is an exploratory study into the potential of integrating research on worked examples and physics games. Students were assigned to either a base version of a physics game, called the Fuzzy Chronicles, or assigned to a version of the Fuzzy Chronicles augmented with worked examples. Students in both conditions demonstrated significant gains on the pre-post-test, but students in the base game version demonstrated significantly greater gains than the students in the worked example version. The results from the current study reinforce results from other studies by our research group demonstrating how important it is that scaffolds based on multimedia research (a) do not over scaffold the student or promote passive, automatic behaviors, (b) do not excessively detract from the student's gameplay time, and (c) do not disrupt game cognition and flow.

Keywords: game-based learning, worked examples, science education, game design, scaffolds, physics

1. Introduction

The current study is an exploratory study into the potential of integrating research on worked examples into physics games to support deeper learning. The theory behind worked examples is that working memory, which is limited in capacity, is heavily utilized when solving problems, such as setting subgoals that require highly focused cognition [1]. Problem solving has been shown to consume cognitive resources that could be better allocated for learning, integration and consolidation. Worked examples free cognitive resources in working memory for learning, specifically, for the assimilation of new knowledge by generative processing [2].

Many research studies have shown the advantages of learning from correct worked examples [1, 3–10]. It is important however to be aware of the "expertise reversal effect" [11], which has shown through numerous studies that an instructional technique that benefits low prior knowledge learners can lose its benefit for, and in some cases be detrimental to, high prior knowledge learners.

Based on the research discussed above, worked examples can enhance learning in multimedia settings. The purpose of the current study was to examine the efficacy of an approach to integrating worked examples into physics learning games. The current study explores this question by comparing two conditions, one that integrates worked examples during into gameplay and one that does not, in order to explore four hypotheses:

1. Students who experienced worked examples of the Fuzzy Chronicles game to support the comprehension and interpretation of game play were expected to show increased pretest-posttest gains compared to students who did not experience worked examples.
2. Students who experienced worked examples would progress significantly farther in the game than the baseline group because they would have an enhanced understanding of gameplay and Newtonian physics concepts.
3. Students in the worked examples condition would display patterns in their gameplay behavior indicating deeper conceptual sophistication than the students in the non-worked examples condition.
4. These effects would be especially pronounced in low prior knowledge learners.

2. Methods

2.1. Participants

Participants consisted of 53 seventh grade students ($F = 24$, $M = 29$) from a Nashville area middle school. Twelve students were removed from the sample due to either missing the pretest (4), a day of gameplay (4), or the posttest (4). One student was also removed from the worked examples condition due to have a difference score over three standard deviations below the mean. This left a total of 40 students ($F = 17$, $M = 23$). A chi-squared analysis revealed equal numbers of males and females distributed between the two groups, X^2 (1, N = 40) = 0.102, $p = 0.75$.

2.2. Materials

The game used for this study was an updated version of the conceptually-integrated educational physics game known as *The Fuzzy Chronicles* [12–14]. During the game, the player takes on the role of the space pilot Surge who is trying to help a group of aliens known as Fuzzies. Detailed descriptions of Fuzzy Chronicles are provided in Refs. [15–17].

Similar to versions of Fuzzy Chronicles use in other studies, each game level in the version used for the current study takes place on a grid with the goal of navigating from a launching point to a goal portal/door while avoiding obstacles. Unlike the previous version, the version of the game used for this experiment only included one level of difficulty for each mission to encourage students to progress through educational content of the game. The levels were broken up into five concepts based on Newton's laws of motion and the game mechanics designed to teach those mechanics. The five concepts included: combination of forces (using rocket boosts), changes in mass (picking up Fuzzies), equal and opposite reactions in 1D (launching Fuzzies while not moving), equal and opposite reactions in 2D (launching Fuzzies while moving), and the law of inertia where an object in motion will stay in motion unless acted upon by an outside force (dropping Fuzzies).

There were 7 levels for each concept, making for a total of 35 levels. Each set of seven levels included one boss level that required the students to use all the skills they developed through the previous six levels to show mastery over the concept. For example, for the boss level for the concept of combining forces, students had to learn how to increase and decrease their speed as well as complete two 90° turns. For the experimental manipulation, the six non-boss levels in each set were grouped in pairs. The first level in each pair for the worked examples group was designed to be split into two isomorphic segments which are separated by a laser. During the first segment there is a preplaced trajectory and preplaced forces that take the ship from the starting launch point to the button that switches off the laser. The first segment thus demonstrates how to complete the target maneuver successfully, and serves as an example that students can use to help navigation from the laser button to the goal.

For the base game group, students are only given the second half of the level and are required to figure out how to complete the maneuver on their own using the basic tips given in the level introductory text. An example of the same level requiring students to move on a diagonal path for the control and the worked examples group can be found in **Figure 1**. For the second level in each pair, both the groups are given the same level which asks them complete a similar maneuver. A table with the level progression for the two groups can be found in **Table 1**.

The pretest and posttest consisted of 18 multiple choice questions. Eight of the items from the test dealt with changes in acceleration in 1D with subsets of those items dealing with: (2) the relationship between force and acceleration when mass is unchanged, (2) balanced forces, and (4) combining forces. Four of the items dealt with adding forces together to create 2D movement. Three of the test items were focused on the F = MA relationship, highlighting changes in mass. Finally, the last three questions dealt with the 3rd law of motion (for every action there is an equal and opposite reaction) and required the students to imagine how throwing an object would affect the speed and direction of another object.

In addition to addressing whether students can learn from the game, this study also examines students' perceptions of the game in terms of enjoyment, difficulty, cognitive effort, and perceived learning. To address this goal, a seven-item game evaluation survey with a five point Likert scale ranging from "1 Strongly Agree" to "5 Strongly Disagree" was developed.

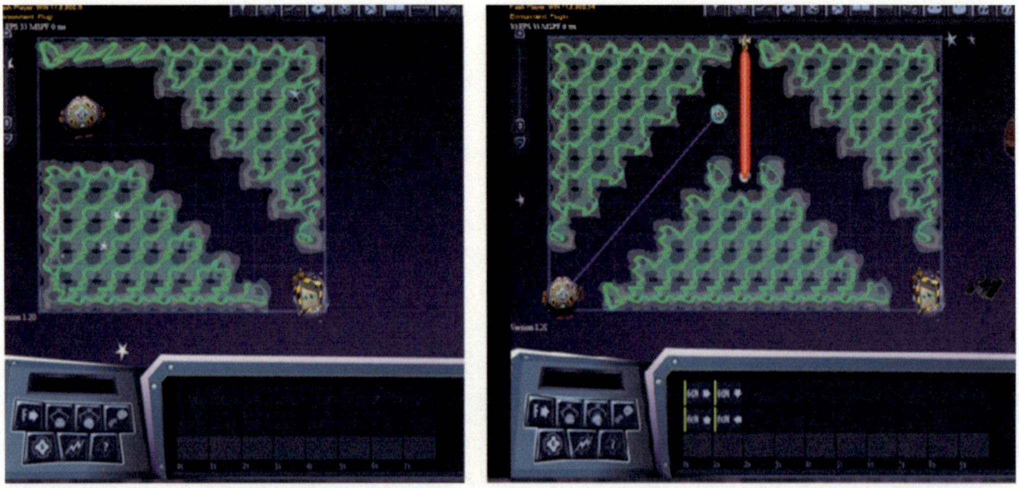

Figure 1. Example screen shots of a base game level (left) and the corresponding worked example level with the worked example in the first half of the level (right).

A second survey was administered to determine the student's level of video game experience. Students were asked how many hours a week they typically played video games, which video game consoles and portable video game devices their families owned and they played regularly, whether they played games on a desktop or laptop computer, and whether they regularly played games on a smartphone or tablet.

Finally, to assess the students' self-efficacy in terms of playing video and computer games, the video gaming subset of items from the Self-Efficacy in Technology and Sciences (SETS) instrument was used [18]. The instrument was included in order to determine whether self-efficacy while playing games could affect the student's play style or if the different versions of the game were more helpful to students with lower video game self-efficacy.

2.3. Procedure

Ten days prior to playing the game, students were given the pretest to determine prior knowledge levels related to the learning goals of the game. Students were given as much time as they needed in order to complete the test. All students were given two full class periods, (90 min) to play the game. On the first day of gameplay students were introduced to the WISE system and given instructions on how to set up their personal game accounts. Students were given hard copy instructions related to their version of the game. The first activity students had to complete in the game was the 15-item video game self-efficacy survey [18]. Upon completing the survey, students were then taken to the in-game tutorial which instructed students on how to place trajectory points, place forces on the timeline, set the direction and magnitude of each force, and how to combined forces.

Students then played the game at their own pace. Students were told that they could assist other students at their lab table, but were instructed not to touch the other student's computer.

http://dx.doi.org/10.5772/intechopen.72152

Concept	Base game	Worked example (WE)	Level
Adding forces horizontally	PS	WE	1
	PS	PS	2
Adding forces to create a diagonal	PS	WE	3
	PS	PS	4
90° turns	PS	WE	5
	PS	PS	6
Force boss mission			7
Adding mass	PS	WE	8
	PS	PS	9
Moving and stopping with mass	PS	WE	10
	PS	PS	11
Moving diagonally with mass	PS	WE	12
	PS	PS	13
Mass boss mission			14
Basic launching	PS	WE	15
	PS	PS	16
Launching a set speed	PS	WE	17
	PS	PS	18
Double launching	PS	WE	19
	PS	PS	20
Launching while stopped boss			21
45° deflection	PS	WE	22
	PS	PS	23
Deflection to straighten path	PS	WE	24
	PS	PS	25
Double Deflection	PS	WE	26
	PS	PS	27
Launching on the move boss mission			28
Basic dropping	PS	WE	29
	PS	PS	30
Mass changes with dropping	PS	WE	31
	PS	PS	32
Dropping and launching	PS	WE	33
	PS	PS	34
Dropping boss mission			35

Table 1. Level progression for base game and worked example groups.

The researchers gave minimal help in terms of game instructions and were instructed to refrain from giving any physics related assistance. The posttest was administered on Friday at the end of the week. Due to the alternating block scheduling, half of the students completed the test 1 day after finishing gameplay while the other half completed the test 2 days after finishing gameplay. After the posttest, students were asked to complete the game evaluation survey and the gaming experience survey.

3. Results

3.1. Learning gains results

Due to a typo on the pretest materials, one question relating to mass was removed from the analysis for both the pre and posttest. There were no significant differences between the two groups on the pretest t (38) = 0.95, p = 0.35. A repeated measures ANOVA examining testing session (pre vs. post) X group (base game vs. worked example), revealed that there was a significant main effect of testing session, $F(1, 36) = 73.30$, $p < 0.001$, $d = 1.27$, with students performing significantly better on the posttest. Students had a mean gain of 4.28 points (SD = 3.21). There was also a significant interaction between testing session and group, $F(1, 36) = 4.38$, $p = .04$, with the base game group showing significantly higher gains between the two testing sessions compared to the worked example group. **Table 2** contains the means and standard deviations for both groups for both the pretest and the posttest.

In addition to looking at overall learning gains, an additional repeated measures ANOVA was conducted to examine which concepts showed gains between the pre and posttest as well as significant differences in gains between the two conditions. For questions dealing with 1D and changes in acceleration, there was a significant main effect of testing session for 1D questions in general, F (1, 38) = 26.65, $p < 0.001$. Within those questions, there was a significant main effect for questions dealing with balanced forces, F (1, 38) = 19.37, $p < 0.001$, and questions dealing with combining forces, F (1, 38) = 19.08, $p < 0.001$. There was no significant difference for questions dealing with the relationship between force and acceleration, F (1, 38) = 0.06, p = 0.80. Students also had significant increases between the pre and posttest for questions dealing with adding forces for 2D movement, F (1, 38) = 38.75, $p < 0.001$, questions dealing with mass, F (1, 38) = 11.56, p = 0.002, and 3rd law throwing questions, F (1, 39) = 29.95, $p < 0.001$. Looking at pretest/posttest differences between the two groups, there was a significant interaction

Condition	Pretest	Posttest
	M (SD)	M (SD)
Base game	7.75 (2.61)	12.95 (3.72)
Worked examples	8.60 (3.03)	11.95 (3.94)
Total	8.18 (2.83)	12.45 (3.82)

Table 2. Means and Standard Deviations for Worked Examples and Base Game groups on Pretest and Posttest.

http://dx.doi.org/10.5772/intechopen.72152

between testing session and condition for questions dealing with dealing with 2D movement, F (1, 38) = 4.64, $p = 0.04$, with the base game group showing larger test gains compared to the worked examples group.

Although there was no significant benefit for providing worked examples in terms of learning gains, one possibility is that worked examples could have been more effective for lower prior knowledge players. Students were ranked as high and low prior knowledge learners using a median split (18 low, 22 high). A chi-squared analysis revealed that there was no significant difference in distribution of high and low ranked prior knowledge individuals between the two conditions, $X^2(1, N = 40) = 0.404$, $p = 0.53$. A MANOVA looking at gain scores between the pre and posttest showed no significant effect of prior knowledge ranking, F (1, 36) = 0.01, $p = 0.93$, as well as no significant interaction between condition and prior knowledge rank, F (1, 37) = 0.08, $p = 0.78$. This suggests that regardless of prior physics knowledge, as measured by our pretest, participants did significantly better when they were in the base game group.

3.2. Game play analysis

Highest game level completed was used to determine how much of the game and learning content was experienced by the students. A significant positive relationship was found between pretest score and highest level completed, $r(40) = 0.48$, $p = 0.002$. There was also a significant positive correlation between the highest level completed during the game and learning gains, $r(40) = 0.33$, $p = 0.04$ suggesting that progression further in the game also helped students learn more. The strongest correlation was between posttest score and highest level completed, $r(40) = 0.63$, $p < 0.001$. Together these results indicate that prior knowledge helped students to progress through the game and that progressing further also helped students improve their scores between the two testing sessions.

To examine whether differences in the number of levels completed affected learning differences between the two groups an ANOVA was conducted. There was significant difference between the two conditions in terms of the average highest level completed by the participants, F (1, 36) = 5.02, $p = 0.03$, with participants in the base game group tending to complete more levels ($M = 19.10$, $SD = 7.21$) than participants in the worked examples group ($M = 15.20$, $SD = 8.61$). Similar to the work of Sweller, this project was also interested in how the two conditions affected play style. To explore this question, the average number of attempts made for each level was computed for the levels that did not include a worked example and was the same across the two conditions (the second level in each pair). This was done for just the first 3 non-worked example levels since all participants had completed those levels. There were no significant differences between the two conditions for average overall attempts, t (31.24) = −.55, $p = 0.59$, although there was unequal variance between the two conditions with the worked examples group showing a larger variance in attempts ($M = 18.92$, $SD = 17.38$) compared to the base game group ($M = 16.43$, $SD = 10.50$).

3.3. Game satisfaction survey

The game satisfaction survey revealed no significant differences between the two groups in terms of whether students enjoyed playing the game ($p = 0.38$), found the game difficult to play ($p = 0.87$), found the interface confusing, ($p = 0.73$), would play again ($p = 0.27$), or reported working hard to complete game missions ($p = 0.57$). In terms of perceived physics learning, there were no significant differences between the two groups in whether they thought they learned a lot about physics from the game ($p = 0.21$) or thought that the game helped them understand physics lessons they had learned in class ($p = 0.19$).

The distribution of responses for all of the participants can be found in **Table 3**. In general, 65% of the students reported that they strongly agreed or agreed that they enjoyed playing the game while only one student said they disagreed. Over half of the students (60%) reported that they agreed or strongly agreed that they would like to play the game or games like it again in the future. In terms of mental effort, 80.4% reported that they worked hard to understand how to play the game and to complete the missions. For difficulty dealing with the game, 32.5% of the students either agreed or strongly agree that they found the game difficult to play, 30% said they neither agreed nor disagreed, while 37.5% said they did not agree with the game being difficult to play. Only 12.5% of the students found interacting with the game to be difficult while the majority were neutral (42.5%). For physics learning, the majority of students agreed to some degree that they learned about physics from playing the game (72.5%) and also thought that the game helped them understand physics lessons they had learned in class (72.5%).

3.4. Video game self-efficacy

The analyses focus on the video game self-efficacy subscale due to the lack of significant relationship between any of the learning measures and the computer gaming self-efficacy scale. There was no significant difference in reported video game self-efficacy scores between the two groups, $t(38) = -1.61$, $p = 0.12$. In addition, there was no significant interaction between game version and self-efficacy ranking (high vs. low created using a median split) on learning gains, $F\ (1, 36) = 0.01$, $p = 0.91$. In general, there was a significant positive relationship between

Question	Survey response				
	Strongly agree (%)	Agree (%)	Neutral (%)	Disagree (%)	Strong disagree (%)
Liked playing game	35.00	30.00	332.50	2.50	0
Play again	37.50	22.50	32.50	2.50	5.00
Worked hard	35.00	47.50	12.50	5.00	0
Game difficult to play	5.00	27.50	30.00	35.00	2.50
Interacting with game was confusing	2.50	10.00	42.50	35.00	10.00
Learned about physics	42.50	30.00	25.00	2.50	0
Helped understand class lessons	40.00	32.50	20.00	7.50	0

Table 3. Student survey responses.

video game self-efficacy and performance on the posttest, $r(40) = 0.33$, $p = 0.04$, although there was no significant relationship with either the pretest or learning gains. There was also a significant positive relationship between the video game self-efficacy score and the highest game level completed, $r(40) = 0.38$, $p = 0.02$, as well as a significant negative relationship with the number of attempts made on the non-worked example levels, $r(40) = -0.37$, $p = 0.02$. This suggests that students with higher self-efficacy were less likely to just use trial and error to solve the levels and completed more levels as a result. This is further supported by a significant positive relationship between perceived game difficulty, $r(40) = 0.44$, $p = 0.005$, and finding the game confusing, $r(40) = 0.51$, $p = 0.001$, with video game self-efficacy. Students with lower self-efficacy were more likely to agree that they found the game confusing to interact with and difficult to play. However, as students' self-efficacy increased they were more like to say they liked the game, $r(40) = -0.52$, $p < 0.001$, and would play the game again, $r(40) = -0.34$, $p = 0.03$. Most importantly, as students' self-efficacy increased, students were more likely to report that they learned physics from the game, $r(40) = -0.37$, $p = 0.02$, and that the game helped them understand lessons from class, $r(40) = -0.50$, $p = 0.001$.

4. Discussion

The highest level completed by each student correlated with how much game and learning content the students experienced while interacting with *The Fuzzy Chronicles*. The measured pretest score served as a positive indicator for how far students were projected to advance in the game, suggesting that students' prior knowledge was a significant component to the number of levels students were able to complete. Pretest scores did not differ between students in the worked example condition and the baseline condition, which suggests that the conditions were balanced in terms of prior knowledge. Students who completed more levels also showed higher learning gains.

Overall, the baseline condition proved to be more beneficial for both high and low prior knowledge learners compared to the outcome of student performance in the worked example condition. This finding was contradictory to our expectation that low prior knowledge participants would perform better after playing through the worked example condition. Highest level completed also correlated positively with students' post test scores, indicating that game play was correlated with increasing or facilitating understanding of game play content. The average highest game level completed differed significantly between the two conditions, with baseline students completing more levels than their counterparts in the worked level condition. This result was unexpected. If anything, we would have expected the same or less time to complete each level in the worked example condition. Instead, however, somehow the inclusion of the worked examples impeded level progression and actually had a negative effect on student performance overall. No significant difference was found between worked example and baseline conditions regarding the overall number of attempts, suggesting that game play behavior between conditions was equivalent even though the amount of level completion between conditions differed.

Self-efficacy of the students was analyzed to determine how individual judgments of performance ability affected game play. Self-efficacy differences were not seen between the two groups and self-efficacy did not appear to have a significant influence on pretest scores or learning gains. However, self-efficacy was revealed to have a significant positive relationship with posttest scores and highest game level completed indicating that the students' perception of their ability to understand the game while playing the game could have influenced their performance and engagement. Self-efficacy and number of attempts made on non-worked example levels were inversely related, suggesting that students with a higher degree of self-efficacy were less likely to approach the levels by trial and error. Students with lower self-efficacy scores were also more likely to perceive the game as confusing and difficult to play, whereas students with higher self-efficacy reported that they enjoyed the game and would play it again. Self-efficacy scores were also positively correlated with students indicating they learned physics concepts from the game and that game help to reinforce content from class. Self-efficacy may have influenced how students perceived the value of the game.

5. Conclusions

The findings show that students in both the base game condition and the worked example condition demonstrated significant pre-post gains. In an earlier study, we included a null condition with only a pretest and posttest but no intervention to determine whether a test/retest phenomenon could account for gains without an intervention [17]. That study showed that gains on the test could not be attributed simply to a test/retest effect. We therefore believe the significant pre-post gains in both conditions in the current study to demonstrate the overall efficacy of the approach enacted in Fuzzy Chronicles. Newtonian concepts can be very challenging for students, and are often resistant to instruction [19–20]. We are pleased that these findings are in line with the overarching disciplinary integrated ideas of the Fuzzy Chronicles.

The findings from the worked examples condition, however, do not support our hypotheses. While these findings are disappointing, we have encountered similar patterns in our prior research when we have attempted to integrate well-documented principles about scaffolding from psychology and cognitive science into digital games for learning. Our research has shown that when scaffolding functionality comes at the expense of time spent in gameplay, it can detract from game cognition and STEM learning [15, 21]. Adams and Clark's findings demonstrated that self-explanation prompts slowed students in the prompt condition so that the students completed significantly fewer levels and scored significantly lower on a learning assessment [15]. Looking across those studies and the current study, we note that the efficacy of implementing well-documented multimedia principles of learning in STEM games may not enhance learning if the design interferes with students' flow, cognitive load, or engagement with the game mechanics. In particular, results suggested that when the worked example approach is overemphasized in a STEM game, it can disrupt or possibly over scaffold learners, resulting in detrimental learning gains and gaming behavior. More specifically, across the current study and the other two studies to which we referred, we have repeatedly found that scaffolds based on multimedia research must not (a) over scaffold the student or promote passive, automatic behaviors, (b) excessively detract from the student's gameplay time, and (c) disrupt game cognition and flow, especially the pace of flow.

http://dx.doi.org/10.5772/intechopen.72152

This does not mean that these well-documented learning and scaffolding principles are incompatible in the design of digital games for learning. It simply means that refining designs that carefully integrate game mechanics and the design of the scaffolding requires careful iteration. In the case of the self-explanation functionality, for example, building on the findings of the Adams and Clark study, we redesigned the self-explanation functionality to adapt to students' level of sophistication in working with abstract prompts [15]. We also adjusted the timing and frequency of the prompts so that the prompts only appear after the player had successfully completed a level. By timing the prompts in this way, they were less intrusive and disruptive to players' gameplay, and more likely to be appropriate to the player's current progress and solution. Our research on this refined approach to self-explanation demonstrated significant pre-post learning gains as compared to a version without the self-explanation functionality [22]. Similarly, we believe that these findings imply the need to refine our approach to worked examples within gameplay rather than implying that worked examples are inappropriate for application in this setting. Essentially, we consider the findings as a reminder of the complexity of integrating scaffolds, an idea which has been developed in other educational contexts and applied to the context of digital games for learning.

Acknowledgements

The research reported here was supported by the Institute of Education Sciences, U.S. Department of Education, and the National Science Foundation through grants R305A110782 and 1119290 to Vanderbilt University. The opinions expressed are those of the authors and do not represent views of the Institute, the U.S. Department of Education, or the National Science Foundation.

Author details

Deanne Adams[1], Douglas B. Clark[2]* and Satyugjit Virk[3]

*Address all correspondence to: douglas.clark@ucalgary.ca

1 Vanderbilt University, Nashville, TN, USA

2 University of Calgary, Calgary, AB, Canada

3 Methinks Technologies, Palo Alto, CA, USA

References

[1] Catrambone R. The subgoal learning model: Creating better examples so that students can solve novel problems. Journal of Experimental Psychology: General. 1998;**127**(4):355-376

[2] Sweller J, Ayres P, Kalyuga S. Cognitive Load Theory. New York: Springer; 2011

[3] Kalyuga S, Chandler P, Tuovinen J, Sweller J. When problem solving is superior to studying worked examples. Journal of Educational Psychology. 2001;**93**:579-588

[4] McLaren BM, Lim S, Koedinger KR. When and how often should worked examples be given to students? New results and a summary of the current state of research. In: Proceedings of the 30th Annual Conference of the Cognitive Science Society. Austin: Cognitive Science Society; 2008. pp. 2176-2181

[5] Paas F, van Merriënboer J. Variability of worked examples and transfer of geometrical problem- solving skills: A cognitive-load approach. Journal of Educational Psychology. 1994;**86**(1):122-133

[6] Renkl A. The worked examples principle in multimedia learning. In: Mayer RE, editor. The Cambridge Handbook of Multimedia Learning. 2nd ed. New York: Cambridge University Press; 2014. pp. 391-412

[7] Renkl A, Atkinson RK. Learning from worked-out examples and problem solving. In: Plass JL, Moreno R, Brünken R, editors. Cognitive Load Theory. Cambridge: Cambridge University Press; 2010

[8] Schwonke R, Renkl A, Krieg C, Wittwer J, Aleven V, Salden R. The worked-example effect: Not an artifact of lousy control conditions. Computers in Human Behavior. 2009;**25**(2009):258-266

[9] Sweller J, Cooper GA. The use of worked examples as a substitute for problem solving in learning algebra. Cognition and Instruction. 1985;**2**:59-89

[10] Zhu X, Simon HA. Learning mathematics from examples and by doing. Cognition and Instruction. 1987;**4**(3):137-166

[11] Kalyuga S. Expertise reversal effect and its implications for learner-tailored instruction. Educational Psychology Review. 2007;**19**(4):509-539

[12] Clark DB. Designing Games to Help Players Articulate Productive Mental Models. Keynote commissioned for the Cyberlearning Research Summit 2012 hosted by SRI International, the National Geographic Society, and the Lawrence Hall of Science with funding from the National Science Foundation and the Bill and Melinda Gates Foundation. Washington, DC; 2012. http://www.youtu.be/xlMfk5rP9yI

[13] Clark DB, Sengupta P, Brady C, Martinez-Garza M, Killingsworth S. Disciplinary integration in digital games for science learning. International STEM Education Journal. 2015;**2**(2):1-21. DOI: 10.1186/s40594-014-0014-4. http://www.stemeducationjournal.com/content/pdf/s40594-014-0014-4.pdf

[14] Clark DB, Virk SS, Sengupta P, Brady C, Martinez-Garza M, Krinks K, Killingsworth S, Kinnebrew J, Biswas G, Barnes J, Minstrell J, Nelson B, Slack K, D'angelo CM. SURGE's evolution deeper into formal representations: The siren's call of popular game-play mechanics. International Journal of Designs for Learning. 2016;**7**(1):107-146. https://scholarworks.iu.edu/journals/index.php/ijdl/article/view/19359

[15] Adams DM, Clark DB. Integrating self-explanation functionality into a complex game environment: Keeping gaming in motion. Computers in Education. 2014;**73**:149-159

[16] Van Eaton G, Clark DB, Smith BE. Patterns of physics reasoning in face-to-face and online forum collaboration around a digital game. International Journal of Education in Mathematics, Science and Technology. 2015;**3**(1):1-13 http://ijemst.com/issues/3.1.1.Van_Eaton_Clark_Smith.pdf

[17] Martinez-Garza M, Clark DB. Data-mining epistemic stances from raw game-play data. International Journal of Gaming and Computer-Mediated Simulations; in press

[18] Ketelhut DJ. Assessing gaming, computer and scientific inquiry self-efficacy in a virtual environment. In: Annetta L, Bronack SC, editors. Serious Educational Game Assessment: Practical Methods and Models for Educational Games, Simulations, and Virtual Worlds. Sense Publishers; 2011. pp. 1-18. ISBN: 978-94-6091-329-7. DOI: 10.1007/978-94-6091-329-7

[19] Hestenes D, Wells M, Swackhamer G. Force concept inventory. The Physics Teacher. 1992;**30**:141-158

[20] Hestenes D, Halloun I. Interpreting the FCI. The Physics Teacher. 1995;**33**:502-506

[21] Virk SS, Clark DB. Signaling in disciplinarily-integrated games: Challenges in integrating proven cognitive scaffolds within game mechanics to promote representational competence. In: Rud AG, Adesope O, editors. Contemporary Technologies in Education: Maximizing Student Engagement, Motivation, and Learning. Palgrave Macmillan; in press

[22] Clark DB, Virk SS, Barnes J, Adams DM. Self-explanation and digital games: Adaptively increasing abstraction. Computers & Education. 2016;**103**:28-43. DOI: 10.1016/j.compedu.2016.09.010

Chapter 5

Game Engine Solutions

Anis Zarrad

Additional information is available at the end of the chapter

http://dx.doi.org/10.5772/intechopen.71429

Abstract

The rapid development of hardware and system platforms provides a favorable foundation for game development. A game engine overview is introduced first. Then, key features and available solutions of game engines are discussed. Typical products of game engines are shown and evaluated. Finally, we summarize our findings.

Keywords: game engine, game builder, 3D game, 2D game, engine architecture

1. Introduction

Game engines are a new way to develop high-quality games easily and rapidly without needing intensive programming skills and computational resources. Today, there is growing interest in game engines due to the rapid development of hardware and system platforms.

3D game engines help game companies reduce their cost, time, and manpower, since game developers can use the available functionalities of the engine. However, with over 100 engines available in the market for commercial and educational purposes, with a wide range of diverse features, each with its own performance levels, license types, and cost structures, selecting an appropriate game engine for a specific purpose becomes a challenging problem.

Game engine systems hit the headlines only a few years ago. Before the appearance of game engine technologies [1, 2], existing systems were often developed as virtual augmented reality systems to handle specific tasks such as NPSNET [3], DIVE [4], and SPLINE [5]. Thus, any modification required a hard change in the programming environment and architecture. As game engine technology matures and becomes more flexible, implementing a 3D environment will become easier. Despite these improvements, programming skills remain a concern, and usually sabotage developers who want to create complex environments.

Game developers usually have advanced programming skills and often block the system from user manipulation or misuse, which further complicates the task. Most game engines are limited to specific tasks and their features are typically coupled with specific game characteristics. Thus, developing extensions or modifications that force a game engine to adopt a new class of applications is almost impossible. Recently, many techniques and programming approaches such as virtual reality modeling language (VRML) [6], OpenGL [7], DirectX [6], X3D [6], and MPEG-4 [8] have been developed to build game applications. However, many of these new methods cannot provide native support to extend existing games. Systems like Bamboo [9] and JADE [10] have been proposed to overcome the limitations, brought about by the interconnected gaming engine and development platform, to offer a better solution.

In this chapter, we evaluate the latest released game engine from a variety of aspects like modularity, performance, usability, library, speed, and the realism. The readers will obtain an overview of game engine research, while becoming familiar with the recent developments and technologies in this area.

2. Existing game engine solutions

As technology moves forward, the need for multiuser game applications is getting more attractive. Before game engines, games were typically written as singular entities. Any modification to a game system required a collaborative effort from graphic designers, game designer, and 3D programmers to develop the required new scenario. Then, a player would need to stop and restart the game to reflect the modifications. Today, most researchers seek to build a gaming platform that facilitates the development and modification of such applications easily and rapidly without having intensive programming skills. For this reason, a game engine concept, which separates the engine and content development, arose in the mid-1990s. By the end of 1998, many games like ID Software's Quake III [11] Arena and Epic Games' 1998 Unreal [12] were designed with a game engine approach in mind.

Currently, there are many modern 3D engine games such as Unity engine [13], Unreal engine [12], Gamebryo engine [14], CryEngine [15], and Software's Source engine [16]. Choosing an adequate game engine depends on the type of game you want to create and the platform you want to use.

Unity engine [13] is a well-known game engine developed by Unity Technologies in Denmark; it is used to create interactive 3D content using JavaScript. Unity does not offer as many features as other tools like Unreal and CryEngine. Therefore, making excellent games without having a full license, which can cost nearly $2000, is very difficult. Unity integrates a custom rendering engine with an NVIDIA PhysX physics engine [17].

The Unreal engine [12] offers a completely royalty-free version with a powerful rendering engine and environment editor. It contains a variety of application programming interface (APIs) and tools to let you create a 3D virtual environment that closely resembles the real world. Unreal comes with partial documentation, while Unity and Source engines provide a complete documentation with detailed examples. Unreal Engine uses C++ while Unity uses C# or JavaScript.

Software's Source engine [16], developed by Valve Corporation, uses Half-Life 2 [18] and Portal. The overall system architecture is based on the popular modular architecture to provide independent updates. It uses an SDK source and a few GUI-based programs to handle complex functions.

Compared to the Unreal Engine [19] and CryENGINE [15], Emergent Game Technologies' Gamebryo engine [14] is used to develop a variety of games, ranging from action games to strategy games like Fallout 3, Empire Earth, and Civilization IV games. Gamebryo also supports a variety of platforms such as Windows, Wii, Xbox 360, and PlayStation.

CryEngine [15] is a game-development tool developed by Crytek Company. It facilitates event scripting, animation, and 3D object creation in the free CryEngine SDK. CryEngine is designed to support PC platforms and consoles, including Xbox 360 and PlayStation. Panda 3D [20] is a complete game and simulation engine with a very rich feature set. It uses advanced shaders and rendering effects, with different techniques. Torque 3D [21] is designed from the ground up to allow developers to make their game abstracted completely away from the underlying hardware. This represents a vast benefit for game developers, allowing them to work on game project without focusing on platform-specific requirements or restrictions.

Before the Game Engine, virtual environments were developed using dedicated systems to implement a specific scenario model. Some of the most well-known systems of this kind include DIVE [4], MASSIVE [22], NPSNET [3], SPLINE [5], and VLNET [23]. These systems focus on specific applications to reduce the overall implementation complexity. The major problems stem from the fact that systems are tightly coupled in terms of implementation. Consequently, any modifications in the application require modifications in the supporting architecture, which occurs because the complexity property is gained through the combination of the internal architecture with the specific application functionalities.

Bamboo [9] uses a microkernel-based architecture to separate the system elements from the kernel in such a way that the add, remove, and modify functions can be performed at runtime. Unfortunately, this highly accredited approach incurs a great deal of complexity, particularly in terms of facilitating communication between components written in different languages. Oliviera et al. [10] developed a Java Adaptive Dynamic Environment (JADE) based on Java architecture. It consists of a lightweight cross-platform kernel that permits system evolution at runtime. The adoption of JADE does not provide an efficient solution to problems that arise from extending virtual reality applications.

In [24], the authors developed the Virtual Environment Mark-up Language (VEML) based on the nonlinear story [24] concept defined by Szilas [25] to build virtual reality applications. This model allows the progress of the story, during the simulation, to be specified independently from the implementation of the 3D object geometry and from the 3D-environment programming.

3. Game engine architecture and principles

An engine is an essential part of a game; it influences the structure and the organization of game graphics, configuration files, and all other inputs such as user inputs, maps, and sounds. **Figure 1** shows a game engine component diagram in a game development context.

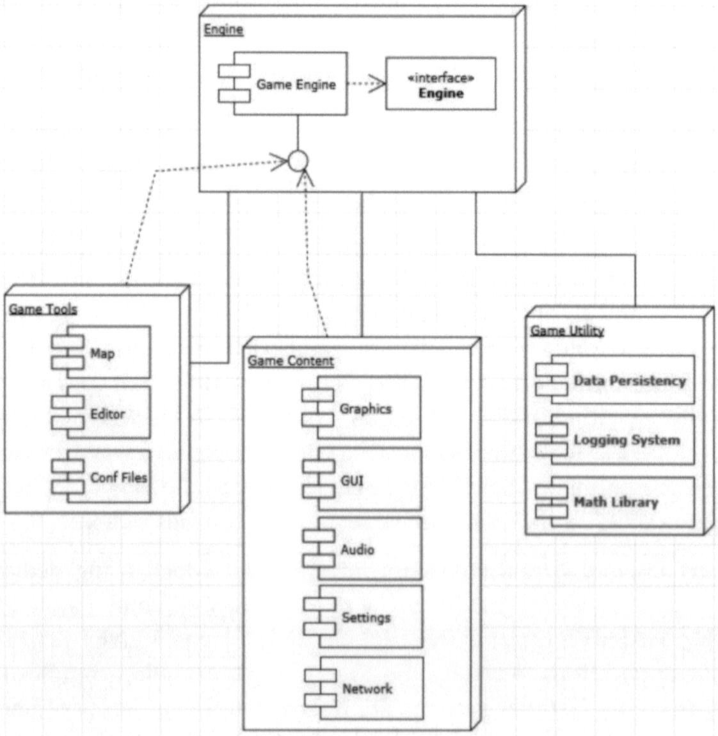

Figure 1. Game engine component diagram.

Game tools, Game Utility, and Game Content are also vital components of a game. Game tools refer to all the tools used to develop a game, such as the character editor, ability editor, configuration files, and game map. Game content refers to all related features in any game. Graphics and audio files are the most important type of data. Network components allow multiple users to connect to each other and access game data. Utility components define all needed data types, message formats, and required files, with respect to the game characteristics. The game tool component plays a bridge role between Game content and the Game engine components.

Currently, no specific standard architecture has been developed in the literature. **Figure 2** shows a detailed game engine architecture. We consider only some features that are most likely important.

Manager components are essential to all games. A physical manger is important for games dependent on physical reactions. For example, car racing needs physical laws, but this is not so important for a card matching game. However, the input manager and the GUI system are important, even for a simple game, to process the user input. The scene manager is required to organize and control the scene content and monitor the game's logic. The game loop is used to control an infinite loop that keeps the game running over-and-over again. The network component is responsible for managing user connections and game data access. The AI System is a special module designed and written by software engineers with specialized knowledge.

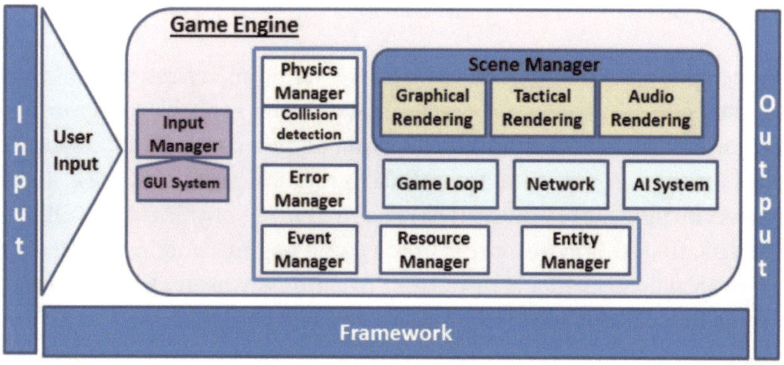

Figure 2. Detailed game engine architecture.

Additional manager components, which depend on programmer and coding approaches like game states, Rule engine, and Speech recognizer, may be needed at specific times.

Designing a game engine solution to fit all game purposes is a challenging problem for an engine developer. There is a need to define key design principles and provide advice to create successful engines. The five principles listed in this section and referred with the acronym MULER are modularity, usability, library resources, efficiency, rendering effects, and picture quality. Each of these features is detailed below and will be used to evaluate available existing popular game engines in Section 4.

3.1. Modularity

Game engine should be implemented via several unique modules. Each manager component is independent much like a single functional unit. Engine developers should invest time in implementing a modular game architecture to reduce the system complexity and offer robustness. Testing process and maintenance becomes easier for the programmer when needed. As shown in the proposed architecture in **Figure 2**, the principle of modularity is satisfied and each component has a unique function.

3.2. Usability

Engine developers are the main actors; therefore, usability of a game engine is an important criterion to evaluate. As defined by [26], usability includes ease of learning, efficiency of use, memorability, error frequency and severity, and subjective satisfaction. Ease of learning and efficiency of use are the main aspects of usability. We evaluated available tutorials, project examples, forum communities, programming languages, and technical support. Information is retrieved from the engine's website. For efficiency of use, we investigated game engine application editors including map editor, GUI editor, animation editor, programming editor, and scene editor. We considered the Debugger as part of the programming editor. This option helps a developer to stop applications at specific lines of the source code and check values. This is helpful for developers because they can easily find the error and fix it.

3.3. Library resources

3D game engine systems are implemented by assembling many resource libraries together. The engine developer selects a game engine based on its available programming resource libraries. A common library for a simple 3D game engine consists of 3D graphics, physics, collision detection, input/output, audio, AI, 3D graphics, and a network library. Modern game engines can include more powerful libraries including physics laws, collision detection, and special effects. In addition, resources in the game engine contain project examples, user guides, and tutorials; these available resources are extremely useful for a game developer. We believe this is the most useful criterion for game engine comparison

3.4. Efficiency

Game engine efficiency refers to the successful use of all inputs and available resources to produce a given game output. It includes memory allocation, CPU usage, rendering process, and other features. We may produce an efficient engine but not an efficient game. This is because the game workflow is designed by the game creator, which has an impact on the game efficiency. Resource managers play an important role for this criterion. It loads the game data and files from disk into the memory to be used for rendering and game scenario creation.

Game designers should consider the reusability and modularity concepts to improve engine efficiency. Single resources can be used to create many instances.

3.5. Rendering effects and picture quality

The rendering process produces 3D animated graphics using specific techniques like rasterization [27], image-based rendering (IBR) [28], ray tracing [27], or any different technique. These techniques are valuable for 3D game engines.

Unlike 2D graphics, the implementation of a 3D graphics rendered requires advanced programming and 3D modeling skills. 3D graphics have countless rendering algorithms from extremely fast to extremely slow. Hardware and software rendering have an impact on the acceleration of the 3D graphics. Most available engines render a scene using the default settings. These features may be good for a quick preview, but not for production work. With modern engines, you can get a very sharp, clear, and high-quality output; this comes at the price of increased rendering time even though the overall final output will be much better.

4. Game engine evaluation

In this section, we evaluate the selected game engines based on the most important principles MULER: modularity, usability, library resources, efficiency, rendering effects, and picture quality. Currently, there are 376 game engines listed in the DevMaster.net database [29]. We set a game engine selection filter based on the following criteria:

- Game engines that lack important features are excluded.
- No high-quality games are implemented.
- No recent update or released versions.

We studied all game engines listed in DevMaster. Only 20 game engines are selected for evaluation. **Table 1** shows the details of the selected engines.

Our goal is to provide a complete evaluation of game engines. Developers want to know which game engine to invest on. Selected engines will have an impact on the game output. **Table 2** will help users to pick the optimal 3D game engine based on their purpose and needs.

The evaluation criteria for each principle are defined as follows:

- Modularity: from "0" to "3" to indicate the modularity level. "0" means modularity is not considered in the game engine architecture.
- Usability: from "1" to "5" to indicate the usability level. "5" represents complete user satisfaction. Score assignment is based on user reviews and forum community responses.
- Library resources: limited resources, acceptable resources, very rich resources.
- Efficiency: poor, good, excellent.
- Rendering effects and picture quality: poor, good, excellent.

4.1. Discussion and general findings

Unity 3D has a poor usability because GUI and AI editor are not implemented. There is also no real demo or technical support provided in the last release. Unity 3D implements a very basic PhysX module, which affects the performance and rendering aspects of the system. Similarly, Jmonkey [30] has a poor performance for heavy games because NiftyGUI library used a JavaBuilder pattern for creating controls on the screen, this way preventing for subclassing elements, which renders the code unreadable. Many users complain about Jmonkey's "very slow engine." Nevertheless, the system-provided documentation covers almost every topic.

Shiva3D's engine can be deployed in more than 10 platforms. It is a quite powerful engine with many features. The dynamic and static shadow management on a custom textured model needs more enhancement, especially for real-time games. Marmalade engine has a poor rendering process since the engine uses limited animation and a mesh library.

One of the best engines available in the community is Unigine. It has a good performance for large-scale games. It also has a full-fledge rendering engine with the latest implemented features (full-dynamic lighting, DX11 tessellation). Recently, a 3D planet system with geographic coordinates is integrated into the engine. Rendering and physics features are comparable to engines like CryEngine and Unreal. However, Unigine's lack of tutorial and example availability is a negative. We cannot decide on the modularity score due to missing information.

Game engine	Language	Supported platforms	2D	3D	License/price
Unity 3D	C# and JavaScript	**Desktop**: Windows, Mac OS, Linux **Mobile**: Android, IOS,	No	Yes	Free for Indie version
Jmonkey Engine	Java, Python, and JavaScript	**Desktop**: Windows, Mac OS, Linux **Mobile**: Android	No	Yes	Free
Marmalade	C/C++	**Desktop**: Windows, Linux, **Mobile:** Android, and IOS	—	Yes	Commercial
LibGDX	Java	**Desktop:** Windows, Mac OS, Linux **Mobile:** Android, IOS, Blackberry, HTML5	Yes	Yes	Free
Panda3D	Python and C++	**Desktop**: Windows and Mac OS	No	Yes	Free/open source
Blender	C/C++, Python	**Desktop**: Windows, Mac OS, Linux	No	Yes	Free
Unreal engine	C++, VisualScripting	**Desktop**: Windows, Mac OS, Linux, HTML5 **Mobile:** NA			Free/open source
CryEngine	C/ C++	**Desktop**: Windows, and Mac OS **Mobile:** Android, and IOS,	No	Yes	Unspecified
Crystal Space	C/C++, Python	**Desktop**: Windows, Mac OS, Linux **Mobile:** NA	—	Yes	Free
CopperCube	JavaScript, Flash, WebGL	**Desktop**: Windows, Mac OS **Mobile:** Android	Yes	Yes	Free
Leadwerks	C++, C#, VB.Net, Python	**Desktop**: Windows **Mobile:** NA			$99.95
Raydium	C/C++	**Desktop:** Windows, MacOS, Linux **Mobile:** IOS	No	Yes	Free
SunBurn	C#	**Desktop:** Windows **Mobile:** Windows Phone	No	Yes	$ 150
UDK	C/C++	**Desktop**: Windows **Mobile:** iOS	No	Yes	$99.00
Corona SDK 61	Lua	**Desktop**: Windows, Mac OS **Mobile:** iOS; Android; Windows Phone	Yes	No	Free
3D Game Studio	C++, C#	**Desktop:** Windows **Mobile:** NA	Yes	Yes	Free for the basic version
Unigine	C/C++	**Desktop:** Windows, and Linux **Mobile:** iOS; Android	No	Yes	$ 25,000
Torque3D	C++, TorqueScript	**Desktop:** Windows, Mac OS, and Linux **Mobile:** NA	—	Yes	Free/open source
ShiVA	C/C++, Lua	**Desktop:** Windows, Mac OS, and Linux **Mobile:** iOS; Android; Windows Phone, and Blackberry	—	Yes	Free for personal use
Irrlicht	C++, C#, VB.Net	**Desktop:** Windows, Mac OS, and Linux **Mobile:** iOS; Android;	Yes	Yes	Free

Table 1. Details of the selected game engines.

Game engine	Modularity	Usability	Efficiency	Library resources	Rendering effects and picture quality
Unity 3D	1	4	Acceptable	Acceptable resources	Acceptable
Jmonkey Engine	3	2	Poor	Rich resources	Acceptable
Marmalade	1	1	Poor	Limited resources	Poor
LibGDX	2	3	Acceptable	Rich resources	Acceptable
Panda3D	3	4	Acceptable	Acceptable resources	Excellent
Blender	3	5	Acceptable	Rich resources	Acceptable
Unreal engine	4	4	Excellent	Rich resources	Excellent
CryEngine	3	5	Excellent	Rich resources	Excellent
Crystal Space	5	1	Poor	Acceptable resources	Acceptable
CopperCube	2	3	Poor	Limited resources	Poor
Leadwerks	4	1	Excellent	Acceptable resources	Excellent
Raydium	1	1	Poor	Acceptable resources	Acceptable
SunBurn	1	2	Good	limited resources	Good
UDK	2	5	Excellent	Very rich resources	Excellent
Corona SDK 61	1	4	Good	Acceptable resources	Acceptable
3D Game Studio	1	4	Good	Acceptable resources	Poor
Unigine	—	4	Excellent	Very rich resources	Excellent
Torque3D	2	3	Good	Acceptable resources	Acceptable
ShiVA	3	3	Poor	Acceptable resources	Good
Irrlicht	—	2	Good	Acceptable resources	Good

Table 2. Game engine evaluation based on MULER.

Unreal engines handle shading in an efficient way by using a DirectX 11 pipeline that includes deferred shading, global illumination, lit translucency, and postprocessing. It also integrates NVIDIA technologies. The physics management component in the CryEngine is excellent. The game engine has built-in rendering paths for OpenGL and DirectX 8/9, allowing to support Linux, Apple, and Microsoft operating systems. The various rendering paths also allow more hardware to be supported by the engine.

SunBurn has a basic physics module and only support windows and windows phone 7. It uses flexible rendering and provides both advanced deferred rendering and traditional forward rendering, allowing you to choose the ideal technique for your project. It does not have a network or AI library. Raydium does not offer a GUI editor, scene editor, and animation editor. It also does not have mapping or AI modules implemented.

UDK [31] is a complete professional development framework. It includes a set of features packed with power and ease of use. UDK has a very easy interface while offering power and flexibility. The rendering process is exceptional due to the use of a multithreaded rendering system. UDK makes the most beautiful graphic games in mobile devices because UDK can transform global illumination to texture.

In Panda 3D [20], the C++ documentation is lacking compared to the Python documentation. It uses C++ to solve the performance issue. Projects developed with Torque can be easily ported to other operating systems and platforms as explained by Nilson and Söderberg [32]. Blender [30] engine is built into an exceptional 3D modeler, which means that "importing" models into your game is as simple as playing it. The Python scripts and game logic are very powerful and easy to use. Blender has a layered architecture including utilities, kernel, computer, render, UI, and applications. LibGDX [33] is mainly developed for 2D mainly with cross-platform tool so you can make games for Windows, Linux, OS X, HTML, Android, and iOS. 3D game Studio engine offers allow developers to build a complete game without knowing C++. In addition, the engine has an integrated 2D engine. However, the engine cannot be used to developed large-scale game with excellent graphics quality.

Irrlicht [34] uses a low-quality rendering model. It supports a wide range of 3D/textures formats. Irrlicht has a very large and friendly community. CrystalSpace [35] requires Cygwin when compiling on windows. Thus, it is too hard for developers to set up modeler and management components. Compared to other engines, CrystalSpace and Jmonkey [34] seem to have the lowermost usability level.

Leadwerks has a very limited support that affects its usability principle. Performance is enhanced with the last release, Leadwerks Game Engine 5. It now decouples the game loop from the renderer. Similarly, usability in CopperCube is not satisfied, the option to drag and move objects into the space is not implemented, and JavaScript API should be extended to include more advanced features.

5. Conclusion

A comparison table shows that there is no best game engine for all games. Each game engine has its own advantages and disadvantages. Cleary Shiva3D and LibGDX are the best in terms of platform deployment criterion. It can be deployed in more than eight platforms. However, when we consider performance and rendering efficiency criteria, UDK, CryEngine, and Unigin are the clear winners.

If you are a developer with mixed skills, then try out UDK and Unreal Engine 4. Making a good game is not risked by choosing a wrong engine. They are just a tool. In my opinion, the best way to find your suitable tool is to play around with the engine and then decide.

Author details

Anis Zarrad

Address all correspondence to: anis.zarrad@gmail.com

Prince Sultan University, Riyadh, Saudi Arabia

References

[1] Cowan B, Kapralos B. A survey of frameworks and game engines for serious game development. In: Advanced Learning Technologies (ICALT): IEEE 14th International Conference on Greece; 2014

[2] Jacobson J, Lewis M. Game engine virtual reality with caveut. IEEE Computer. 2005; **38**(4):79-82

[3] Michael RR, Macedonia M, Zyda J, David R, Pratt R. NPSNET: A network software architecture for large scale virtual environments. Presence: Teleoperators and Virtual Environments (USA). 1994;**3**:256-287

[4] Hagsand O. Interactive MUVEs in the DIVE system. IEEE Computer. 1996;**3**(1):30-39

[5] Waters R, Anderson D, Barrus J, Brogan D, Casey M, McKeown S, Nitta T, Sterns I, Yerazunis W. Diamond Park and Spline: A Social Virtual Reality System with 3D Animation, Spoken Interaction, and Runtime Modifiability TR-96-02a November; 1996

[6] Xie W, Yanrong L. The virtual furniture store constrution based on VRML/X3D. In: 2012 International Conference on Computer Science and Information Processing (CSIP), China. 2012

[7] Lee H, Baek N. Implementing OpenGL ES on OpenGL. In: ISCE '09: IEEE 13th International Symposium on Consumer Electronics, Japan; 2009

[8] Battista S, Casalino F, Lande C. MPEG-4: A multimedia standard for the third millennium 1. IEEE MultiMedia. 1999;**6**(4):74-83

[9] Magerko B, Laird JE. Building an interactive drama architecture. In: 1st International Conference on Technologies for Interactive Digital Storytelling and Entertainment, Germany. 2003. pp. 24-26

[10] Oliveira M, Crowcroft J, Slater M. Component framework infrastructure for virtual environments. In: Proceedings of the third international conference on Collaborative virtual environments. USA. 2000. pp. 139-146

[11] Mamei M, Zambonelli F. Motion coordination in the Quake 3 arena environment: A field-based approach. In: International Workshop on Environments for Multi-Agent Systems, 2004. pp. 264-278

[12] Lewis J, Brown D, Cranton W, Mason R. Simulating visual impairments using the unreal engine 3 game engine, In: IEEE 1st International Conference on Serious Games and Applications for Health (SeGAH), Portugal. 2011. pp. 45-53

[13] Polančeć D, Mekterović I. Developing MOBA games using the unity game engine. In: 2017 40th International Convention on Information and Communication Technology, Electronics and Microelectronics (MIPRO), Croatia. 2017

[14] Emergent: Gamebryo Game Engine, Available from: http://www.emergent.net/

[15] Juarez A, Schonenberg W, Bartneck C. Implementing a low-cost CAVE system using the CryEngine2. Entertainment Computing. 2010;**1**:157-164

[16] Kovacs D, Mitchell J, Drone S, Zorin D. Real-time creased approximate subdivision surfaces with displacements. IEEE Transactions on Visualization and Computer Graphics. 2010;**16**(5):742-751

[17] Zhonghua L, Sankaranarayanan G, Deo D, Chen D, Suvranu D. Towards physics-based interactive simulation of electrocautery procedures using PhysX. In: IEEE Haptics Symposium, USA. 2010. pp. 125-137

[18] Cricenti L, Branch A. A generalised prediction model of first person shooter game traffic. In: IEEE Local Computer Networks, LCN 34th Conference, Switzerland. 2009

[19] Ferreyros C, Wendorf M, Juárez P. Developing a Videogame Using Unreal Engine Based on a Four Stages Methodology. Peru: IEEE ANDESCON; 2016

[20] Goslin M, Mine MR. The Panda3D graphics engine. Computer Journal. 2004;**37**(10): 112-114

[21] Shiratuddin F, Fletcher D. Development of southern Miss's innovation and commercialization park virtual reality environment. Proceeding Sixth Conference on Construction Applications of Virtual Reality, USA; 2006. pp. 278-285

[22] Benford S, FahlŽn L. A spatial model of interaction in large virtual environments. In: Proceedings of the 3rd conference on European Conference on Computer-Supported Cooperative Work, Italy. 1993. pp. 109-124

[23] Pandžić S, Tolga K, Elwin L, Thalmann N, Thalmann D. A flexible architecture for virtual humans in networked collaborative virtual environments. Proceedings Eurographics, Hungary; 1997. pp. 177-188

[24] Boukerche A, Duarte D, Araujo R, Andrade L, Zarrad A. A novel solution for the development of collaborative virtual environment simulations in large scale. Ninth IEEE International Symposium on Distributed Simulation and Real Times DS-RT Proceedings, Canada; 2005. pp. 86-97

[25] Szilas N. IDtension: A narrative engine for interactive drama. In: Proceedings of TIDSE'03. Frauenhofer: IRB Verlag; 2003

[26] Williges T, Hartson R. The effectiveness of usability evaluation methods: Determining the appropriate criteria. In: Proceedings of the Human Factors and Ergonomics Society 43rd Annual Meeting, USA. 1999. pp. 1090-1094

[27] Davidovič T, Engelhardt T, Georgiev I, Slusallek P, Dachsbacher C. 3D rasterization: A bridge between rasterization and ray casting. Proceedings of Graphics Interface, Canada; 2012. pp. 201-208

[28] Lai J, Chen C, Chien Y. Architecture design and analysis of image-based rendering engine. In: 2011 IEEE International Conference on Multimedia and Expo (ICME), Spain

[29] DevMaster.net. Game Development. 2017. Available from: http://devmaster.net

[30] Navarro A, Vicente Pradilla J, Rios O. Open source 3D game engines for serious games modeling. Book Chapter ISBN 978-953-51-0012-6, March, 2012

[31] Shiratuddin M, Thabet W. Virtual office walkthrough using a 3D Game Engine. International Journal of Design Computing. 2002;**4**(10):24-28

[32] Nilson B, Söderberg M. Game engine architecture. Mälardalen University 2007. Available from: http://www.idt.mdh.se/kurser/cd5130/jgms/2007lp4/report9.pdf

[33] Scacchi W. Practices and technologies in computer game software engineering. IEEE Software. 2017;**35**(1):110-116

[34] Rocha RV, Rocha RV, Araújo RB. Selecting the best open source 3D games engines. In: Proceedings of SBGames. 2010

[35] DeChiara R, Erra U, Andreoli R, Scarano V. Interactive 3D environments by using videogame engines. In: 17th International Conference on Information Visualisation. Vol. **1**(2). 2013. pp. 515-520

Chapter 6

Multiplayer Disciplinarily-Integrated Agent-Based Games: SURGE Gameblox

Douglas B. Clark, Paul Medlock-Walton,
Raúl Boquín and Eric Klopfer

Additional information is available at the end of the chapter

http://dx.doi.org/10.5772/intechopen.73051

Abstract

Early work on disciplinary-integrated games (DIGs) focused on Cartesian time-series analyses as the formal representations through which the game communicates challenges and opportunities to the players as well as the formal representations through which the players control the game. In our earlier work, we explored the potential generalizability of the DIG genre in terms of hypothetical examples in physics, biology, chemistry, and the social sciences as well as in terms of multiple model types including constraint-system analyses, system dynamics models, situation-action models, and agent-based models. In particular, Sengupta and Clark and Krinks, Sengupta, and Clark explored the integration of computational modeling, physical models, and Cartesian models. Building on that work, we began outlining theoretical frameworks and arguments highlighting the affordances of moving DIG design more deeply into agent-based modeling. In the current paper, we present the actual design process and rationale through which we developed prototypes of two multiplayer DIG prototypes with agent-based models as the mode of control wherein players create, trade, and elaborate on one another's code as part of gameplay. We close with a discussion of implications for the design of disciplinary-integrated games leveraging agent-based modeling as the focal formal representation for communication and control.

Keywords: science education, science as practice, modeling, agent-based modeling, disciplinary-integrated games, digital games

1. Introduction

Over the past decade, digital games have been the object of substantial research and interest for approaching the difficult task of reorganizing students' conceptual resources [1–3]. Developing environments from Science as Practice perspectives [4–7] that engage students in modeling would seem to hold great promise. Toward these goals, we have proposed Disciplinarily-Integrated Games as one such approach [8–9]. As proposed in Clark et al. [8], disciplinary integration is an approach to designing games in terms of a science as practice perspective. More specifically, disciplinary integration can be thought of in terms of "model types" and "modeling strategies" [10], which Collins and colleagues have termed "epistemic forms" and "epistemic games" in earlier work [11–13]. Collins and colleagues argue that the professional work of scientists can be understood in terms of model types (epistemic forms) that are the target structures guiding scientific inquiry and modeling strategies (epistemic games) that are the sets of rules and strategies for creating, manipulating, and refining those model types.

DIGs are designed to engage students more deeply in specific modeling and representational practices of developing, interpreting, manipulating, and translating across specific model types. Essentially, all DIGs have the following characteristics: (a) formal representations for controlling the game, (b) formal representations for communicating challenges and opportunities, (c) a phenomenological representation presenting the phenomenon being modeled, (d) an intermediate aggregating representation, and (e) game mechanics and goals focused on engaging the player in interpreting, creating, modifying, and translating across these formal and phenomenological representations.

Early work on DIGs focused on Cartesian time-series analyses as the formal representations for communicating challenges and opportunities as well as the formal representations through which players control the game [8–9]. To have value, the proposed DIG genre must be generalizable. In our earlier work, we explored this claim of generalizability in terms of hypothetical examples of DIGs in physics, biology, chemistry, and the social sciences as well as in terms of multiple model types including time-series analyses with Cartesian formal representations, constraint-system analyses with Cartesian formal representations, and other model types and non-Cartesian formal representations such as system dynamics models, situation-action models, and agent-based models [14]. In particular, Sengupta and Clark [15] and Krinks et al. [16] explored the integration of computational modeling, physical models, and Cartesian models. Clark et al. [17–19] outlined theoretical frameworks and arguments highlighting the affordances of moving DIG design more deeply into agent-based modeling as the formal representational form through which the game communicates challenges and goals to players as well as the formal representational system through which players control the game. In the current paper, we present the actual design process through which we developed prototypes aligning with those ideas for SURGE Gameblox. More specifically, we introduce and describe the design process through which we developed two multiplayer DIG prototypes with agent-based models as the mode of communication and control wherein players create, trade, and elaborate on one another's code as part of gameplay.

2. Technical design

2.1. Gameblox and Starlogo integration to create hybrid SURGE Gameblox

The current project, which we call SURGE Gameblox, is built upon the integration of two pre-existing robust programming environments for students. This process of integration to create the hybrid SURGE Gameblox environment was funded by the SURGE grant from the US National Science Foundation. Essentially, when the project began, there were two preexisting platforms that each had pieces of functionality that were required for the creating the models that we wanted students to modify. These two environments, Gameblox and Starlogo Nova, had been created under prior funding by the MIT Scheller Teacher Education Program. Gameblox is a blocks-based programming language that makes it easy to create 2D multiplayer games. Gameblox is targeted toward making games with a moderate number of sprites, often using a physics engine for games like platformers and mobile experiences including scavenger hunts and participatory models. Gameblox was not built to handle large models with hundreds of agents running simultaneously. Gameblox, however, already has a robust infrastructure for creating multiplayer games. There are blocks that allow for variables to be shared across multiple computers and updated in real time, procedures that can be called on a remote machine, and the ability to create separate instances of a game, allowing independent games to occur between multiple computers.

Starlogo Nova allows students to create 3D agent-based models by programming breeds using a blocks-based language. These agent-based models allow hundreds or thousands of agents to move simultaneously, with each following its own sets of programming instructions. While Starlogo Nova provides a system for handling the complex systems well, it did not have a way to easily connect two models together over a network.

After evaluating the complexity of integrating the two platforms, it was decided to take the 3D renderer from Starlogo and integrate it into the multiplayer framework of Gameblox to allow models to work across multiple computers.

2.2. Collaboration

When the project began, neither Gameblox nor Starlogo had support for allowing more than one user to edit a project at a time. Through a separate funding source, Gameblox was already working on multi-user collaboration in the editor, where two people can edit a project simultaneously, like Google docs. For the SURGE Gameblox project, we set up a separate server that contains this code, which allows users to work on only one block page. Gameblox projects are organized into block pages, similar to how large coding projects are separated into multiple files. The collaboration code is set up so that all editors can view the code on all of the block pages, but each editor can modify only one block page. The projects are set up in such a way that Player 1 can edit only Player 1's code, but can view Player 2's code as it is being changed. This functionality is central to how both the complex systems and physics model activities work.

3. Ecology complex system prototype design

When building this model, we wanted to build on the complex system models that have been developed over the years with Starlogo and to have the model include elements where students are reading data from graphs, using code to modify the model, and having the model meaningfully work across multiple devices.

3.1. Existing Starlogo models

We started by looking at Starlogo models that are used now for complex systems, with two exemplars being the colored butterflies and the fish and algae model. In both of these models, students are able to modify how the models run by changing the values on sliders that affect particular breeds and their environment. In the butterflies model, the sliders are used to set the initial conditions for the model. For the SURGE Gameblox project, however, the variability achieved in the models needs to occur through manipulation of code when the model is designed instead of through the on-screen widgets while the model is being run. In addition, given that many of the graphs students are reading occur over time, unlike the existing Starlogo models, it is important that values change throughout the running of the model as opposed to only during the setting of initial conditions.

An important functionality that we carried over from more complex models, like the fish and algae model, is the use of traits, properties that are associated with the instances of classes of objects that are used to store information about the agents as the model runs.

3.2. Prototype #1: Positioning plants to maximize animals on a farm

3.2.1. Design

Players compete to get as many animals living on their farms as possible (**Figure 1**). The animals roam between the two farms, pause to eat grass, and get varying levels of energy from each type of grass. Each player programs how much grass of each type to add to his or her farm by reading graphs that inform the user how much energy each animal gets, and the percentage of type of animals in each level. Players have graphs of the seasonal changes in sunlight and rainfall. Each type of grass does better in different climate conditions. Players need to account for the seasonal changes represented in these graphs to

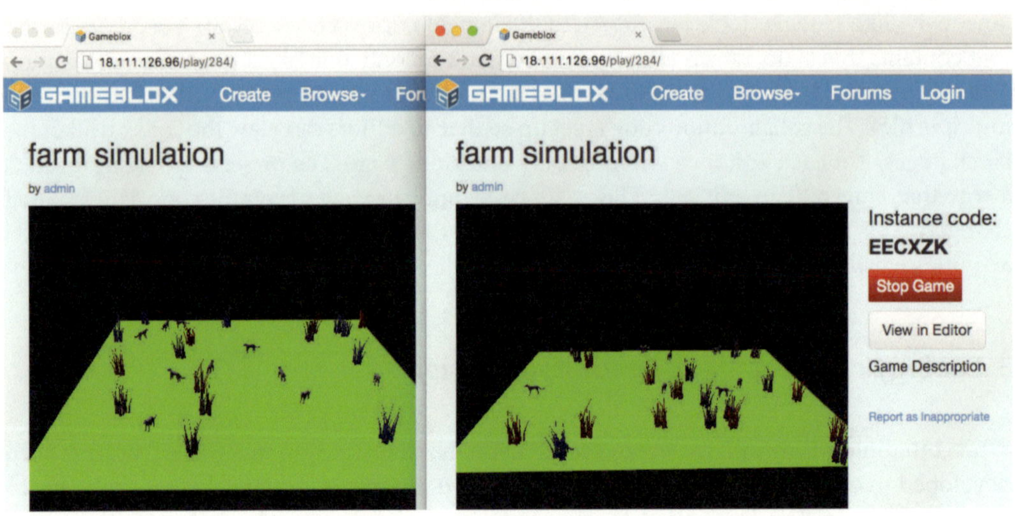

Figure 1. Screenshot of farm game for two players.

maximize their populations. In our initial version of the prototype, we focused on a competitive structure for this prototype so that we could compare competitive and collaborative structures. The player who maintains the largest number of animals on his or her side wins (**Figures 2** and **3**).

3.2.2. *Feedback*

The two largest pieces of feedback we received were that it was hard to know what location was best and that you could not react dynamically to weather changes.

Strategy behind setting positions not apparent. When playing the game, the animals walk randomly from one screen to another, and the plants are placed at random y locations at the particular x value selected by the user. Given that the animals are randomly placed on the board, the locations where the animals go are almost at random. This led to there being no good strategy for optimizing where a player places plants to grow more effectively. One could imagine a future version having a heat map that showed the climate in different areas of the board and allowing the players to read that map to make strategic decisions around where to plant, but this version was not implemented.

Cannot react dynamically to weather changes. The coding in this prototype was limited to planting different types of grass based on the time that had passed. This not only limited the complexity of the code that could be written, but also meant that the model could run only for the limited period of time on the graphs, and players could not extrapolate their knowledge to handle situations that were not available on a graph.

3.3. Prototype #2: Generalizing rules from the graphs

The two main changes that occurred for the second version of the prototype were to (a) remove the position selection from the plant block, so all plants would generate in random locations and (b) include a block that would allow the player to get data from the graph about a particular point in time, as shown in **Figure 4**.

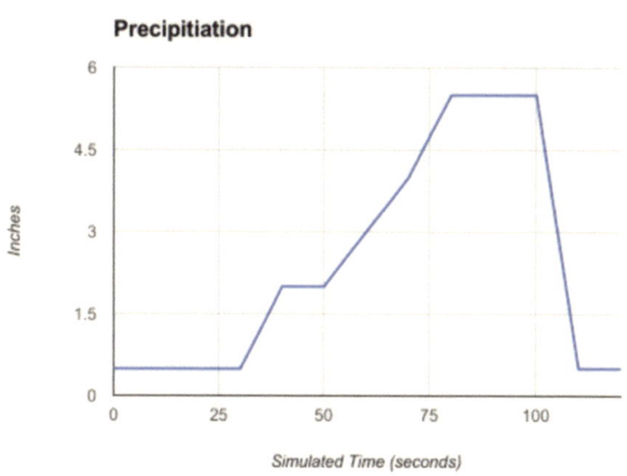

Figure 2. Graphs of precipitation and sunlight.

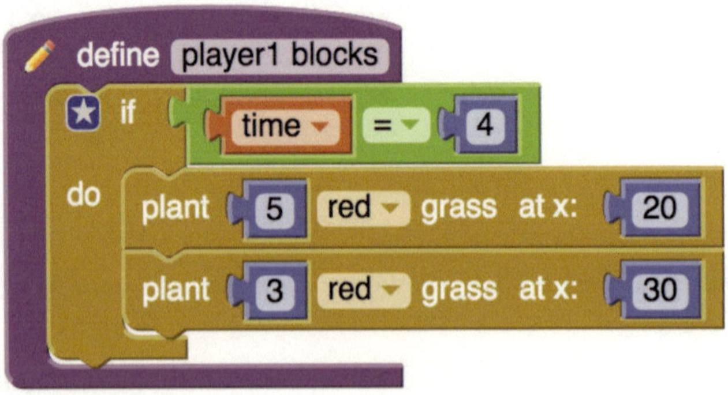

Figure 3. Screenshot of simple blocks to place grass on a location.

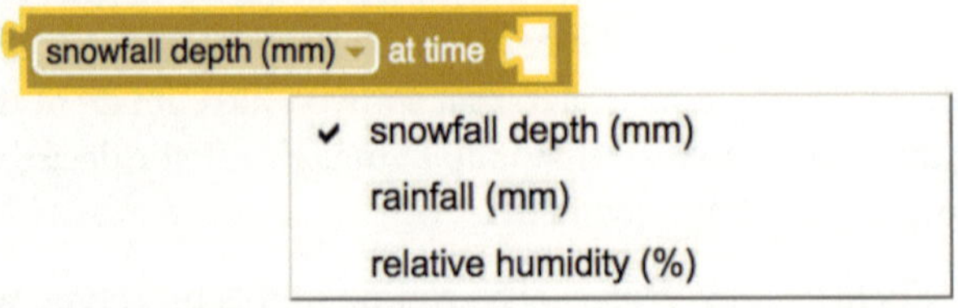

Figure 4. Block used to get data from graph.

The addition of these changes allows the activity to be broken up into two parts. The first part of the activity is run similar to the first prototype, where different colored grass is placed randomly on the ground by choosing specific times to plant. The second part of the activity, however, allows for more complicated coding strategies, enabling the user to decide what to plant based on the values of the rainfall and sunlight instead of simply choosing static times.

3.4. Prototype #2: Next steps

The next iteration of the prototype will focus on revising features of the game activity structure to focus on a collaborative game rather than a competitive game. Our initial goals involved creating one competitive prototype (ecosystems) and one collaborative prototype (kinematics) to be able to explore the affordances and trade-offs between competition and collaboration. We therefore created the competition version of ecosystems first, but our ultimate commitments are toward building collaborative environments. Recent meta-analyses of digital games and learning suggest that collaborative structures tend to be more effective for learning [20–21], and collaborative structures align very well with perspectives framing students as modelers [4–5] and computational thinkers [22–23]. As Kafai et al. [24] articulate, CT can and should be framed in terms collaborative design and production within communities. Therefore, while we believe that comparison analyses between competition and collaboration are of value, we ultimately think that the research and theoretical foundations around games for learning as well as computational participation and science as practice provide greater support for collaborative approaches.

4. Newtonian kinematics prototype design

We chose Newtonian kinematics as the domain for the second prototype, and we chose a collaborative structure. We made these choices so that we could compare differences in collaborative versus collaborative structures as well as compare across domains. When creating the physics model, we had three goals in mind: 1) students should use code to collaboratively modify the model based on reading graphs, 2) the model spans the screens on two computers, and 3) the graphs should describe a phenomenon in physics that students would study in class.

4.1. Prototype #1: Coloring cubes

Our first prototype had cubes moving based on speed vs. time graphs given to the player. The player needs to predict the location of the cube at a particular point in time.

4.1.1. Gameplay

Players work collaboratively to turn all of the moving cubes purple. Each of the cubes moves based on position or velocity graphs given to the students. Students then need to predict when the cubes will cross the center of screen. When the cube reaches the right side of one player's screen, it will appear on the left-hand side of the other player's screen. Player 1 uses the blocks to fire the red laser, which turns cubes red, and player 2 controls the blue laser. When a cube is already red and is hit by the blue laser, it turns purple. Players win by turning all of the cubes purple in the most efficient way (**Figures 5–7**).

4.1.2. Limitations

The two largest problems that we noticed through testing this prototype were that (a) the prototype did not incentivize collaboration sufficiently, depending on the pairs working on it, and (b) the absence of numbers on the 3D renderer caused confusion.

Not collaborative. The largest problem with this prototype was that each player could independently solve for the location of the cube and did not need to talk to the other player. This defeated one of the large goals of the project, and we knew therefore that we needed to push the prototype in a different direction.

Tick marks. The 3D renderer that we are using from Starlogo is limited in that we can put only 3D objects in the model. Although we were able to verbally inform the players about the axis on the green floor, it was hard for a player to plan and adjust their strategies and code without markings and numbers to know exactly where the cubes are at a particular time. We therefore chose to move to a 2D environment where we could label the positions in our next iteration.

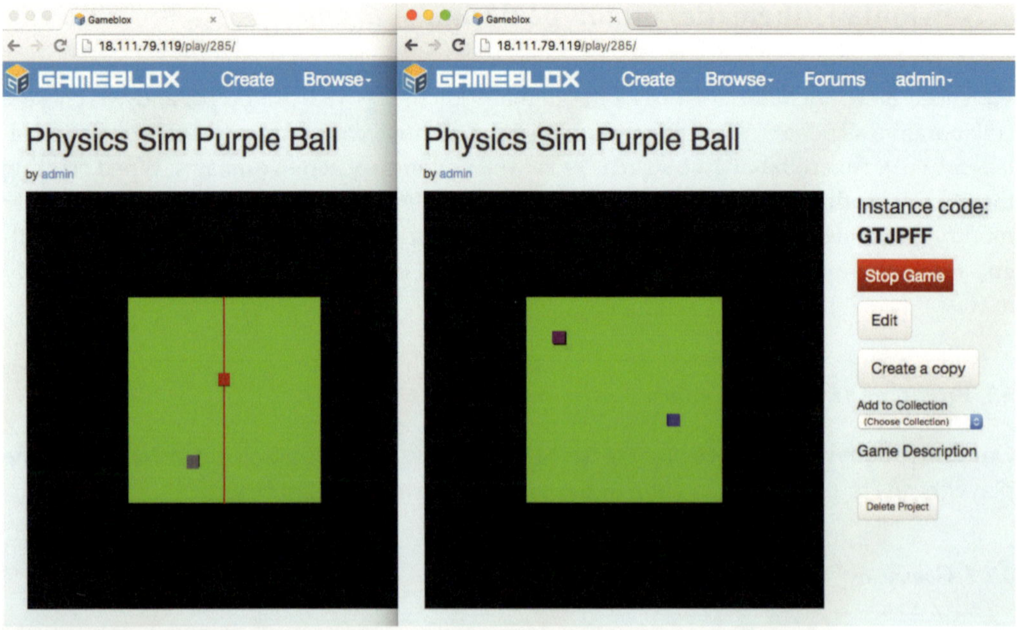

Figure 5. Running simulation.

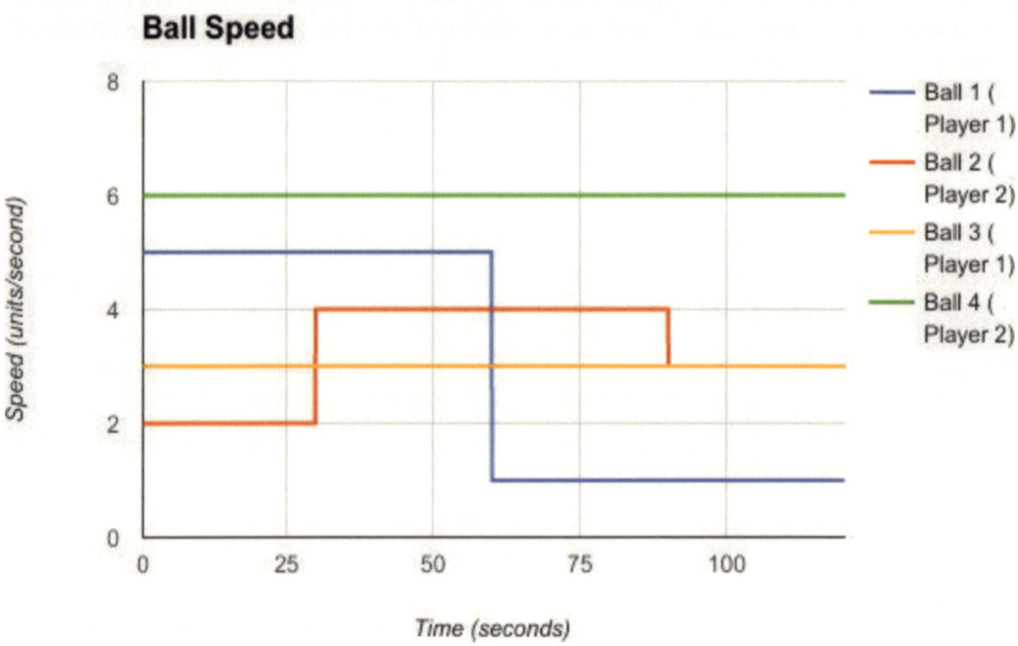

Figure 6. Graphs of the speed of the balls over time.

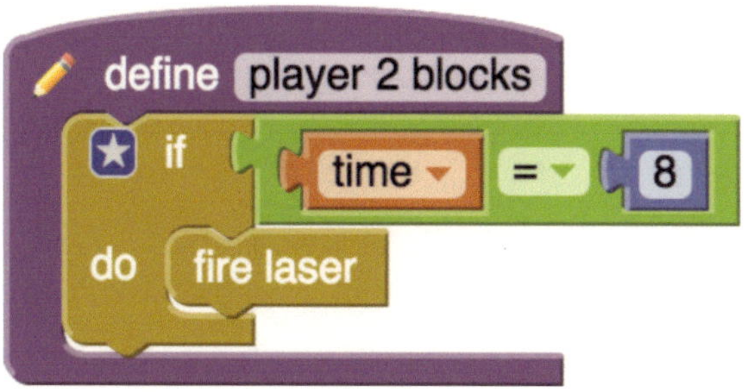

Figure 7. The simplest block needed for a player to color a single cube at a particular point in time.

4.2. Prototype #2: Moving across a marked line

Given that the underlying gameplay was not collaborative, we shifted to creating paper prototypes that would lead to better dynamics within the model. After several rounds of designing and playtesting various prototypes, the one described below became the starting point for the next digital version of the project.

4.2.1. Gameplay

Each player has a timeline and a graph. At the beginning of the game, the player learns where the ball should land at a particular time. In the figures, for example, the ball should be at $x = 10$ when $t = 10$. Player 1's speed vs. time graph applies only when the ball starts moving on the line controlled by player 1 (when x is between 1 and 5). The same is true for player 2 (when x is between 6 and 10). Players can choose to add a "Speed Up" or a "Slow Down" when the ball starts moving on their part of the line. The "Speed Up" or "Slow Down" will increase or decrease the speed of the ball by 2 (**Figures 8** and **9**).

4.2.2. Feedback

When testing the game, the three pieces of feedback we consistently saw were that (1) collaboration naturally occurred as both players were trying to solve the problem, (2) the game was harder than expected, and (3) there was confusion on how to read the graphs (**Figure 10**).

Collaboration. One problem with the previous prototype was that each player could individually solve for the location of the cube without needing to speak with the other player in order to succeed. In this prototype, that is no longer the case, because by adding a "speed up" the ball will appear in a different location at a different time on the other player's screen, which will cause him or her to change strategy.

Harder than expected. The same benefit that made collaboration happen, where a small change would affect the strategy of the other player, made the game significantly harder than we

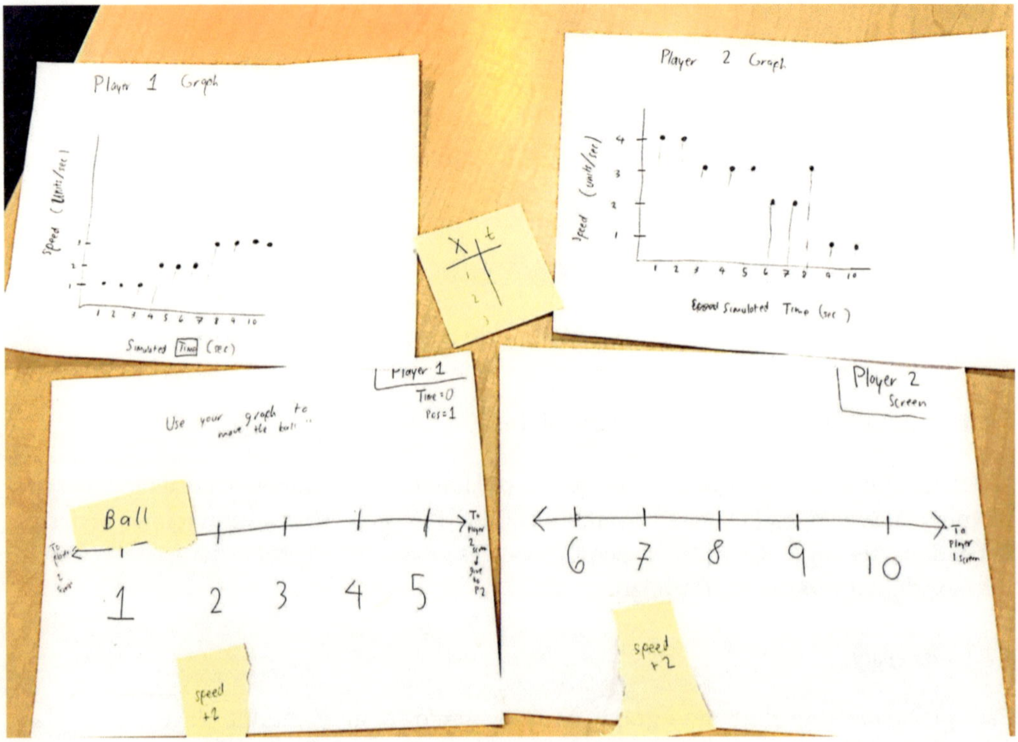

Figure 8. Game setup in paper prototype.

expected. This had both unexpected benefits and drawbacks: students could spend a very long time (20+ minutes) trying to find a solution, and if they did not solve it systematically, it could lead to frustration. The most successful players wrote a table of times and locations of the ball over time. Having the players generate a table that leads to a position graph achieved an outcome we did not expect.

Confusion reading the graph. Some students were confused by the points on the graph representing the speed at a particular point as shown in **Figure 8**. Other students were confused by graphs in **Figure 11** because they were trying to find the velocity at a point with a vertical line (the instantaneous change) but were not sure which value they should choose. Ultimately, we used the graphs in **Figure 11** because they are both more accurate and are more similar to the formal Cartesian representations that students encounter in other science contexts.

4.2.3. Moving to a digital prototype

While we were originally expecting to use the paper prototypes to simply test the interactions before moving to a digital version, testing demonstrated that working and coordinating on paper first was important to the learning experience, especially given the difficulty of the challenge. After

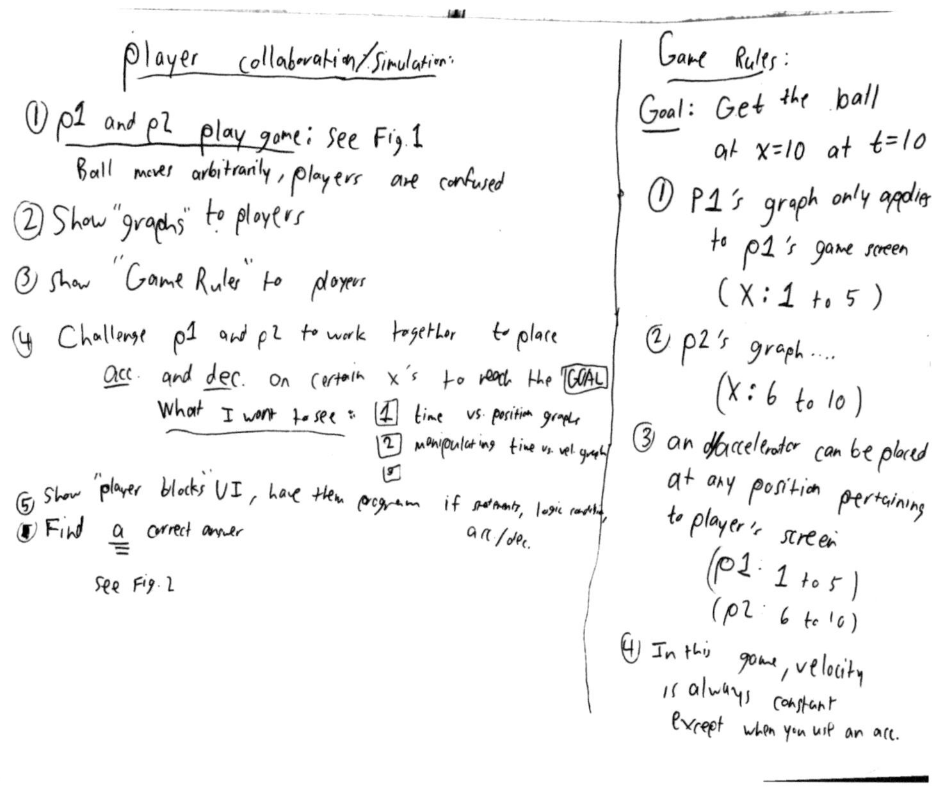

Figure 9. Instructions from paper prototype.

the students believed they had found a solution of "speeds ups" and "slow downs," we would provide them a sheet where each player would write his or her solution, like the one in **Figure 12**.

The students would then see a Gameblox model like the one below, which simulates the same scenario that they saw on paper (**Figure 13**).

Each player would then be presented with a limited set of blocks to program the "speed ups" and "slow downs" that they discovered from solving the paper version. If the students got the answer correct, then the dinosaur would arrive at the desired location after 10 seconds had passed. If not, then the students would know that their solutions were incorrect (**Figure 14**).

4.2.4. Expanding the game

After we had the basic mechanic of getting the ball to go to a particular location at a particular time, there were several changes we made to expand the work the players had already done, including graphing how the ball moves, and calculating the distance it covered.

Graphing actual speed vs. time. As the ball moves from one half of the line to the other (between 0 and 5 and 6–10), the speed is dependent on the graph of the particular player who is

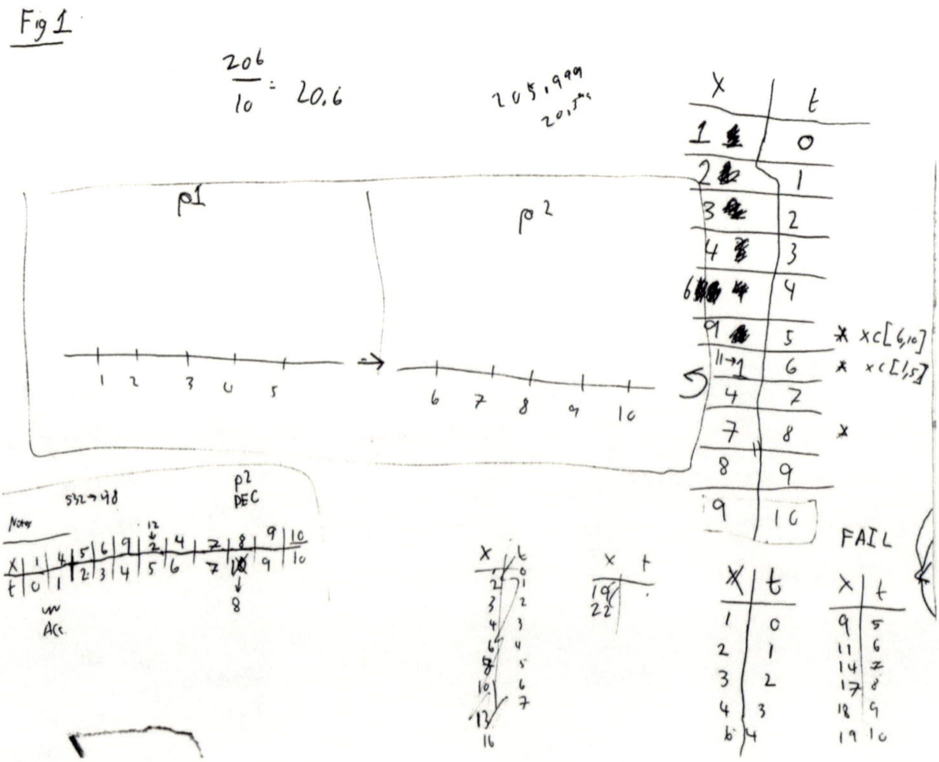

Figure 10. Table of time and position values.

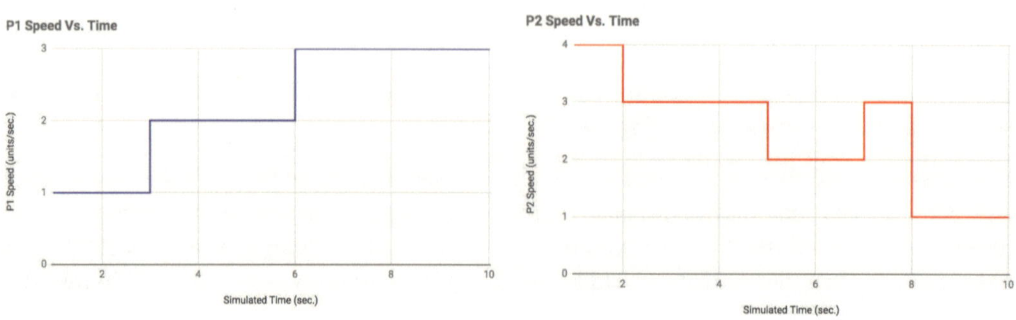

Figure 11. Speed vs. time graphs for player 1 & 2.

programming for that part of the line. After the students have programmed their solutions in Gameblox, they create the graph of the speed vs. time of the ball. This means following where the ball is and knowing whether to reference Player 1's or 2's graph in order to find the ball's speed at the appropriate time.

Calculating distance. With a graph of the actual speed of the ball over time, it is possible to calculate the total distance the ball has traveled by calculating the area underneath the

Figure 12. Time and "speed up"/"slow down" table.

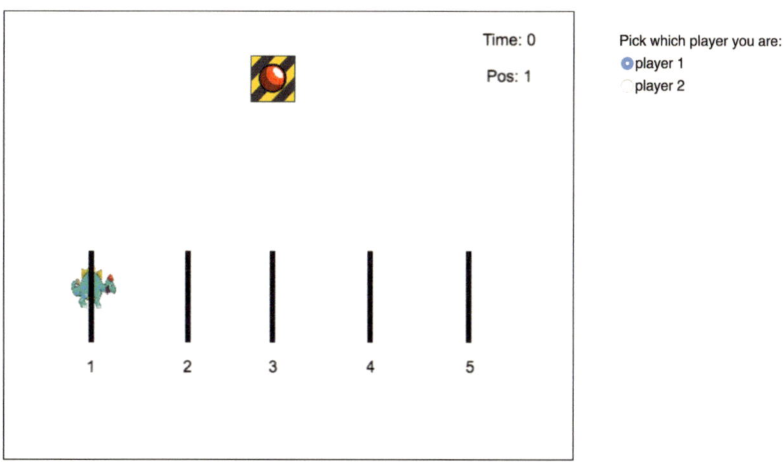

Figure 13. Gameblox version of physics simulation.

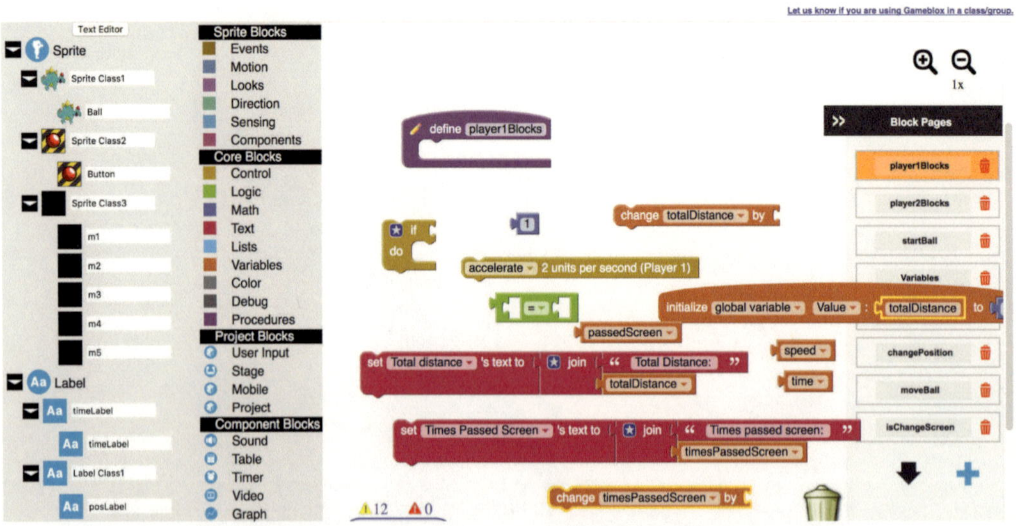

Figure 14. All of the blocks that the users are able to choose from to construct their solutions.

graph. In early versions of the prototype, we had speeds that could be 1 or 0. This meant the player could use a "slow down" and the speeds would be −1 or −2. The model would correctly have the character move backward on the line, demonstrating a negative speed. There was confusion, however, regarding whether the negative area on the graph should be added or subtracted from the total distance sum when calculating the distance. This can help lead to discussions around the difference between distance and displacement, as the decision of how one handles the area with a negative speed changes the quantity that the players obtain.

Programming the distance. After the students determined the distance that the ball traveled through calculating the area underneath the combined graph, we had the players program a short script in Gameblox to programmatically determine the distance covered. Since $d = vt$, and $t = 1$ for every step, the equation simplifies to $d = v$, so each player needs to add the speed that the ball is traveling every time his or her script is triggered. By doing this, each player can calculate how far the ball traveled from their screen. By adding the distances from both players, they are able to see the total distance the ball has traveled. If the players are then asked about how to calculate the displacement, they would need to take the absolute value of the speed. Below is an example of a solution that has two "slow downs" and calculates the distance traveled (**Figure 15**).

4.2.5. Simplifying the experience

Finding the solution to the original problem we proposed took too long for all of our original testing teams and was discouraging to some teams. In order to create an easier on-ramp to the activity, we created a "Level 0," which helps the students understand the mechanics of the problem though an easier set of graphs as shown in **Figure 16**.

http://dx.doi.org/10.5772/intechopen.73051

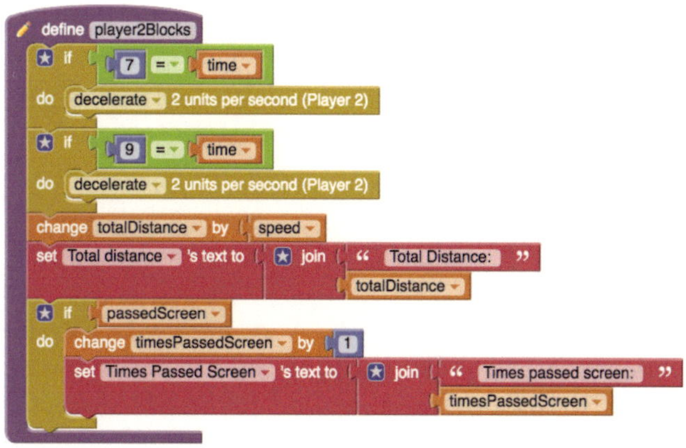

Figure 15. A sample solution of the blocks.

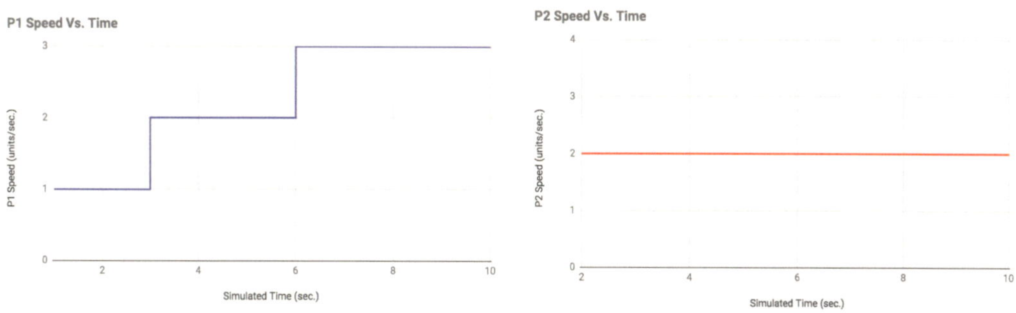

Figure 16. Level 0 graphs for simpler solutions.

The graphs are notable not only for having constant speed but also for having speeds that are two and above. Speeds that are two and greater mean that if a player uses a "Slow down," then the speed will not be negative, which will eliminate possible confusion when calculating distance. Students would go through the entire process of the game with these simpler graphs (finding a solution, programming the solution, creating a combined speed graph, calculating the distance, and programming the distance), before doing the same activity with the more complex graphs.

4.2.6. Next steps for the kinematics prototype

Our sense is that the current structure of this prototype potentially focuses more heavily on a specific solution than we might like. Another related perspective on designing games for science education is the constructible authentic representations (CARs) perspective [25]. CARs is highly related to the DIG perspective in that CARs focuses on (a) meaningful construction, (b) conceptually integrated primitives, and (c) authentic representations. One aspect that the CAR perspective emphasizes very heavily is the "sandbox" aspects of the game, in the sense of incentivizing more open-ended experimentation, than sometimes results in DIGs, where the puzzles at the heart of a level or game can be more focused. We would like for future versions of this prototype to be more "CARs-like" and we will explore structures that incentivize open-ended exploration to a greater degree than in the current prototype, and structures that may feel more game-like than the current prototype.

5. Implications and conclusions

To have value, the proposed DIG genre must be generalizable. As described in the introduction, our earlier work has discussed this claim of generalizability in terms of hypothetical examples of DIGs in physics, biology, chemistry, and the social sciences as well as in terms of multiple model types including time-series analyses with Cartesian formal representations, constraint-system analyses with Cartesian formal representations, and other model types and non-Cartesian formal representations such as system dynamics models, situation-action models, and agent-based models [14]. Sengupta and Clark [15] and Krinks et al. [16] conducted our foundational work on integrating agent-based modeling into DIGs, and Clark et al. [17–19] have outlined theoretical frameworks and arguments highlighting the affordances of moving DIG design more deeply into agent-based modeling. In this current paper, we have presented the actual design process through which we developed prototypes aligning with those ideas for SURGE Gameblox. More specifically, we introduced and described the design process through which we developed two multiplayer DIG prototypes with agent-based modeling as the formal representational form through which the game communicates challenges and goals to players as well as the formal representational system through which players control the game.

We would argue that there are five main implications to draw from our work developing these two prototypes and the SURGE Gameblox environment. Each of these five implications focuses on different aspects and kinds of generalizability.

First, at the most basic level, these prototypes serve as proofs of concept that such games and environments are indeed technically possible. We certainly would not argue that these prototypes represent the only way that such games or environments might be structured, but these prototypes show the potential viability and possibilities of such games and environments.

Second, these prototypes demonstrate the generalizability of the multiplayer agent-based modeling DIG approach pedagogically. Ecosystems and kinematics as domains hail from different disciplines and represent very different kinds of agent-based models in the sense that the ecosystems models focus on complex system dynamics whereas the kinematics model focuses more on discrete systems of single agents. These two prototypes therefore suggest that pedagogically this approach can be generalized across multiple domains and types of systems.

Third, these prototypes demonstrate the generalizability of such an approach economically and pragmatically in the sense that both of these prototypes are built on top of the same core SURGE Gameblox environment. It is certainly true that SURGE Gameblox is built upon the robust infrastructure of MIT's Gameblox and Starlogo Nova software environments, but the resulting hybrid SURGE Gameblox environment is indeed capable of supporting cost-effective and time-effective development of similar DIGs across multiple domains and topics.

Fourth, while the development of DIGs for new topics in disciplines can be cost-effective and time-effective, such development will still always require iterative refinement and testing through the design and development phases. Neither of the two prototypes was completed in the first round of development. Both prototypes required multiple rounds of development from their initial conceptualization to their current structure. Furthermore, the designs will benefit from multiple additional iterative rounds of design, testing, and refinement. This is more than just refining the software code. This iterative development and testing and refinement are also requisite parts of the design process for the activity structures themselves. As discussed in our recent meta-analysis of digital games for learning [20], this implication highlights the fact that design, rather than medium alone, determines the efficacy of a learning environment, whether it be a classroom lab, a textbook, a lecture, or a recreational digital game or a disciplinary-integrated game.

Fifth, and finally, these prototypes provide proof of concept for the broader DIG genre in terms of generalizability. While early work on DIGs focused on Newtonian kinematics with Cartesian timeseries analyses as the formal representations of control and communication, we have argued in our earlier work for the generalizability to other topics and formal representational systems [8, 14, 15]. These prototypes provide proofs of concept of such generalizability of the broader DIG conception of developing disciplinary-integrated games wherein manipulation and translation across formal representational systems provide the means of communication and control within the game as players engage in modeling and computational thinking from a science as practice perspective.

Acknowledgements

This material is based upon work supported by the National Science Foundation under Grant No. 1119290. Earlier development of Starlogo Nova was supported by the National Science Foundation under Grant No. 1508911 and 1639069. Any opinions, findings, and conclusions or recommendations expressed in this material are those of the author(s) and do not necessarily reflect the views of the National Science Foundation.

Author details

Douglas B. Clark[1]*, Paul Medlock-Walton[2], Raúl Boquín[2] and Eric Klopfer[2]

*Address all correspondence to: douglas.clark@ucalgary.ca

1 University of Calgary, Calgary, AB, Canada

2 MIT, Cambridge, MA, USA

References

[1] Honey MA, Hilton M, editors. Learning Science through Computer Games and Simulations. National Research Council. Washington, DC: National Academy Press; 2010

[2] Martinez-Garza M, Clark DB, Nelson B. Digital games and the US National Research Council's science proficiency goals. Studies in Science Education. 2013;**49**:170-208. DOI: 10.1080/03057267.2013.839372

[3] Young MF, Slota S, Cutter AB, Jalette G, Mullin G, Lai B, ... Yukhymenko M. Our princess is in another castle: A review of trends in serious gaming for education. Review of Educational Research. 2012;**82**:61-89. DOI: 10.3102/003465431243698

[4] Lehrer R, Schauble L. Cultivating model-based reasoning in science education. In: Sawyer RK, editor. The Cambridge Handbook of the Learning Sciences. Cambridge, England: Cambridge University Press; 2006. pp. 371-388

[5] Lehrer R, Schauble L. Scientific thinking and science literacy: Supporting development in learning in contexts. In: Damon W, Lerner RM, Renninger KA, Sigel IE, editors. Handbook of Child Psychology. 6th ed. Vol. 4. Hoboken, NJ: John Wiley and Sons; 2006

[6] Pickering A. The Mangle of Practice: Time, Agency, and Science. Chicago: University of Chicago Press; 1995

[7] Duschl RA, Schweingruber HA, Shouse AW, editors. Taking Science to School: Learning and Teaching Science in Grades K-8. National Research Council Board on Science Education, Center for Education, Division of Behavioral and Social Sciences and Education. Washington, DC: The National Academies Press; 2007

[8] Clark DB, Sengupta P, Brady C, Martinez-Garza M, Killingsworth S. Disciplinary integration in digital games for science learning. International STEM Education Journal. 2015;**2**(2):1-21. DOI: 10.1186/s40594-014-0014-4. http://www.stemeducationjournal.com/content/pdf/s40594-014-0014-4.pdf

[9] Clark DB, Virk SS, Sengupta P, Brady C, Martinez-Garza M, Krinks K, Killingsworth S, Kinnebrew J, Biswas G, Barnes J, Minstrell J, Nelson B, Slack K, D'Angelo CM. SURGE's evolution deeper into formal representations: The siren's call of popular game-play mechanics. International Journal of Designs for Learning. 2016;**7**(1):107-146. https://scholarworks.iu.edu/journals/index.php/ijdl/article/view/19359

[10] Collins A. What's Worth Teaching?: Rethinking Curriculum in the Age of Technology. New York: Teachers College Press; 2017

[11] Collins A. A study of expert theory formation: The role of model types and domain frameworks. In: Khine MS, Saleh I, editors. Models and Modeling: Cognitive Tools for Scientific Enquiry. London: Springer; 2011. pp. 23-40

[12] Collins A, Ferguson W. Epistemic forms and epistemic games. Educational Psychologist. 1993;**28**:25-42

[13] Morrison D, Collins A. Epistemic fluency and constructivist learning environments. Educational Technology. 1995;**35**(5):39-45

[14] Clark DB, Sengupta P, Virk SS. Disciplinarily-integrated games: Generalizing across domains and model types. In: Russell D, Laffey J, editors. Handbook of Research on Gaming Trends in P-12 Education. Hershey, PA: IGI Global; 2016. pp. 178-194. DOI: 10.4018/978-1-4666-9629-7

[15] Sengupta P, Clark DB. Playing Modeling games in the science classroom: The case for disciplinary integration. Educational Technology. 2016;**56**(3):16-22

[16] Krinks K, Sengupta P, Clark DB. Benchmark lessons, modeling, and programming: Integrating games with modeling in the curriculum. International Journal of Gaming and Computer-Mediated Simulations. in press

[17] Clark DB, Sengupta P. Reconceptualizing Games for Integrating Computational Thinking and Science as Practice: Collaborative Agent-Based Disciplinarily-Integrated Games; (submitted)

[18] Clark DB, Medlock-Walton P, Sengupta P, Brady C, Klopfer E. Prototypes of Collaborative Agent-based Disciplinarily-Integrated Games for Integrated STEM Education. Presentation at International Society for STEM in Education (ISSE) Symposium 2017; Banff, Canada; 2017

[19] Clark DB, Medlock-Walton P, Brady C, Sengupta P, Klopfer E., Duncan F, Krinks K, Virk S. Multi-Player Disciplinarily Integrated Games As C-Thinking. Poster Presented at the Annual Meeting of the American Educational Research Association; San Antonio, TX; 2017

[20] Clark DB, Tanner-Smith EE, Killingsworth SS. Digital games, design, and learning: A systematic review and meta-analysis. Review of Educational Research. 2016;**86**(1):79-122

[21] Wouters P, van Nimwegen C, van Oostendorp H, van der Spek ED. A meta-analysis of the cognitive and motivational effects of serious games. Journal of Educational Psychology. 2013;**105**:249-265. DOI: 10.1037/a0031311

[22] NRC. Report of a Workshop on the Scope and Nature of Computational Thinking. Washington, DC: National Academy Press; 2010

[23] Grover S, Pea R. Computational thinking in K–12: A review of the state of the field. Educational Researcher. 2013;**42**(1):38-43

[24] Kafai YB, Burke Q, Resnick M. Connected Code: Why Children Need to Learn Programming. Cambridge, MA: MIT Press; 2014

[25] Holbert N, Wilensky U. Constructible authentic representations: Designing video games that enable players to utilize knowledge developed in-game to reason about science. Technology, Knowledge and Learning. 2014;**19**(1-2):53-79. DOI: 10.1007/s10758-014-9214-8

Section 2

Modelling and Educational Simulations

Chapter 7

Interaction Design in Virtual Reality Game Using Arduino Sensors

Juin-Ling Tseng and Chia-Wei Chu

Additional information is available at the end of the chapter

http://dx.doi.org/10.5772/intechopen.71016

Abstract

Virtual reality (VR) is the use of computer simulation to produce a virtual world, providing users with a variety of sensory simulation, which enables users to feel as though they are in the virtual world. Currently, mature three-dimensional (3D) computer graphics technology can present realistic 3D visual effects. However, system interaction is still mainly through specific interactive devices for system control, such as the Vive controller for HTC Vive. In order to enable the user to control the game intuitively, this study employed a currently popular Arduino technology to carry out design of interactive control devices for virtual reality. The interaction design in this study is based mainly on a virtual reality baseball game. To let users carry out swings more intuitively in the baseball game, this study used actual baseball bat–installed sensors, called "Arduino baseball bat," as a replacement for the VR joystick. The implemented system was roughly divided into two components: a transmitter system module on the bat and a receiver system module connecting to the server host. According to the results, our system cannot only realistically display 3D visual effects, but the Arduino baseball bat can also provide intuitive real-time game interaction for the user.

Keywords: virtual reality, interaction design, Arduino sensors, game design, unity

1. Introduction

Today, most games require specific devices for implementation, such as personal computers, mobile phones, tablets, and video game consoles. Although the special effects and image processing are captivating for the games designed for these devices, two major issues exist between the games and the game users. First, users can watch the game scenes only through the display screen, which makes it challenging to produce an immersive gaming experience. Second, users are allowed to manipulate the games only through traditional interactive devices such as the rocker, keyboard, and mouse and not intuitively. To address these two issues, this study used the virtual reality (VR) headset and Arduino somatosensory interaction mechanism for three-dimensional (3D) game development.

1.1. VR headset

Three-dimensional technologies [1–4] with a wide variety of applications including movies [5], games [6], art [7], and education [8] are commonly used. Among these, 3D VR is the most popular one [9, 10]. To induce users to become more immersed in a VR system, the system generally presents the required 3D scene information through a VR headset. At present, Oculus Rift [11, 12], 3Glasses [13], and HTC Vive [14, 15] are the most popular VR headsets, as shown in **Figure 1**.

1. Oculus Rift [11, 12]

   Oculus Rift is a VR head-mounted display (HMD) system developed by Oculus VR. Rift is equipped with a 7-inch screen, with substantially reduced latency and motion blur incurred by pixel switching in the original prototype and by rapid turning of the user's head. The field of view (FOV) is more than 90° horizontal, and the image resolution is 2160 × 1200. Rift also provides a three-axis gyroscope, accelerometer, and magnetometer, allowing the users to interact with the 3D scene content. Oculus Rift provides a wireless controller called Oculus Touch, which allows users to manipulate 3D scene information. However, Oculus Touch is operated similarly to the general rocker, displaying an absence of the intuitive control concept to a certain extent.

2. 3Glasses [13]

   Compared to Oculus Rift, 3Glasses exhibits a large visual angle (110°) and a delay of less than 13 ms. Its resolution is as high as 2560 × 1440, satisfying the requirement of the mainstream VR headsets. With respect to the operation, plug and play is supported, and an intelligent light sensor is incorporated to adapt to variations in screen brightness. Moreover, the system incorporates a gyroscope mechanism, albeit without a space-tracking function. Therefore, users are not allowed to move freely to interact in fields through 3Glasses.

3. HTC Vive [14, 15]

   HTC Vive is a highly popular VR HMD at present. It is capable of utilizing the room scale technology to set the real-world room environment as a 3D interactive virtual space in which users are allowed to move freely and use a handheld controller with the motion tracking function to manipulate 3D virtual objects. The whole system is equipped with more than 70 sensors, which include the gyroscope, accelerometer, and laser position sensor, for positioning and sensing purposes. The spatial positioning technology of HTC Vive, which is dissimilar to the image collection approach of Oculus Rift, calculates the light emitted from the lighthouse and uses the sensor in the Vive system to receive the light information. Therefore, it can efficiently calculate the position of a user and the handheld controller in the space. Oculus Rift uses a camera to detect a user's position, which is also prone to space limitation. For example, when a user shifts away by a significant distance, it is not feasible to identify the user's position, owing to the unclear image. In contrast, the Lighthouse used by HTC Vive can irradiate to a larger range (up to 15 × 15 feet of space tracking). This implies that HTC Vive incorporates a space-tracking mechanism superior to that of Oculus Rift.

Figure 1. Oculus rift, 3Glasses, and HTC vive.

1.2. Arduino somatosensory interaction

Our routine life involves various interactive devices such as air conditioner thermostats and car-reversing radars. The air conditioner thermostat uses a sensor to detect the ambient temperature for automatically adjusting the indoor temperature. The car-reversing radar uses a sensor to detect the distance from an object located behind the car; when the car is reversed excessively close to the object, a tone is produced to warn the driver. In the past, it was challenging to develop such electronic devices; however, the present use of Arduino technology substantially reduces the threshold for development.

Arduino is an authorized interactive environment development technology, wherein both the software (open source) and hardware are open. The software development environment can be downloaded free of charge from the Arduino website; this implies that the software development process is straightforward and is supported by numerous references. In the traditional hardware environment, developers of a microcontroller are generally required to have a background in electronics, electrical machinery, or related fields. For common personnel, it is time-consuming to gain a complete understanding of the development environment. The threshold for learning Arduino is relatively more straightforward: personnel without a background in electronics, electrical machinery, or related fields can conveniently learn to develop Arduino-based interactive devices. As Arduino is based on public sharing, most developers share their creative works, and a number of creative projects are available on the Internet, enabling developers to complete their creative works in a significantly short time.

The Arduino development system mainly includes Arduino development boards, Arduino development software, and Arduino extended components, as shown in **Figure 2**. They are briefly introduced as follows:

1. Arduino development board

   The Arduino development board is the motherboard for development of systems such as Uno, Leonardo, Due, Mega, and Nano. Consider the Arduino Uno development

Figure 2. Arduino development board and its components.

board as an example. It includes an ATmega328 microcontroller chip, a USB port, and an input/output pin. The ATmega328 microcontroller chip is the main processing chip. The USB port is a port through which the power supply is provided, and the developed PC program is uploaded to the development board. The input/output pin can be connected to the required sensor. Owing to its affordability and convenient development, Arduino Uno is one of the most popular development boards.

2. Arduino development software

The Arduino Integrated Development Environment (IDE), based on AVR-GCC and a few open-source software, supports Java and C/C++ programming languages. This allows developers to get started conveniently. The IDE software is available for free download on the Arduino website and can be used immediately after the downloaded package is decompressed. This IDE can run on Windows, Mac OS X, and Linux. On the main interface of Arduino IDE, the white area in the middle is used for program editing, whereas the black area at the bottom is used to provide information tips. The main programs include both the setup () and loop () functions. The setup () function is executed only one time, when the program starts. Therefore, the code written in the setup () function is generally responsible for initialization. The loop () function is executed repeatedly and is also the main programming area. After the programming is complete, the program can be compiled. If the compiling process is successful, the program can be uploaded to the development board. The sensors or indicators connected to the development board reflect the results of program execution.

3. Arduino extended components

Arduino extended components refer to the extended boards (shields) or sensors connected to the development board. The main function of a shield is to reinforce the specific requirements of the original development board. For example, if Arduino is expected to exhibit the capability to connect to the WiFi network, WiFi Shield can be directly superposed on the Arduino Uno. In a similar manner, Ethernet Shield, GSM Shield, and Motor Shield can satisfy various expansion requirements. The Arduino development board is equivalent to the motherboard of the entire Arduino system. Sensors such as the temperature sensor, three-axis accelerometer, gyroscope, power sensor, bending sensor, and button sensor are the key equipment of the Arduino system for sensing environmental variations. Through these sensors, the Arduino development board can read information associated with the environment or objects, such as the ambient temperature, object movement or rotation, force endured, and bending degree.

2. Related works

2.1. VR headset-related work

VR headset has become the most recent development trend of the information and communication technology (ICT) industry. At present, an increasing number of experts and researchers have been assigned to the relevant studies and applications, including medical care and entertainment. The following sections provide a brief introduction to relevant applications:

2.1.1. Medical care

Juanes et al. [16] used the Oculus Rift headset to construct a 3D virtual environment vision system with stereoscopic imaging effect for hospital operating rooms. This system provides users with an immersive experience and enables learners to become familiar with the operation of various devices and medical monitoring systems in operating rooms to provide more effective practical training. To achieve this purpose, Juanes et al. used Maya to construct 3D models for the relevant equipment in operating rooms, Oculus Rift SDK and Unity3D to construct control and display mechanisms, and Oculus Rift to present relevant information, as shown in **Figure 3**.

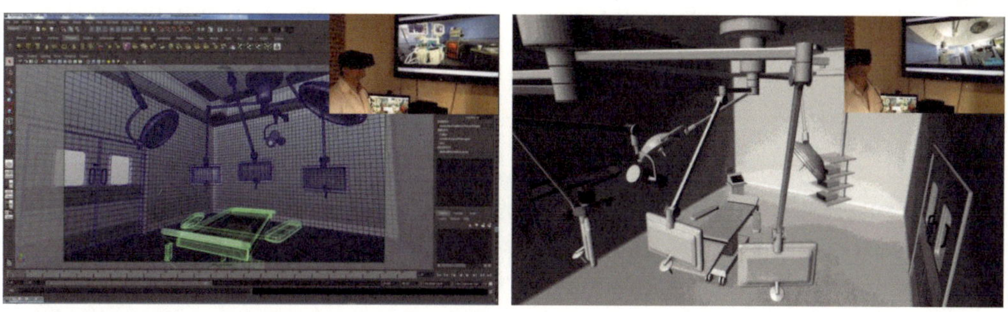

Figure 3. VR application in medical care.

2.1.2. Entertainment

In order to understand the impact of the headset on the gamer, Tan et al. [17] took Half-Life 2 first-person shooter as the experimental environment to explore the experience of ten players (P1–P10) as a result of wearing the Oculus Rift headset. Before the experiment, Tan et al.

analyzed the fundamental information about the ten players, including their age, gender, game interests, gameplay habit, and whether they played Half-Life before. In the experiment, Tan et al. compared the Oculus Rift and the desktop computer screen modes and used the questionnaire to analyze the variations in the immersive experiences among the ten players in the above two game modes, as illustrated in **Figure 10**. The questionnaire analysis results demonstrate that the average score for immersive experience of Half-Life through the traditional desktop computer screen was 142.5 and that through Oculus Rift was 147.2. This implies that Oculus Rift produces a better immersive experience than the traditional desktop computer screen, as shown in **Figure 4**.

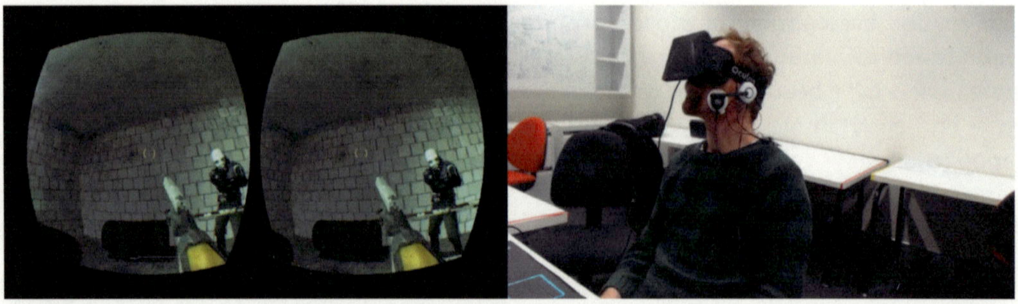

Figure 4. VR application in entertainment.

2.2. Arduino somatosensory interaction

Arduino uses small-size development boards as the implementation platforms and connects to various sensors through development boards such that the users can interact with live objects in the real world. Arduino has a wide variety of applications, including medical care, 3D virtual environmental interaction, and wearable devices. These applications are briefly introduced in the following sections.

2.2.1. *Medical care*

Dasios et al. [18] designed a remote monitoring system for elderly care by using the Arduino device. Installed in the elderly's home, this system has Arduino's detection nodes available at routinely used locations such as the bedroom, living room, bathroom, and dining table. It also incorporates a wearable node on the elderly's body to detect the regional temperature, humidity, light intensity, and the elderly's activity status. The system uses the coordinator node to transmit the data of each detection node to the server through the Internet; these data are recorded in the server's database. The caretakers can understand the elderly's living environment and activity status directly through web pages. This enables the caretakers to expeditiously identify an abnormal situation and further undertake related care activity, as shown in **Figure 5**.

2.2.2. *3D virtual environment interaction*

Wang and Yu [19] proposed a project called Virtual Spine in 2013. The main purpose of this project is to help common personnel avoid incorrect or overly fixed sitting postures over long periods and prevent the endangering of physical health. The 3D Virtual Spine interactive system developed in this project is divided into the Sedentary-Sensory Unit, Advisory Unit, Interactive 3D Unit, and Messaging Unit.

In the Sedentary-Sensory Unit, Wang and Yu installed Arduino pressure sensors on the seat to collect pressure data, which is transmitted to the Advisory Unit and Interactive 3D Unit to calculate the pressure burden accumulated on the spine and perform 3D rendering and interaction. The red area in the virtual seat indicates an area acted upon by a relatively larger pressure; therefore, it can be observed that two red circular areas with larger pressure are present in the 3D virtual spine. The Advisory Unit uses the Messaging Unit to transmit the comprehensive information instantly to users through media such as mobile devices, computer screens, or smart TVs to prevent physical injuries because of long periods of sitting or incorrect sitting postures, as shown in **Figure 6**.

Figure 5. Arduino application in medical care.

2.2.3. Wearable device

Sugathan et al. [20] developed a wearable health monitoring system in 2013, as shown in **Figure 7**, which primarily used Arduino and biosensors in clothing. When a patient wears this system, sensors to detect the patient's heartbeat frequency, electronic skin activity, and noninvasive skin temperature are started. By integrating these devices, we can instantly understand the overall situation of the patient. Such patients generally fall down due to heart disease, resulting in an alteration in the lifestyle or physical failure. This system can instantly detect variations in the patient's body and thus help avoid more serious illness.

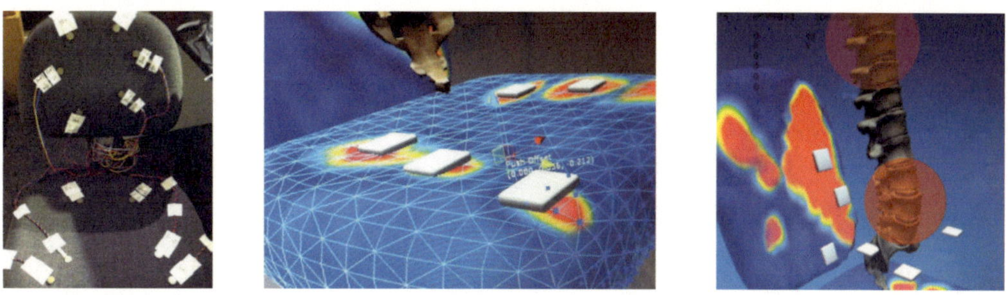

Figure 6. Arduino application in 3D virtual environment interaction.

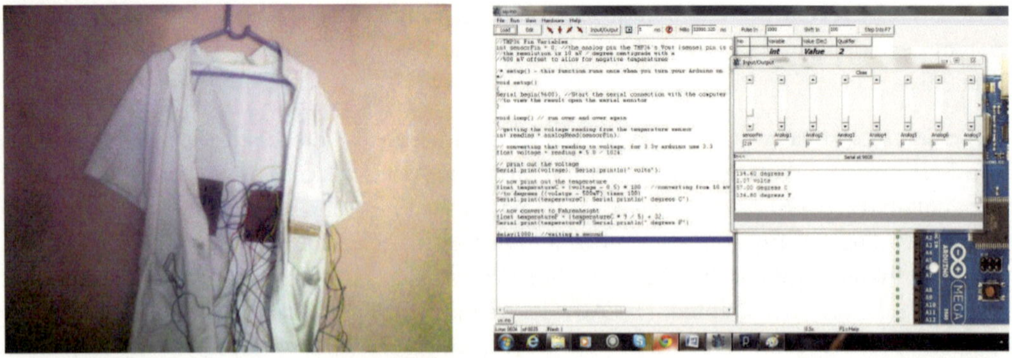

Figure 7. Arduino application in wearable devices.

3. System design

Although Arduino has been used in numerous applications, the main applications involve the use of sensors to detect the environment or the user's physical condition, such as in medical care, sports, and clothing-like wearable devices. 3D interactive applications have rarely been developed. In this study, VR technology was integrated with the Arduino somatosensory interaction mechanism, and the theme of baseball game was used to develop a "wearable VR somatosensory interactive game system," as shown in **Figure 8**.

The interaction architecture of this system generally includes the batting-sensing module, batting-information transmission module, batting-information receiving module, game control reaction module, and VR display module, as shown in **Figure 9**.

- Batting sensing module:

The main function of this module is to use the MPU-6500 six-axis sensor to detect the batting data.

- Batting information transmission module:

The main function of this module is to use the NRF24L01 communication device to transmit the batting data to the computer.

- Batting information receiving module:

This module corresponds to the batting information transmission module. Therefore, this module also uses the NRF24L01 communication device to receive the batting data from the batting information transmission module.

- Game control reaction module:

This module, deployed in the Unity3D software development environment, reads the data from the batting information receiving module to examine whether the bat has been swung and generates corresponding control reactions in the game system.

- VR display module:

This module is developed mainly for the required VR devices. The VR devices developed for this system are Oculus Rift and HTC Vive. Therefore, this system supports the VR display of Oculus Rift and HTC Vive.

In view of the above interactive architecture, this study divided the implementation of the system into two parts: one is the design of the hardware VR bat, and the other is the development of the VR baseball game. The former is completed using the Arduino technology, whereas the latter is developed mainly using the Unity3D environment.

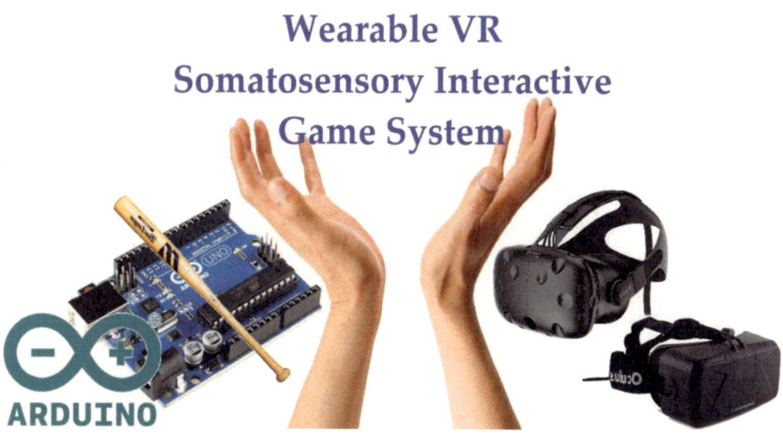

Figure 8. Wearable VR somatosensory interactive game system.

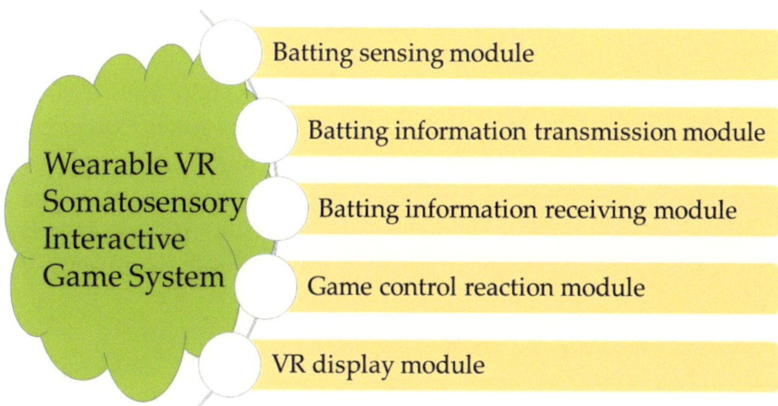

Figure 9. System architecture.

3.1. Hardware VR bat design

The system is designed with two sets of Arduino to detect the transmission and reception of batting information: one is located on the bat (transmission end), and the other is located on the computer (receiving end). The baseball game system is also installed on the computer to simultaneously reflect the batting actions in the game based on the information received by Arduino. Users can watch 3D VR scenes of the VR baseball game system via Oculus Rift or HTC Vive for an immersive experience. In order to complete the Arduino bat, we installed an InvenSense MPU-6500 six-axis sensor and NRF24L01 high-power wireless receiving device on the Arduino Nano development board. These devices, as shown in **Figure 10**, are introduced as follows:

Figure 10. Arduino Nana, MPU-6500, and NRF24L01.

- Arduino Nano:

In the design of Arduino Nano, the DC power interface is replaced with the Mini-B USB interface to connect the computer. Apart from the alteration in the appearance, all other interfaces and functions remain identical. The controller also uses ATmegal 68 or ATmega328.

- InvenSense MPU-6500:

The InvenSense MPU-6500 replaces the older MPU-6050. The new MPU-6500 incorporates a gyroscope and accelerometer to reduce significant installation space. Compared to the older MPU-6050, the new MPU-6500 offers an SPI protocol and reduces the energy consumption of action sensing and tracking by ~60%. InvenSense's motion processing database can process complex data of motion sensing, reduce the burden of motion processing operations on the operating system, and provide a structured API for application development.

- NRF24L01:

NRF24L01 is a wireless receiving device that runs in the 2.4–2.5 GHz universal ISM band. The wireless transceiver includes the frequency generator, enhanced equipment, SchockBurstTM, mode controller, power amplifier, crystal amplifier, modulator, and demodulator. The output power channel selection and protocol settings can be set through the SPI to achieve significantly low current consumption. For example, the current consumptions are 9.0 mA and 12.3 mA in the transmission and receiving modes, respectively, and the consumption is the lowest in the standby mode.

This system primarily uses the Arduino IDE as the firmware inside the Arduino bat. Because the system must determine whether a user has swung the bat, the Arduino bat in this system is required to read the bat rotation and acceleration data detected by the MPU-6500 and transmit it to the computer; moreover, the receiver must be capable of receiving the data to determine whether the bat has been swung.

3.2. VR baseball game development

In addition to 3D baseball scene production, the following modules were developed for the VR baseball game system on the computer, involving the pitcher, batting, and score counter:

- Pitcher:

This module includes ball speed control and pitch-type control. The ball speed is generated randomly, whereas there are mainly fastball and curveball. According to the various pitch types, this module automatically generates the motion trajectory of the Bezier curve. To make the pitching more convenient, this system also marked the strike. When the baseball: following the trajectory: finally arrived at the strike area, either a strike or bad ball occurs.

- Batting:

This module consists of the game-side Arduino data reading module, batting control module, and bat collision detection module. The main function of the game-side Arduino data reading module is to read the data of bat rotation and acceleration in the Arduino at the receiver end and send the data to the batting control module to determine whether it is necessary to swing the bat. Upon swinging, this module calls the bat collision detection module to determine whether the bat collides with the baseball. As the game-side Arduino data control module is the main function module that connects the Arduino device with the Unity game system, this module is developed with the Arduino for Unity kit.

- Score counter:

The system scores points by determining whether a home run is hit. Therefore, the system calculates the movement distance of each baseball after it is hit. When the distance exceeds the warning track, the system scores one point. To display the score results, the system incorporates a scoreboard in the baseball field to display the number of home runs and the distance to which the baseball is hit.

4. Implementation results

The test environment is Intel Core i7-6700HQ CPU 2.6 GHz, 8 GB memory, Nvidia Geforce GTX 960 M, and Windows 10. However, in order to achieve an enhanced performance experience, this study recommends that the performance level of the display card be at least that of Nvidia Geforce GTX 980. The function implementation and display results are as follows:

- Hardware VR bat implementation results and its firmware development:

In this study, Arduino Nano, InvenSense MPU-6500, and NRF24L01 were integrated, as illustrated in **Figure 11**. On the receiving end, Arduino Nano and NRF24L01 were combined. The receiving end can receive bat information immediately after it is connected to the USB port of the computer.

With regard to the development of the firmware on the transmitter, the system uses the accelgyro to read the acceleration values ax, ay, and az and the gyroscope values gx, gy, and gz on the x-, y-, and z-axes of the MPU-6500 and uses the Serial.write () instruction to transmit the data through the NRF24L01. On the receiver, this system uses the Mirf to receive the data transmitted by the NRF24L01.

- VR baseball game development:

When the game starts, the virtual pitcher in the game automatically detects whether the player faces the pitcher. When the player wearing Oculus Rift or HTC Vive faces the pitcher, the pitcher starts. Before the virtual pitcher throws a baseball, the system randomly sets the destination in the vicinity of the strike area for the ball to touch base and calculates the required motion trajectory. When the ball is thrown, it advances along the specified trajectory at the specified speed. The red arrow in **Figure 12** refers to the trajectory of the ball, and the red circle marks the ball moving on the trajectory.

When the ball is thrown, the player is free to determine the batting time. When the virtual bat in the system collides with the ball, the ball begins to detect when to touch ground. When the ball touches the ground, the system calculates its motion distance. If the distance exceeds the warning track for home runs, one home run is accumulated. Each game has ten times of pitching, as shown in **Figure 13**.

- VR display module:

In this system, two VR display modules were developed for Oculus Rift and HTC Vive, respectively. For Oculus Rift, this system introduced the Oculus SDK for Unity kit. Through this kit, a TrackCamera was developed to track the images for both the eyes, required by the Oculus Rift display. For HTC Vive, this system imported a SteamVR for Unity and implemented a SteamVR_Camera to integrate SteamVR such that the system's image information can be displayed on the HTC Vive headset, as shown in **Figure 14**. The player's use of the system is illustrated in **Figure 15**.

In this study, the Unity Profiler was also used to detect the implementation performance of this system. When executing this system, the CPU running speed was maintained at 60 FPS or higher, whereas most GPUs achieved a speed of ~100 FPS. This implies that this system can achieve the timeliness for interactive implementation of the game (30 FPS or higher), as shown in (**Figure 16**).

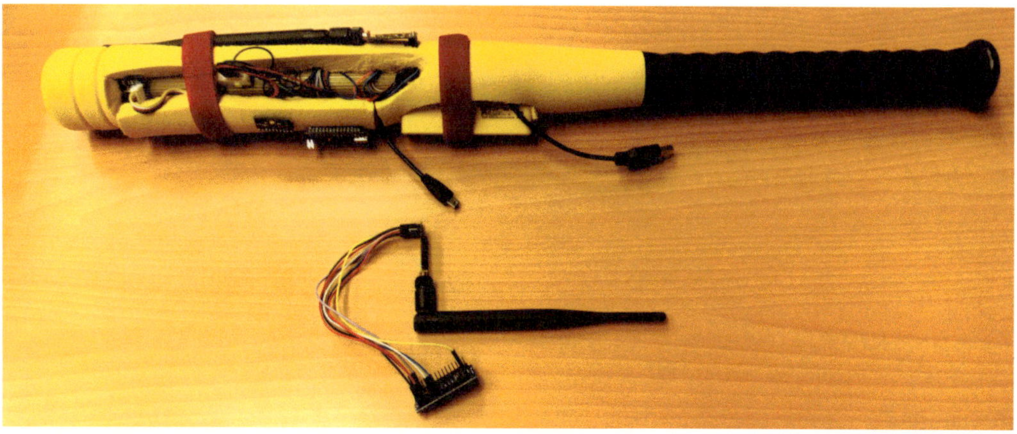

Figure 11. VR bat implementation results.

Figure 12. The strike area and ball motion trajectory.

Figure 13. Counting the number of home runs and calculating their motion distance.

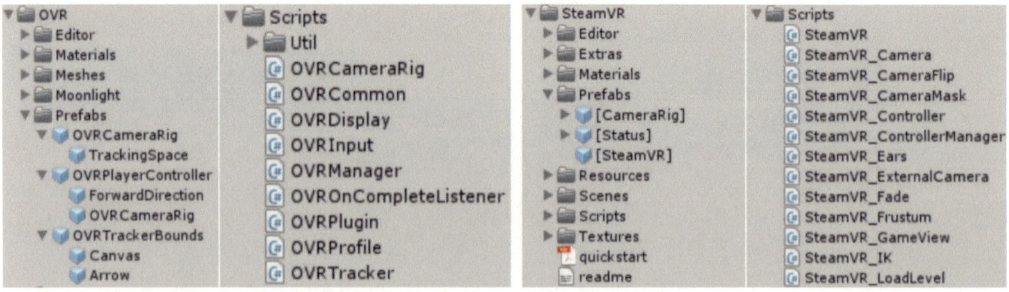

Figure 14. Oculus SDK for Unity kit and SteamVR for Unity.

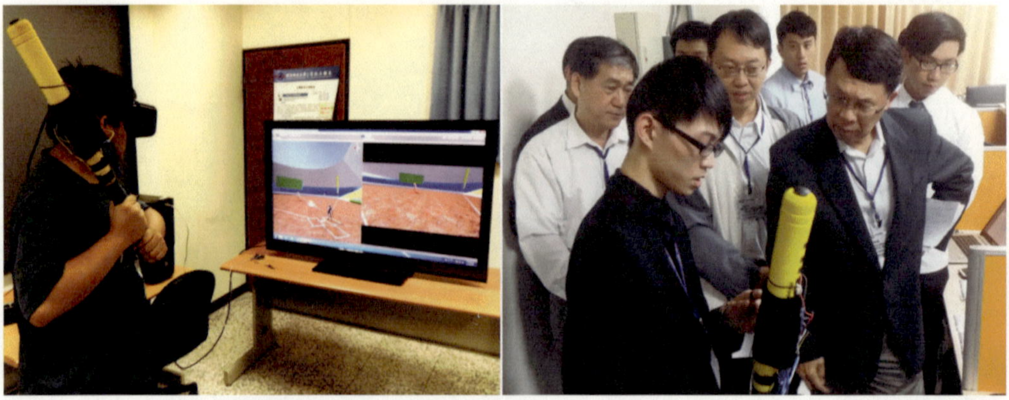

Figure 15. The player's use of the system.

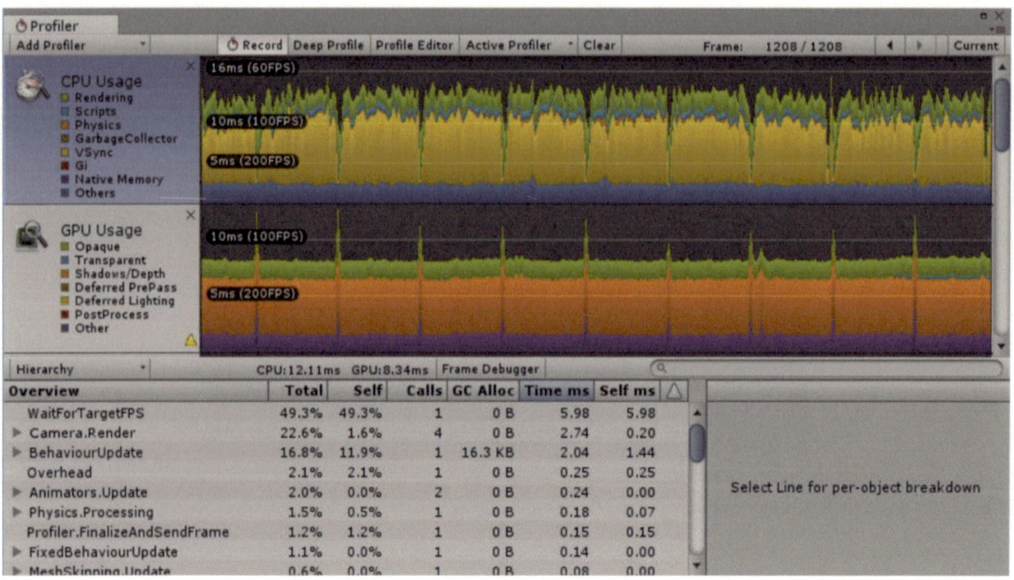

Figure 16. The performance of our system.

5. Conclusion

This study focused on the combination of Arduino and VR technology and used the interactive design characteristics of Arduino to provide a more intuitive manipulation mode for VR games. The experimental results demonstrated that Arduino sensing devices are of a wide variety and convenient to be combined with VR games and provide adequate execution performance. Therefore, it is likely that in the future, Arduino will be capable of providing more varied creative studies and combinations for VR developers. In addition, it is noteworthy that Arduino is the main development technology of the Internet of Things (IoT), and IoT and VR are both the development trends of information technologies in the next 10 years. Therefore, this study focused only on the VR games. The aforementioned technology projection also implies additional opportunities to further integrate these two trends. Moreover, this is highly likely to serve as a flourishing creation space for studies on these two trends.

Acknowledgements

We would like to thank Axis 3D Technology, Inc., for industry cooperation. This work was supported by the Ministry of Science and Technology, Taiwan, under contract no. MOST 105-2622-E-159-001-CC3 and MOST 106-2622-E-159-002-CC3. Additionally, we would also like to thank the support of Regional Industry-University Cooperation Center, Ministry of Education, Taiwan.

Author details

Juin-Ling Tseng[1]* and Chia-Wei Chu[2]

*Address all correspondence to: flysun@must.edu.tw

1 Minghsin University of Science and Technology, Taiwan

2 City University of Macau, Macau

References

[1] Tseng JL. Development of a low-cost 3D interactive VR system using SBS 3D display, VR headset and finger posture motion tracking. International Journal of Advanced Studies in Computer Science and Engineering. 2016;**5**(8):6-12

[2] Xu S, Lyu W, Li H. Optimizing coverage of 3D wireless multimedia sensor networks by means of deploying redundant sensors. International Journal of advanced studies in Computer Science and Engineering. 2015;**4**(9):28-33

[3] Tseng JL. An improved surface simplification method for facial expression animation based on homogeneous coordinate transformation matrix and maximum shape

operator. Mathematical Problems in Engineering. 2016;**2016**. Article ID: 2370919. DOI: 10.1155/2016/2370919

[4] Tseng JL. Surface simplification of 3D animation models using robust homogeneous coordinate transformation. Journal of Applied Mathematics. 2014;**2014**. Article ID: 189241. DOI: 10.1155/2014/189241

[5] Karunaratne S, Yan H. 3D animated movie actor training using fuzzy logic. In: IEEE Computer Graphics International. 2001. p. 23-30. DOI: 10.1109/CGI.2001.934654

[6] Bangquan L, Yun M. A facial animation based on emotional model for characters in 3D games. In: IEEE International Conference on Computer Science and Information Processing. 2012. p. 1304-1307. DOI: 10.1109/CSIP.2012.6309101

[7] Janarthanan V. Innovations in art and production: Sound, modeling and animation. In: IEEE Ninth International Conference on Information Technology: New Generations. 2012. p. 879-882. DOI: 10.1109/ITNG.2012.80

[8] Aoki M, Koning W, Miyai A, Kamihira T. 3D animation education in the US and Japan: Different environments, similar issues. In: ACM SIGGRAPH Asia Sketches. Article No. 34. 2011. DOI: 10.1145/2077378.2077421

[9] Laver KE, George S, Thomas S, Deutsch JE, Crotty M. Virtual Reality for Stroke Rehabilitation [Internet]. 2015. Available from: http://www.cochrane.org/CD008349/STROKE_virtual-reality-for-stroke-rehabilitation

[10] Cheng LP, Roumen T, Rantzsch H, Köhler S, Schmidt P, Kovacs R, Jasper J, Kemper J, Baudisch P. TurkDeck: Physical virtual reality based on people. In: Proceedings of the 28th Annual ACM Symposium on User Interface Software & Technology. 2015. p. 417-426. DOI: 10.1145/2807442.2807463

[11] Gordon R. Oculus Rift Will be Cheaper Thanks to Facebook; Aiming for 2015 Release [Internet]. [Updated]: 2014. Available from: https://gamerant.com/oculus-rift-cheaper-after-facebook-buyout/

[12] Wikipedia. Oculus Rift [Internet]. [Updated]: 2017. Available from: https://en.wikipedia.org/wiki/Oculus_Rift

[13] Chang CM, Hsu CH, Hsu CF, Chen KT. Performance measurements of virtual reality systems: Quantifying the timing and positioning accuracy. In: Proceedings of the ACM on Multimedia Conference. 2016. p. 655-659. DOI: 10.1145/2964284.2967303

[14] Soffel F, Zank M, Kunz A. Postural stability analysis in virtual reality using the HTC vive. In: Proceedings of the 22nd ACM Conference on Virtual Reality Software and Technology. 2016. p. 351-352. DOI: 10.1145/2993369.2996341

[15] McGhee J, Bailey B, Parton RG, Ariotti N, Johnston A. Journey to the centre of the cell (JTCC): A 3D VR experience derived from migratory breast cancer cell image data. In: SIGGRAPH ASIA 2016 VR Showcase. 2016 Article No. 11. DOI: 10.1145/2996376.2996385

[16] Juanes JA, Gómez JJ, Peguero PD, Lagándara JG, Ruisoto P. Analysis of the oculus rift device as a technological resource in medical training through clinical practice. In: ACM Proceedings of the 3rd International Conference on Technological Ecosystems for Enhancing Multiculturality. 2015. p. 19-23. DOI: 10.1145/2808580.2808584

[17] Tan CT, Leong TW, Shen S, Dubravs C, Si C. Exploring gameplay experiences on the oculus rift. In: ACM Proceedings of the 2015 Annual Symposium on Computer-Human Interaction in Play. 2015. p. 253-263. DOI: 10.1145/2793107.2793117

[18] Dasios A, Gavalas D, Pantziou G, Konstantopoulos C. Wireless sensor network deployment for remote elderly care monitoring. In: Proceedings of the 8th ACM International Conference on PErvasive Technologies Related to Assistive Environments. 2015. DOI: 10.1145/2769493.2769539

[19] Wang SJ, Virtual-spine YD. The collaboration between pervasive environment based simulator, game engine (mixed-reality) and pervasive messaging. In: Proceedings of the 7th International Conference on Pervasive Computing Technologies for Healthcare. 2015. p. 45-48. DOI: 10.4108/icst.pervasivehealth.2013.252108

[20] Sugathan A, Roy GG, Kirthyvijay GJ, Thomson J. Application of Arduino based platform for wearable health monitoring system. In: 2013 IEEE 1st International Conference on Condition Assessment Techniques in Electrical Systems. 2013. p. 1-5. DOI: 10.1109/CATCON.2013.6737464

Chapter 8

Developing Educational Simulation for Rockwell Hardness Test Machine

Ahmed Hadi Shubber, Amirmudin Bin Udin and
Asnul Bin Minghat

Additional information is available at the end of the chapter

http://dx.doi.org/10.5772/intechopen.71430

Abstract

The purpose of this paper is to analyze, develop, design, implement, and evaluate the engineering simulation model in metallurgy subject [Rockwell hardness test simulation (RHTS)], according to analyze, design, develop, implement, and evaluate (ADDIE) model and the Mechanical Engineering students of Babylon Institute in Iraq are chosen for case study. This paper presents the various steps involved in the simulation procedures. The detail simulation development process and its significant characteristics are highlighted. The flowchart of the model is rendered, displaying the different components used to develop the simulation algorithm using Microsoft Studio 2010 computer programming language. The advantages and limitations of the simulation model are identified by interviewing experts. The findings resulted from the simulated model reveal that the learners can learn easily and effectively. The developed software package is expected to provide valuable tool for both students and instructors. Furthermore, the same package in the form of a bi-product can also be used as a "research tool" together with the application for engineering education.

Keywords: RHTS, education simulation, Rockwell hardness test, metallurgy, ADDIE

1. Introduction

Modeling and simulation go hand in hand. Definitely, model building is a well-recognized way toward the understanding of the real world. Truly, it is a simplification of some complex structure or a system. Conversely, it may be for prediction, a substitute for experiential learning or simply for entertainment. The major difference between simulation and experimentation must be mentioned. In simulation, one experiments with a model and not with a phenomenon. The use of simulations represents the natural way of "learn by doing." Alike students' role playing, we use computer simulations to understand intricate systems, real situation, or dynamic processes. Computer simulations allow us to mimic situations or processes that would be difficult, impossible, dangerous, too long, or too expensive to perform in reality [1–3].

Undoubtedly, the purpose of an educational simulation is to motivate the learner to engage in problem solving, hypothesis testing, experiential learning, scheme construction, and development of mental models [4, 5]. Lately, these new information technology tools are changing the learning environment in engineering education from primarily teacher-centric to student-centric. Unfettered access to web-based or computer educational materials are highly useful [6].

In order to meet the growing demand for engineers those well versed with computer tools for problem solving and metacognitive skills, engineering educators are increasingly incorporating in curricula information technology-based learning tools. Consequently, web-based multimedia modules, virtual collaborative environments, virtual laboratories, software for simulation, and visualization of engineering phenomena [7] are developed. The twofold objective of this ongoing transformation is: (i) to improve the quality of instruction with innovative course materials that cater to the learning styles of present generation students and (ii) to provide students exposure to computer problem solving tools so as to facilitate their transition from academia to industry [8].

In this research, we attempt to design a simulation model for Rockwell hardness test machine to enhance the metacognitive skills of metallurgy lesson for mechanical engineering students of Iraq. The model is tested, implemented, and analyzed, and the results are compared and understood.

2. Theoretical background

In the past, overall education in Iraq has suffered from severe deterioration due to the decrease in spending, lack of supplies, collapse of infrastructure, and overcrowded schools. These are compounded by the continuing prevalence of classical teaching methods that focus on lectures and memorization. The stress analysis and deductive skills, the spirit of initiative, and creativity are all failed to optimally encourage student engagement. Much educational necessities such as libraries, laboratories, modern teaching techniques, smart boards, roving laboratories, electronic library, and computers and their accessories to a considerable percentage of schools and institutions of higher education are already rendered. Despite many efforts since 2003 to develop courses for all levels of education, there is still a need to develop study courses and provide additional supports to maintain international standards [9–11].

Metallurgy is considered as one of the most important branches of engineering materials. The emergence of various metal industries enforced the students teaching more significant for their work. Particularly, technicians in factories producing various types of engineering materials require knowledge of integrated types of metallic materials. In addition to their knowledge on physical, thermal, and chemical properties, they must be aware of the conditions for the manufacturing process [12]. Metallurgy is always considered as one of the hardest lessons taught in the Department of Mechanics in Iraq because many students fail to succeed in the first attempt [13]. Consequently, metallurgy is proven as a difficult subject for many students [14].

The present research aims to find ways that may transform the engineering curriculum of Department of Mechanics in Babylon Technical Institute into simulation-enhanced engineering curricula. It emphasizes on the incorporation of simulation-based interactive modules to enhance student learning. The pedagogy of "learning-by-doing in virtual environments" is being employed in the development of modules. In fact, one of the practical and efficient way in which engineers can learn is through hands-on activities in computer laboratories. The Rockwell hardness test module being a part of the metallurgy lesson is expected to complement student learning achieved through computer laboratories and conventional classroom instruction. However, our emphasis is not directed toward distance learning. It is rather focused for on-campus classes in enhancing the quality of student learning by embedding computer simulation in conventional mode of teaching and learning processes.

3. Rockwell hardness test

This hardness machine is the most popular one due to its accuracy, swiftness, and precision capacity to differentiate between small or large hardness in hardened steel. This has the ability to subject pressure on apparatus or materials under test without being damaged or destroyed. The advantages of the Rockwell tester [15] are the following:

a. Widely applicable in the industry due to the rapid and simplistic performance.

b. Highly accurate because the produced impression is small in size.

c. Easy conversion of Rockwell hardness number to Brinell number using special table or chart.

d. Suitable for testing both hard and soft materials.

4. Methodology

4.1. Objectives

The identification of goals for the construction of lesson is considered as the important standard to determine their contents, nature, activities and exercises accompanying the methods. Furthermore, the modes of using particular teaching methods and the goals for lessons are categorized into general and specific one. General goals primarily focus to enhance Engineering

Education and improve the metacognitive skills. Conversely, special goals intend to administer students having following perspectives:

a. Students identify when, where, and how to use the Rockwell hardness test.

b. Students identify the parts and components of the Rockwell hardness test.

c. Students identify the sequence of steps involved in the Rockwell hardness test.

d. Students identify the advantages and disadvantages of the Rockwell hardness test.

e. Students know how to safely use the machines.

f. Students know how to measure Rockwell hardness correctly.

g. Students know how to recognize the differences between the Vickers test and the Rockwell hardness test.

4.2. Simulation design and development

The researcher followed simulation model development process depended on the analyze, design, develop, implement, and evaluate (ADDIE) model (developing instructional model steps) in designing and developing the simulation according to the following procedures: analyzing, designing, developing, implementing, and evaluating.

ADDIE is considered a guide in designing and effectively tracking a project's progress. "ADDIE" stands for Analyse, Design, Develop, Implement, and Evaluate. This sequence, however, does not impose a strict linear progression between each step. Rather, each stage is a clear instruction on its own. This means that even if the individual applies ADDIE at the middle of the project, it will still retain its value and be able to provide a sense of structure to the whole program. Educators find this approach very useful having stages clearly defined which makes implementation of instructions effectively. As an Instructional Design (ID) Addie Model has found wide acceptance and use [16–18].

To conclude, using ADDIE model is the best tool to simulate the machine model. By revising such design model, the researcher found that ADDIE design model best suits the simulated model in the present study as it considered a generic process that is traditionally used by instructional designers and training developers. Moreover, the five phases applied in this model namely analysis, design, development, implementation, and evaluation are dynamic and flexible guidelines for building effective training and performance support tools. In this model, each design step has an outcome that feeds into the subsequent step that makes the final product more flexible and accurate. What differentiates this model from others is the accepted improvement using rapid prototyping. During each step of designing, the model received continual or formative feedback while instructional materials are being created. In a nut shell, such model could save time and money by identifying the problems while they are still easy to fix [19–21].

The simulation process is developed for RHTS models in the metallurgy lesson as described hereunder.

RHTS development involves the underlined steps:

1. Identification of general and special goal of the model.
2. Use of metals group such as stainless steel, mild steel, steel, brass, and aluminium in conducting the real test.
3. Manufacturing specimens from these metals by machines turning and milling, wire cutting, and polishing suitable for the apparatus specified in the research.
4. Conducting the test on real apparatus. In addition to the registration of the real data and results during the test, capturing pictures of each step, movement, and reading of apparatus is also considered.
5. Modification and calibration of pictures for the measurements are performed with the real equipment and specimen using a set of computer programs such as Photoshop and other image processors.
6. Designing a computer program using Microsoft Studio 2010 to simulate the model and conversion of data and images to the software codes. Devising the computer interfaces representing the real test steps.
7. Acquiring data from the program alike a real machine when running the simulation or executing the program.

The user is responsible for checking the statement true or false with the possibility of re-trying it several times, data collection, and storage in specific places to be audited.

4.2.1. Simulation Design Process

The development processes of RHTS are illustrated in **Figure 1** [22, 23]. The computer language Microsoft Studio 2010 is used to design and develop the RHTS model. An evaluation of the proposed model is carried out to identify their strengths and weaknesses through pilot test. A group of experts with mechanical engineering and teaching methods background are chosen to get their consensus and confirm the content validity.

The researcher reviewed the previous literature related to the characteristics of designing the simulation. Previous studies [3, 24] identified the main characteristics of simulation, which were fit for engineering education that could be summarized as the following:

1. Simulation program offers a series of clear events to the students allowing them the opportunity to participate actively in the program.
2. It offers the learner many suitable choices.
3. It helps the students to learn using the sound, images, and animation drawing.
4. It directs the students using the proper guidance to the study depending on their control in the learning environment.

5. It provides a large base of information to the learner useful in understanding the subject matter under consideration.
6. The simulation program assists the learner to understand the reality, thought, and emotions.
7. It allows the learner to commit mistakes without affecting the results adversely.
8. It permits the learner to achieve great freedom in the learning process.
9. It proffers a new style to the learner which is very different from traditional approaches.
10. It grants a chance to the learner to apply some of the learned skills.
11. It generally creates appropriate conditions for learning and skills training with the computer which are very similar for the real world.

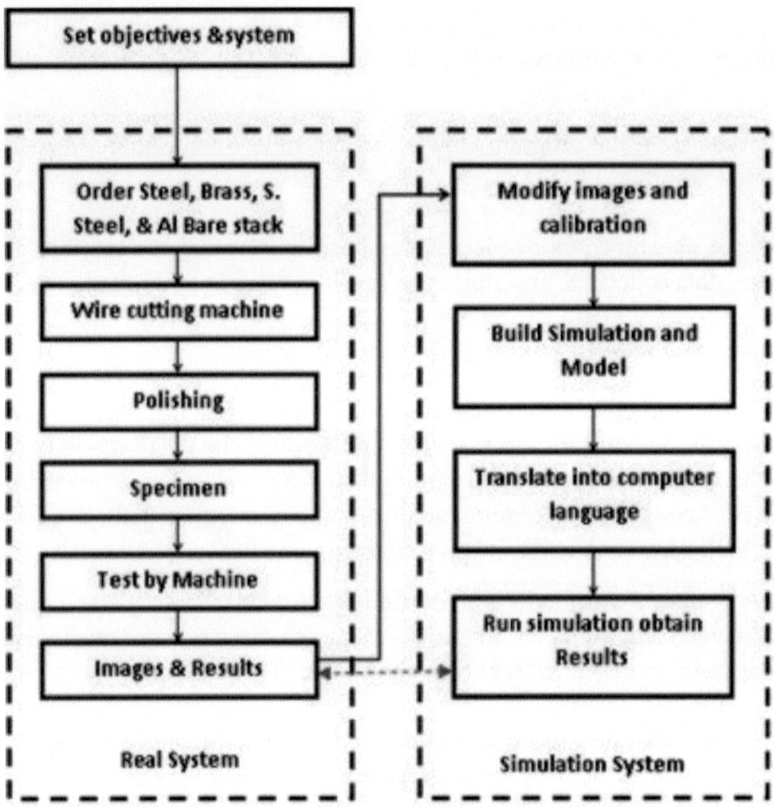

Figure 1. Block diagram for the simulation development processes.

4.2.1.1. RHTS design

The RHTS designed by [22, 23, 25] is performed using thc following stages:

A. Design of Screen 1 as depicted in **Figure 2** is comprised of the following options:

1. ABOUT ROCKWELL TEST: Review the information related to the Rockwell Test.
2. ABOUT SIMULATION: Review the information relating to how to use the simulation model.
3. TEST STEPS: Review the information related to the test steps.
4. SIMULATION TEST: Move to the next screen to use the simulation model for the Rockwell Test.
5. EXIT: End of simulation model.

B. Design of Screen 2 as shown in **Figure 3** includes the following options:

1. Aluminum Al: Use Aluminum specimen and the next screen.
2. Steel: Use Steel specimen and move to the next screen.
3. Brass: Use Brass specimen and move to the next screen.
4. S-Steel: Use S-Steel specimen and move to the next screen.
5. EXIT: End of simulation model.
6. Back: Back to the previous screen.

C. Design of Screen 3 as illustrated in **Figure 4** contains the following choices:

1. Load operating lever: Click on lever to apply the load.
2. Capstan hand wheel: Click on it to increase or decrease elevation.
3. Image of hardness dial gauge: To show that the value of hardness is clear.
4. Dial adjusting hard wheel: Click on it to rotate the large needle dial to the "C"
5. Input text "Rockwell hardness number": To input the hardness value.
6. "Enter" Key: Click on it to show whether the hardness value is true or not.
7. Label: To show whether the result is true or not.
8. Back: Back to the prior screen.
9. EXIT: End of simulation model.

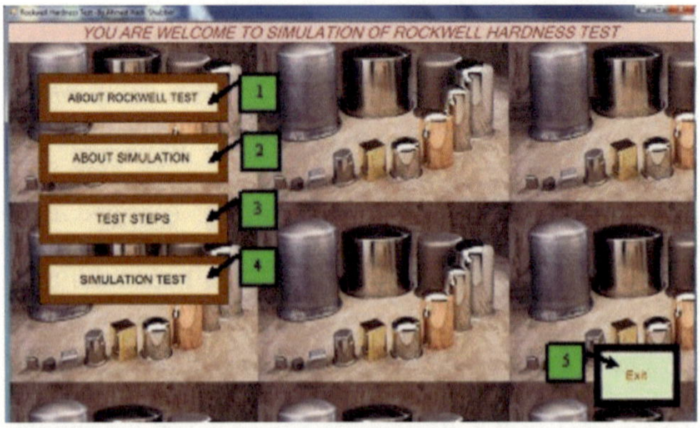

Figure 2. Schematic diagram displaying the design of screen 1 for simulating Rockwell hardness test.

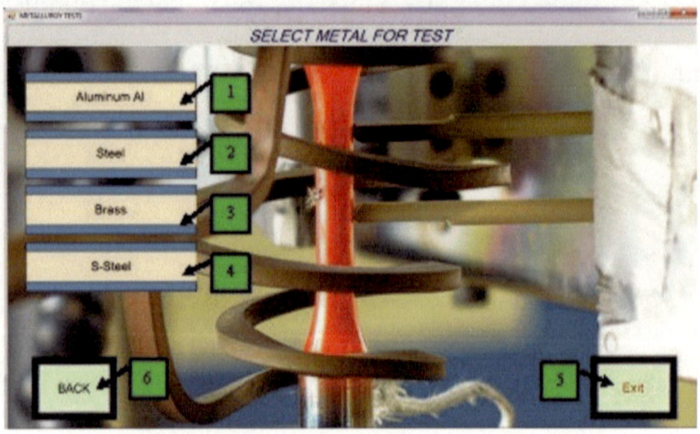

Figure 3. Schematic diagram displaying the design of screen 2 for simulating Rockwell hardness test.

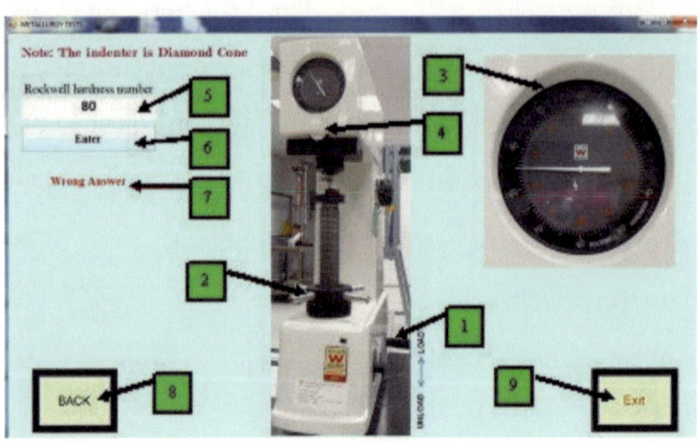

Figure 4. Schematic diagram displaying the design of screen 3 for simulating Rockwell hardness test.

4.2.1.2. RHTS procedures

1. In the screen 1, click on (Simulation test (4)) to move to the next screen to use simulation for Rockwell Test.
2. In the screen 2, click on one of the options (Aluminum Al (1), Steel (2), Brass (3), and S-Steel (4)) to choose material and move to the next screen.
3. In the screen 3, follow the following options:
   a. Two clicks on Load operating lever (1) to become unload.
   b. Click on Capstan hand wheel (2) to up elevating screw rod then continuous clicks until you watch the touch marker.
   c. Click on Capstan hand wheel (2) clockwise until the hardness scale needle (large needle) rotates three revolutions and the preliminary load needle (small needle) points to the red marker (3).
   d. Click on dial adjusting hard wheel (4) until the needle position deviates to the "C" zero point (3).
   e. Two clicks on load operating lever (1) to the tester applies the total load and the needle begins to move (3).
   f. Waiting until the hardness scale needle stops moving (3).
   g. Two clicks on Load operating lever (1) to remove the main load.
   h. Waiting until the hardness scale needle stops moving (3).
   i. After the main load has been relieved, you can read the Rockwell hardness value at which the needle points to the dial scale (3).
   j. Input the Rockwell hardness value in Input Text (5)
   k. Click on Enter (6) to watch result is true or false.

The flowchart illustrating the entire modeling and simulation process of the proposed algorithm is shown in **Figure 5**.

4.2.2. Simulation model development

In order to develop the simulation model, the researcher seeks the opinions of experts, specialists, teachers, and the laboratory supervisors in order to modify and develop the model to be more clear, easy, content accurate, and suitable for the students.

4.2.3. Simulation model implementation

The model was applied on a group of experts and specialists in metallurgy laboratory course on the mechanics Department students at the Al-Furat Al-Awsat Technical University.

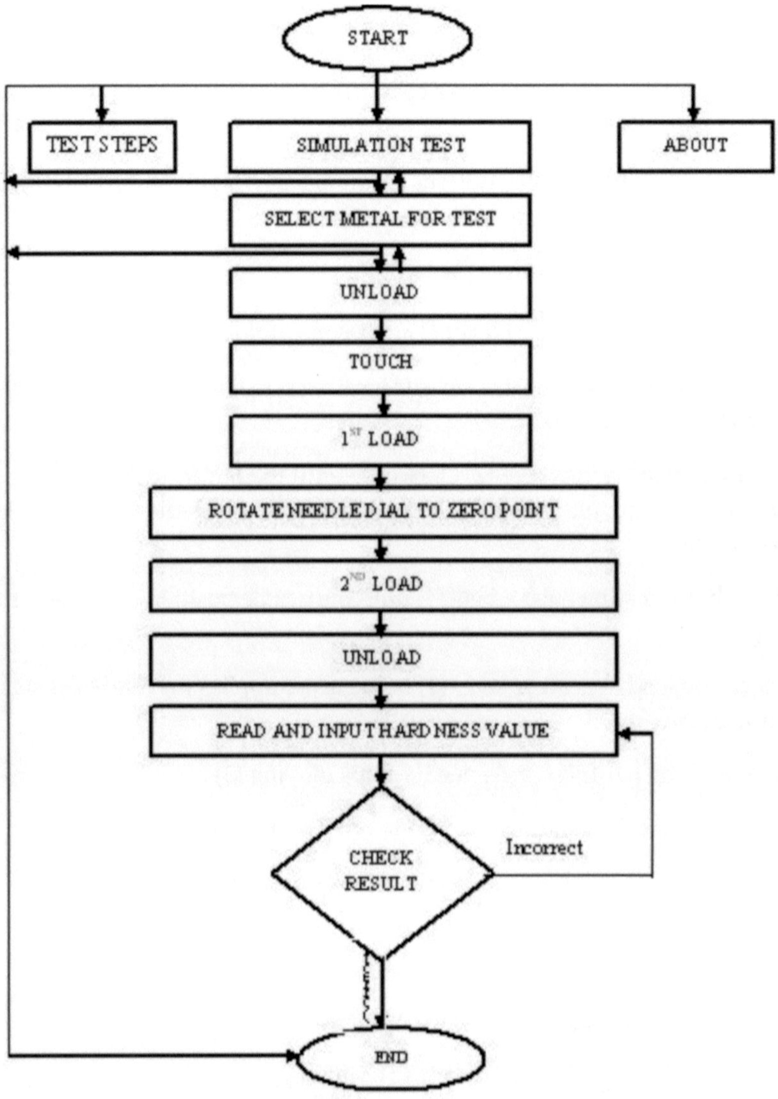

Figure 5. Flow chart of all the events in the proposed algorithm for the Rockwell test machine.

4.2.4. Simulation model evaluation

For validity purpose, the simulation model exemplified to 12 experts and specialists in the Department of Mechanical Engineering and the Faculty of Education in the Al-Furat Al-Awsat Technical University and the University of Babylon during the interview with them in their Departments. Also, Tokmak et al. [26] work in terms of evaluating the simulation system was found to be consistent with the purpose of designing the model in the present study. Additionally, the experts' discussion resulted in four main points. Firstly, with respect to the curriculum matching and procedures, they all emphasized that the model was matching the planned curriculum for the students in the Department of mechanics. This included the experiment procedures, which were screened in a manner similar to the machines in the real word. One of the experts indicated the possibility of developing and adding some vocabulary to the model to be applicable to other similar colleges, institutes, and universities.

Secondly, with respect to accuracy and modernity, all the experts indicated that the results of the simulated model was found to be accurate, and based on their knowledge they had not seen such model before. Thirdly, with respect to the clarity of the used language, some linguistic corrections have been identified and some terms have been modified. All of the language corrections and terms modifications were taken into consideration by the researcher. Finally, with respect to the motivation, learners' participation, and the clarity of the design, all the experts emphasized that the model was rich soil for learning motivation. This is because the model contained exciting images and movements for the students, which could raise the possibility of engaging all the students in the tests and which could not be achieved by the traditional method. The experts also emphasized the clarity of the model's designation purpose. In general, the experts stressed that designing such model will support and facilitate education in engineering and educational laboratories. After taking into consideration all of the experts' suggestions and after modifying the model, the researcher reinterviewed the experts and they expressed full agreement on the model. As such, the model was ready to be applied to the students.

5. Conclusions

The influences of Rockwell hardness test simulation in achieving enhanced metacognitive skills are inspected. The researcher designed RHTS relying on established approaches is clearly able to identify striking simulation characteristics. Researchers are expected to employ the simulation design to evaluate the increased reliability and validity of the study instrument in identifying the presence of possible deficiencies during actual implementation [27, 28]. The simulation is executed to determine the effectiveness of metacognitive skills on mechanical engineering students of Iraq as test sample. Simulation design suggests that the developed model may serve as a research tool for both students and instructors in metallurgy lesson to improve their metacognitive skills. Laboratory experiments are carried out, data are collected, and computer algorithms are developed using Microsoft Studio 2010. Relevant theoretical background and formulae related to the RHTS are designed via user-friendly approach. The simulation model contains meticulously executed steps including the generation of metacognitive tasks, its goals, and effective tools that promote overall ability and efficiency in education. It is hoped that the capability of students in understanding metallurgy lesson will improve via the acquisition of metacognitive skills. It may also enable learners in controlling their cognition, emotion, and motivation in addition to solve complex problems in mechanical engineering. The present model simulation is highly instructive for successful process of cognition and learning. This simulation will definitely enhance the susceptibility of students to understand and solve multifaceted problems in metallurgy. Finally, it may be applied to the students of technical institutes in Iraq to know the influences on the enhanced metacognitive skills in engineering education.

The findings related to the proposed simulation model indicate that the simulated model was suitable for undergraduate Iraqi students majoring in Mechanical Engineering and they were appropriate for teaching metallurgy lessons to students. After examining the interview findings, the experts indicated that the curriculum and procedures in the simulated model matched the planned curriculum for the students. With respect to accuracy and modernity, all the experts indicate that the results of the simulated model were accurate. With respect to the clarity of the language, most of the experts identified linguistic corrections and modified a few terms. Finally, with respect to the motivation, learner participation and the clarity of the design, all the experts agreed that model is fertile soil for motivating learners.

The students were attracted by the simulated model as the instructions are written in a clear way and associated images and active interfaces were indicated using color. In addition, the students conducting the experiments on their own and at their own pace were easy and considered individual learning differences. This was consistent with Stančić and Yilmaz, who studied the features of effective simulated model such as user suitability, applicability, attraction to users, clear instructions, clear images and motions, and ease of use. The proposed simulated model was relevant, suitable, and applicable to the teaching medium.

The simulated model was designed using the ADDIE model that found to be applicable and efficient. ADDIE model provides clear instructions for each design step and calculated the errors for each stage before circulating to the next stage, which makes the final product more accurate and applicable. It also saves time, effort, and money if the product is fully designed at once, then found there are deficit in the product. In this case, the product was drawn from the market and reworked. Each simulated model for the metal machines was simulated according to the characteristics of each machine. Students using these simulated models found them to be easy and effective as each simulated model offered flexible options.

Author details

Ahmed Hadi Shubber[1]*, Amirmudin Bin Udin[2] and Asnul Bin Minghat[2]

*Address all correspondence to: ahmed.shuber@gmail.com

1 Al-Furat Al-Awsat Technical University, Technical Institute of Babylon, Iraq

2 Universiti Tecknologi Malaysia, Johor Bahru, Malaysia

References

[1] Shubber AH, Udin AB, Minghat AB. Vickers test simulation to improve metacognitive skills. Procedia – Social and Behavioral Sciences. [Internet]. 2015;**204**(November 2014):45-53. Available from: http://www.sciencedirect.com/science/article/pii/S1877042815047564

[2] Shubber AH, Udin AB, Minghat AB. Tensile test machine simulation for improving metacognitive skills. EDULEARN14 Proc. 2014:3473-3483

[3] Stančić H, Seljan S, Cetinić A, Sanković D. Simulation models in education. Međunarodna Znan Konf Futur Inf Sci. 2007 (Digital Information and Heritage (1; 2007))

[4] Winn W. Cognitive perspectives in psychology. In: Jonassen D, editor. Handbook of Research on Educational Communications and Technology. Routledge/Taylor & Francis Group; 2003. p. 79-112

[5] Duffy T, Cunningham D. Constructivism: Implications for the design and delivery of instruction. In: Jonassen D, editor. Handbook of Research on Educational Communications and Technology. New York: Simon & Schuster; 1996

[6] Donovan MS, Bransford JD. How people learn: Bridging research and practice. National Academy of Science [Internet]. 1999;**88**. Available from: http://www.nap.edu/catalog/9457.html

[7] Chaturvedi SK, Akan O. Simulation and visualization enhanced engineering education. In: International Mechanical Engineering Education. China: ASME and CMES; 2006. p. 1-8

[8] Bourne JR, Brodersen AJ, Ccampbell JO, Dawant MM, Shiavi RG. A model for on-line learning networks in engineering education. Journal of Engineering Education [Internet]. 1996;**85**(3):253-262. Available from: http://doi.wiley.com/10.1002/j.2168-9830.1996.tb00241.x

[9] Ministry of Higher Education & Scientific Research of Iraq. The strategic framework and the general policies of technical and vocational education in Iraq. In: Third International Congress on Technical and Vocational Education and Training [Internet]. China. 2012. p. 2-12. Available from: www.tvetoman.net/PDF/PDF_AR_7.pdf

[10] Ministry of Planning Republic of Iraq. National Development Plan 2010-2014 [Internet]. Baghdad; 2010. Available from: http://www.mop.gov.iq/mop

[11] United Nations Human Settlements -UNHABITAT. Country Programme Document 2009-2011 :Iraq. Iraq; 2009

[12] FTE. Metallurgy Curriculum, Mechanics Depart. Iraq: Foundation of Technical Education; 2010

[13] Al-Mosawi A. Learning difficulties in metallurgy lesson: A case study in technical Institute of Babylon. Education Research International. 2013;**2**(1):116-119

[14] Black P, Harrison C. Science inside the Black Box: Assessment for Learning in the Science Classroom. London: NFER Nelson; 2004

[15] Low SR. NIST Recommended Practice Guide: Rockwell Hardness Measurement of Metallic Materials. special Pu. U.S.: U.S. government printing office; 2001. p. 116

[16] Piskurich GM. Rapid Instructional Design: Learning ID Fast and Right. New Jersey: John Wiley & Sons, Inc.; 2015. p. 444

[17] Alajmi M. E-learning and ADDIE model. In: Proceedings of World Conference on E-Learning in Corporate. 2009. p. 37-42

[18] Allen WC. Overview and evolution of the ADDIE training system. Advances in Developing Human Resources. 2006;**8**(4):430-441

[19] Hays RT, Singer MJ. Simulation fidelity in training system design: Bridging the gap between reality and training. Springer Science & Business Media; 2012

[20] Molenda M. In search of the elusive ADDIE model. Performance Improvement [Internet]. 2003;**42**(5):34-36. Available from: http://doi.wiley.com/10.1002/pfi.4930420508

[21] Reinbold S. Using the ADDIE model in designing library instruction. Medical Reference Services Quarterly [Internet]. 2013;**32**(3):244-256. Available from: http://www.ncbi.nlm.nih.gov/pubmed/23869632

[22] Scheinman DE. Discrete Event Simulation and Production System Design for Rockwell Hardness Test Blocks. California; 2009

[23] Heath B, Hill R, Ciarallo FA. Survey of agent-based modeling practices (January 1998 to July 2008). Journal of Artificial Societies and Social Simulation. 2009;**12**(4):9

[24] Yilmaz L, Davis P, Fishwick AP, Hu X, Miller JA, et al. What makes good research in modeling and simulation (M&S): Sustaining the growth and vitality of the M&S Discipline. In: Winter Simulation Conference 2008. IEEE/ACM; 2008. p. 671-676

[25] Chang GC. Strategic planning in education: Some concepts and methods. In: Directions in Educational Planning: Symposium to Honour the Work of Françoise Caillods. 2008

[26] Tokmak HS, Incikabi L, Yelken TY. Differences in the educational software evaluation process for experts and novice students. Australasian Journal of Educational Technology. 2012;**28**(8):1283-1297

[27] Cooper DR, Schindler PS. Business Research Method. 7th ed. New York: McGraw-Hill; 2000

[28] Hair JFJ, Black WC, Babin BJ, Anderson RE, Tatham RL. Multivariate Data Analysis. 6th ed. Upper Saddle River, NJ: Pearson Prentice Hall; 2006

Chapter 9

An Evaluation of Open Digital Gaming Platforms for Developing Computational Thinking Skills

Andoni Eguíluz, Pablo Garaizar and
Mariluz Guenaga

Additional information is available at the end of the chapter

http://dx.doi.org/10.5772/intechopen.71339

Abstract

Due to business needs and the growing importance of technology in society, in recent years, the concept of computational thinking has emerged, especially focused on its inclusion in compulsory education as a relevant complement, transversal to traditional subjects. In parallel, various initiatives have developed interactive digital tools for learners to meet this type of thinking through a series of activities commonly framed as games. In this chapter, we evaluate many of the existing free access platforms to propose pedagogical, design, and content approaches with which they can be compared.

Keywords: computational thinking, learning, resources, school, videogames, visual languages

1. Introduction

Computational thinking (CT) allows you to solve problems in a way that a computer (human or machine) can execute. In just a decade, since Wing [1] introduced the concept to the technological community, the movement has been very intense, both in the scientific community and the educational world, as well as in the tools and content available [2]. Thanks to all these efforts, we begin to see signs that the situation is changing, but there are many challenges [3], starting with the still insufficient definition of the concept of CT and its structuring in the classroom [4, 5], which involves multiple initiatives by national and international organizations.

Considering the ubiquity of computers in our digital society, CT appears to be a fundamental skill not only for computer specialists but also for many other professionals. It is still a topic of debate how important and transversal CT should be in compulsory education [5]; however, for practical reasons, the educational world has been paying it increasingly more attention. In recent years, many initiatives have been developed to promote CT in primary and secondary education due to both the social boom in CT and the lack of computer professionals in the present and near future. The Hour of Code, Code Week, or Scratch Day are some of the well-known global events that promote changes in curricular design toward this new digital formation. Most of these initiatives are based on digital platforms where learner programmers can develop and improve their CT skills through games.

It is not this chapter's goal to discuss the advantages of incorporating CT into education, but to analyze the tools, their possible uses, and their limitations.

To delimit the study, we see that there are many common features among most of the current tools geared to developing CT skills like code.org, Alice, Scratch, or Kodable: they are open and free for general use; they focus mainly on primary and secondary school students; and there is an explicit gaming characteristic, which facilitates the use by these learners and applies the proven benefits of games in education [6].

It is also important that all these tools seek to avoid novice programmers having to confront the complexity of text-based computer coding and to improve the learnability [7]. There are several ways to address this problem such as narrative tools, flow-model tools, or specialized output realizations [8]; in this chapter, we focus on the most common tools, which are those that use the block-based visual programming. These tools employ user interfaces based on visual blocks that are moved and placed constructively as an assembly game, usually with the visual abstraction of a puzzle with its pieces and fitting ways. These blocks work as an abstraction of programming components: sentences, data, control structures, procedures, and so on. Consequently, they considerably limit the prior knowledge required to program and reinforce the program structure, eliminating the possibility of syntax errors and focusing only on the logic that exists in the activity that is to be undertaken.

In this chapter, we review a number of existing platforms with features mentioned above. There are articles which discuss some of them [9–11]; our intention is to propose an objective analysis, reviewing their possibilities from different perspectives. From a pedagogical point of view, we study different dimensions that can affect the learning process in or out of class (such as the richness of the proposed interaction, the time that can be invested, and the depth of the exploration). From the point of view of the game, the fun and engagement generated. From a CT point of view, we will analyze what concepts involved in CT each platform covers and to what extent. Finally, we will analyze the degree of adaptation to the personal characteristics of programming learners, their skills, and knowledge. We will consider, among others, aspects such as feedback and interaction, registration possibilities, and learning design.

2. Review of platforms

In our study, we include those platforms accessible online in July 2017 that can be used through the computer, mobile, or tablet without a paid commercial license that do not require additional hardware or devices, that are at least available in the English language, with international and open distribution, that contain some relevant part of visual programming and that incorporate some game characteristics. In this section, we describe them in an alphabetical order and then analyze them according to their features in the comparison.

2.1. Alice (http://www.alice.org/)

Alice is a free creation tool for small games, animations, and interactive resources in 3D. It is also an interactive animated story development tool that proposes a visual programming interface strongly linked to the development of object-oriented code, with explicit concepts such as methods, event listeners, objects like characters, or classes such as scenes. In its version 3, it also allows a parallel development in which each block movement displays the corresponding Java source code. It is one of the few 3D–oriented environments, making it possible to create games and animations, while adding a degree of complexity to the need to elaborate the scene with its models, skeletons, terrains, or cameras. Its alliance with Disney, Pixar, and EA has facilitated the inclusion of elaborated graphics, which enrich the experience of the project. It was created by the University of Virginia and taken over and maintained by Carnegie Mellon University since 1997.

2.2. App Inventor (http://appinventor.mit.edu/)

App Inventor is a free creation tool for small games, animations, and interactive resources. This tool has a closer approach to professional development than most platforms analyzed and it is probably the least close to a game because its goal is to build apps for an Android device. Users visually design the graphic user interface (GUI) on the one hand and its logical operation on the other, simulated in execution on the device itself or in an Android emulator included. System and development dependency for mobile devices causes event orientation (sensors, button clicks, etc.) to be very present in App Inventor and determines the control flow. It is also important to design the user interface, which has a specific section of the tool (Designer) in addition to code editing (Blocks). It was originally created by Google in 2010 and taken over by MIT in 2012 and oriented to youth and adult audience, not to children.

2.3. Bee-Bot (https://itunes.apple.com/es/app/bee-bot/id500131639?mt=8)

Bee-Bot is a game of successive challenges to learn programming for iPad. Bee-Bot is a bee robot, a physical toy for children of 4 years and above, which also has a free App for iPad that can be used without the toy, geared to preliterate children. It allows children to learn programming concepts about directional motion primitives, while taking their virtual robot through a series of scenarios. It has 12 levels with labyrinths of progressive difficulty. There is also a more complex paid app for children of 7 years and above.

2.4. Beetle Blocks (http://beetleblocks.com/)

Beetle Blocks is a free 3D model creation tool. It is a visual programming environment that allows for modeling three-dimensional shapes. Like a Logo language with its 3D tortoise, you can program the movement of a virtual beetle to generate geometric shapes of all kinds that are chained with repetitive and alternative control structures and programmable routines. The block language is based on Snap!, which is analyzed in Section 2.20.

2.5. Blockly Games (https://blockly-games.appspot.com/)

Blockly Games is a game of successive challenges to learn programming based on a generalized visual programming library. Blockly (https://developers.google.com/blockly/), developed by Google as open source in 2012, is really a library to make Web applications based on visual programming by blocks (hence its name). Starting from this, other tools have been made such as App Inventor, Microsoft MakeCode, or OzoBlockly. Here we analyze Blockly Games, which is a Blockly-based Google development, proposing a series of educational games to learn how to program in a directed and progressive mode, in a series of levels that are structured into seven sections: Puzzle, Maze (movement to exit a maze with repetitive and alternate structures), bird (continuous 2d motion with twists and x-y displacement based on conditions and boolean expressions), turtle (logo style drawing with repetition over angles and distances), movie (movement of geometric shapes based on a time value that ranges from 0 to 100), pond tutor (a shooting game with angles and forces that introduces text programming corresponding to the visual), and pond (a shooting game with players to be controlled by the computer). It also incorporates two free challenges that can be published on Reddit.

Blockly's development technology is web-oriented (in Javascript), but it also has native support for Android and IOS.

2.6. Cargo-Bot (https://itunes.apple.com/es/app/cargo-bot/id519690804)

Cargo-Bot is a game of successive challenges to learn programming. It is also a game for iPad where children can teach a robot to move boxes inside a factory by using visual programming structures. The game contains 36 puzzles and has the peculiar feature of having been the first game entirely developed on the iPad itself based on Codea (a Lua code editor for iPad). It uses encoding with icons with motion primitives for the crane (down, up, and move box) and calls to repeat procedures as well as box color codes for alternative actions.

2.7. Code.org (https://code.org/) and Code Studio (https://code.org/educate/gamelab)

Code.org is a nonprofit organization created by Harvard computer scientist Hadi Partovi in 2013 having diverse games of successive challenges to learn programming, and tool of creation free of small game, animation, or interactive resource. He has been able to intensively energize the need to bring CT to young people through the activities promoted from his website and, in particular, the creation of a movement called "Hour of Code" that proposes simple digital activities in the form of programming challenges that can be achieved in one hour (or a few more hours) with Blockly-based visual programming. By attracting personalities of the technological world to the promotion, like Mark Zuckerberg and Bill Gates, and later President Barack Obama himself, the movement has been a success not only in the USA but at the global level, managing to mobilize more than 100 million children and adults who use their resources for free to learn to code. Another of the successes of Code.org has been to use elements of existing video games or films to contextualize the challenges of code; and negotiating with corporations to use characters from Plants vs. Zombies, Flappy Bird, Frozen, Star Wars, or Minecraft, which makes the project much more attractive, as well as an important graphic, design, and logic quality. After 4 years of Hour of Code editions, Code.org and its partners have more than 170 different activities identified and accessible on the web (https://code.org/learn).

In addition to the online programming activities, Code.org also deals with the full computing curriculum content in primary and secondary education, provides training materials and resources of different types for free use of schools, and promotes training activities for schoolchildren and teachers (with special attention to women and underrepresented minorities). It has developed a blocks-based visual language, Code Studio (https://studio.code.org), that, Scratch-style, makes it possible to create multimedia resources or video games. This tool distinguishes four types of projects: Draw Something, App Lab (to simulate mobile apps), Play Lab (games or simple stories), and Game Lab (more elaborate games).

All the technology developed by Code.org is open source. The web also incorporates a section for teachers with management features for student groups and a complete dashboard page with detailed control of the development of each student.

2.8. Daisy the Dinosaur (http://www.daisythedinosaur.com/)

Daisy the Dinosaur is a game of successive challenges to learn programming. It is a small game for the iPad aimed at the first contact with programming for the youngest children, who can solve it in a few minutes. Its concept is very simple: the learner moves Daisy the Dinosaur by using some of the nine motion commands in the appropriate sequence. When the challenges are over, you can play in free-play mode to freely move the character.

2.9. Kodable (https://www.kodable.com/)

Kodable is a game of successive challenges to learn programming. Kodable is one of tools with the strongest focus on teachers and classes. It envisages a progression of levels oriented to the whole age of primary education. It has a number of free levels and many more accessible through pay-by-school licenses. The approach is an icon-based visual programming language that allows you to move a character (Fuzz) through an orthogonal maze by collecting the stars. To the motion instructions in all four directions, conditionals are added using colored boxes, loops with counters, and functions to repeat the same code several times. Another series of worlds provide conceptual training complements in programming using games, although they do not use visual programming such as a Tetris-style game for strings and integers, a tower defense for object-orientation, and so on. Teachers have a dashboard with full access to the progress information of their classes and students. In addition, there is a creation mode to generate custom levels, which both teachers and students have access to.

2.10. Kodetu (http://kodetu.org/)

Kodetu is a game of successive challenges to learn programming. It is a maze-solving game that allows an astronaut to be guided to the target in a space station by using visual blocks of motion and rotation, and repetitive and alternative structures. It is based on Blockly Maze and proposes a sequence of 15 levels of progressive difficulty, being the last maze a challenge even for people who already know how to program. It is designed to be able to play in an hour or two. Teachers can generate their own groups and access the information about the learning path covered by their students.

2.11. Kodu Game Lab (http://www.kodugamelab.com/)

Kodu Game Lab is a free small 3D game creation tool. Kodu, originally called Boku, is a visual programming environment developed by Microsoft in 2009, for the Xbox console and Windows OS. Like Alice, the execution environment is in 3D, but the programming orientation is quite different and is not block- but event-oriented. The concept is quite original with respect to other tools: the user can modify the world with a visual editing system of ground and 3D objects and add characters on which rules are created (in when-do form, with what is called in Microsoft Tile-Based Coding): If an event occurs, an action is executed. The events and rules are very oriented to an arcade type game (move, shoot, and collide) in a fixed gravity context. It does not incorporate control structures because the event system itself generates an infinite repetition in a real-time loop, and each rule (when) functions as an alternative.

2.12. Hopscotch (https://www.gethopscotch.com/)

Hopscotch is a free creation tool for small games, animations, or interactive resources. Hopscotch, available only for iOS, is a visual programming language specifically designed to be used on Apple touch devices and is oriented to very simple games. Although the payment license allows you to personalize characters and other improvements, in the free mode you can develop the entire gameplay. Hopscotch also has an online community to share creations, and a web player so that anyone can play the games created from a browser. Hopscotch makes a significant effort to use the resources of the tablet, both to ensure that the entire editing system can be done in a tactile way and to incorporate all the possibilities of the device in programming (tilt, vibration, and acoustic sensors).

2.13. Lightbot (https://lightbot.com/)

Lightbot is a game of successive challenges to learn programming. It is a commercial game for mobile platform (also with a version for Windows and Mac), with a free demo version (code hour) that allows users to play the first levels. The approach of the game modernizes the classic movement puzzles like Robozzle (explained later), with successive challenges of small labyrinths in which you have to illuminate the blue squares with the only instructions to advance, turn, jump, and ignite. To repeat, you can define several subprograms and make recursive calls. The game proposes a staggering of several levels of complexity and has two apps differentiated by difficulty for the age bands of 4–8 and 9 + .

2.14. Made with Code (https://www.madewithcode.com/)

Made with Code is a game of successive challenges to learn programming. It is a Google initiative created in 2014 to encourage school-age girls to develop their first experiences in CT. It includes a lot of educational materials with textual and audiovisual contents, and proposals of projects and activities by using various tools. As far as our analysis is concerned, it has a specific area of visual programming projects (https://www.madewithcode.com/projects/) proposing a series of short activities with Blockly-based visual programming. Some of these activities are programming challenges with basic concepts (like the ones based on *Inside Out* or *Wonder Woman*), and there are more open and creative ones that simply seek to provide tools for girls to propose their own elements based on computational abstractions such as designing a costume pattern (*LED dress*), playing a musical rhythm (*beats*) or creating a visual message based on its components (*code for equality*), with a clear intention to show how many everyday activities and objects have computational components in their design, construction, or use.

2.15. MakeWorld (https://makeworld.eu/)

MakeWorld is a context and path-free creation tool to define programming challenges related to other STEM areas. MakeWorld is one of the few platforms created in Europe, in the framework of a European Union innovation project. It targets primary school children for a first-learning CT environment. Therefore, it minimizes textual aspects and proposes an icon-based action interface, with two levels: worlds (a programming challenge) and stories (a set of challenges linked to a learning sequence). Through these, programming challenges are sought to work concepts of other subjects (mathematics, languages, science …) where they include computational elements such as enumeration, sequencing, identification, classification, cycles, processes, systems, and so on. The concepts of CT are limited to the most basic context: movements in a grid, repetitions through recursive subprograms, and scoring events to manage progress. MakeWorld allows both solving worlds by posing a game with goals and creating worlds (hence its name) to go a step further in the level of abstraction. These worlds can be published and shared in the social community.

2.16. Minecraft (https://education.minecraft.net/)

Minecraft is a free construction game. It is a game based on three-dimensional blocks that allow users to create constructions in a free world, with the intense expression of the creativity of the user. Although its initial objective was only to be a constructionist game, it has evolved and allows users to incorporate complex logics within the objects of the game, including from 2017 a visual programming language and environment, Code Builder (with equivalence in JavaScript). It can be programmed with the Microsoft Visual programming tool (MakeCode) or with the existing Scratch and Tynker tools and allows game elements to change and behave according to the programmed code. After Microsoft bought the original product, it has developed a whole line of education aimed at raising problems and challenges of computational thinking and allowing them to be shared among users in the community. Although Minecraft is a commercially licensed product, educational use has been dropping in price and can be used partially free.

2.17. Robozzle (http://www.robozzle.com/)

Robozzle is a game of successive challenges to learn programming. Robozzle, published in 2009, is, according to its creator Igor Ostrovsky, a "social puzzle game." It poses a very basic programming environment in a maze in which you have to capture the stars with the only instructions to move forward and rotate. To repeat, you can define several subprograms and make recursive calls, and for the concept of alternative you use up to three colors that determine whether the statement is executed or not. The result is a little game of challenges to solve the puzzles that each level poses. The game itself does not propose a staggering of levels of complexity (a priori there are only the basic difficulties of the small tutorial), but it leaves the creation of new challenges to the users themselves, and their evaluation by difficulty and taste, in a community that has created about 10,000 puzzles. It allows CT to be introduced with a simple game, without considering longer control structures or programs, with very few, primitive elements, close to the low level that is behind the programs.

2.18. Scratch (https://scratch.mit.edu/)

Scratch is a free creation tool for small games, animations, and interactive resources. Scratch is a visual programming language created by MIT's Lifelong Kindergarten Lab in 2002, with an editing and execution system in the cloud. With an important orientation to the user community and an open approach, it allows to share and derive programs from others. Due to its significant history and implementation, there are many tutorials for users, teachers, and parents. The structure of programming components differentiates elements such as control structures, events, operators, data, or sensors. The elements that are manipulated by Scratch are configurable images and sounds, allowing you to set up 2D animations and video games of a certain level of complexity.

Scratch was one of the first tools to be established and has therefore greatly influenced most of the ones listed in this chapter. It uses the visual puzzle metaphor for the programming pieces, where each block has a shape that can only be combined with other compatible blocks, and a color that determines the block type.

2.19. ScratchJr (https://www.scratchjr.org/)

ScratchJr is a free creation tool for small games, animations, and resources. It is a visual programming language developed as a derivation of Scratch by the same MIT department, aimed at younger users without reading skills. The interface concept changes (from vertical blocks to simplified horizontal blocks, reducing the number of blocks, and using icons instead of texts) and is aimed at mobile devices, being available for free for Android, IOS, and Chromebook. There is also a version launched in collaboration with PBS Kids, which uses characters from the animated series.

2.20. Snap! (http://snap.berkeley.edu/)

Snap! is a free creation tool for small games, animations, and interactive resources. Snap! is a visual programming language very similar to Scratch, inspired by it in its appearance and type of interaction, but with a series of improvements that make it interesting for a greater range of users: it runs in HTML and JavaScript so that it does not depend on Flash and does not limit the platforms that can be used, allows you to define custom blocks, manage multiuser sessions in real time, nested sprites, generate projects such as executables, undo option, top-level functions, and so on. However, there is a much smaller community of users and projects, and the documentation available for teachers is very inferior.

2.21. SpriteBox (http://spritebox.com/)

SpriteBox is a game of successive challenges to learn programming. It is a game developed for Code Hour by the LightBot company. It has a similar approach, but it raises the level of CT a little by incorporating loops rather than jumps to routines. It also includes a game element in proposing a platform game in which users have to overcome programming challenges that affect the game (create platforms, open gaps, and rebuild the stage). It takes approximately an hour and raises progressive difficulty levels in three consecutive worlds.

2.22. The Foos (http://thefoos.com)

The Foos is a game of successive challenges to learn programming. It is a tablet-oriented game for preschool and primary children (no need for reading). It is based on the idea of a platform game that, in addition to being played as a traditional game, allows the movement to be configured with a block code. Progressive leveling that introduces sequences, repetition, events, and alternatives and ends with possibilities of free play and creation of personalized levels.

The App, created by the Pasadena CodeSpark company in 2014, is commercial, but educational use is free and must be managed by a teacher who will set up the class, invitations, and devices. It has a specific version of code hour that is a subset of the whole game and can be played in a Web browser without installation.

2.23. Tynker (https://www.tynker.com)

Tynker is a free small game creation tool, which includes several successive challenge games to learn programming. It is a commercial project that has a series of free levels and also a school model that can be subscribed to without cost with a set of six phases (each composed of a series of progressive levels), and you can order additional paid phases. The visual environment has vertical blocks similar to Scratch or Code.org, with a lot of context variation and games to choose from. Our analysis deals with the free levels and a specific section defined for code hour, Tynker Hour of Code (https://www.tynker.com/hour-of-code) with a multitude of different levels. Tynker also has a free programming environment, which allows editing games with a Scratch-style editor, allowing for customizing both scenery and objects, as well as the codes that these objects use with all the available blocks, making it one of the most complete tools.

2.24. Waterbear (http://waterbearlang.com)

Waterbear is a free creation tool for small games, animations, and resources. Waterbear is a visual programming language created by Dethe Elza, a Canadian professional (in an open source development environment), inspired by Scratch but with a language developed to be able to program in a visual way closer to textual programming languages, incorporating elements such as arrays, dates, or diversity of mathematical functions. There is no community of users, and the environment is very self-learning-oriented, practically without didactic material available.

2.25. Platforms not covered

There are many other services and products aimed at learning CT or some of its skills, which we have not considered in this study as they fail to meet the specified conditions. In the first place, there are a whole series of games that require the acquisition of physical devices. Based on classic toys, these include robots and similar devices. Through their connection to the physical world, they enrich the possibilities of previously analyzed tools, limited by a screen and the need of Internet connection. They are an important niche market for companies in the educational toys sector. This is the case of LEGO Mindstorms (https://www.lego.com/mindstorms/), which was already commercialized in 1998 as a result of the collaboration between MIT and the LEGO construction toys company, to incorporate new robotic parts (different types of engines and sensors) controllable by children, using a visual programming language that is installed on the computer or device and that allows the user to write a program that is transmitted to the construction. The FIRST LEGO League began in 1999: an annual international competition with scientific and technological challenges based on this game, with more than 200,000 schoolchildren participating.

In this same line of products, we also find many others that have been appearing the last decade, such as Bee-Bot (https://www.bee-bot.us/), BlocklyProp (https://www.parallax.com/product/program-blocklyprop), Cubelets (http://www.modrobotics.com/cubelets/), Dash the Robot (https://www.makewonder.com/), Edison (https://meetedison.com/), Lego WeDo (https://education.lego.com/en-us/elementary/shop/wedo-2), mBot (http://makeblock.com/), microbit (http://microbit.org/), OzoBlockly (http://ozoblockly.com/), Robbo (https://www.robbo.world/), Sphero (http://www.sphero.com/), and many others.

There are also some mixed physical/digital toys that include a simple but necessary physical part (usually pieces to be placed), connected in some way (Bluetooth) with a digital application that needs the "program" created in the physical world in order to beat the virtual challenge: what is called "tangible programming." This is the case of Puzzlets (http://www.digitaldreamlabs.com/), with several games aimed at primary education or KIBO (http://kinderlabrobotics.com/kibo/), commercialized in dozens of countries.

We should also mention an important category represented by GameMaker Studio (https://www.yoyogames.com/gamemaker), GameSalad (http://gamesalad.com/), Stencyl (http://www.stencyl.com/), Unity (https://unity3d.com/), or Unreal (https://www.unrealengine.com/). These are video game authoring tools which include some possibilities of visual programming. Some of them have been used to learn programming [12], but they are not aimed at learning programming as such, nor are they specifically aimed at children or young people, nor are they commonly used in this type of activity. However, they are not far from this area, and this is already happening with some initiatives such as the Stencyl Educational

Kit (http://www.stencyl.com/education/overview/), GameMaker for Education (https://www.yoyogames.com/education) or GameSalad for Education (http://edu.gamesalad.com/), in all cases with paid licenses.

It is also important to note that text-based programming learning environments continue to exist, as in the 1990s when programming began to be introduced in schools: Basic (such as http://smallbasic.com/) or Logo (e.g., MSW Logo: http://www.softronix.com/logo.html).

There is a growing set of activities for lower educational levels called "unplugged." For example, Computer Science Unplugged (http://csunplugged.org/), a collection of free activities that teaches CT through games and puzzles with cards, paper and pen, strings, and school or household materials, without considering technological tools. Other examples with a more commercial focus are Hello Ruby (http://www.helloruby.com/), Code Monkey Island (http://codemonkeyplanet.com/), CodeMaster and other CODE games (http://www.thinkfun.com/), or Robot Turtles (http://www.robotturtles.com/).

We also find on the market a series of games that do not fit properly with the programming model that is usually classified as visual programming, but which do use concepts of abstraction, algorithms, and resolution of problems that promote CT. This is the case, for example, of SpaceChem (http://www.zachtronics.com/spacechem/), which proposes a series of puzzles in the form of chemical elements that must be manufactured with a specific combination of pathways and operators on atoms and molecules.

Finally, there is another large group of tools like Code Combat (https://codecombat.com/), Code Hunt (https://www.codehunt.com/), CodeHS (https://codehs.com/), CodinGame (https://www.codingame.com/), Colobot (https://colobot.info/), Minetest (http://www.minetest.net/) or Swift Playgrounds (https://www.apple.com/swift/playgrounds/), games for learning programming with text-based languages like JavaScript, Java, Python or Swift, without considering visual programming. They are usually a widely used resource for older students who have spent a few years with visual programming tools.

3. Analysis of platforms

We have analyzed these 24 tools, which we extend to 26, as both Code.org and Tynker really encompass two different approaches that require independent measure. Here we present the information considered about these platforms.

3.1. Classification

The vast majority of the tools can be differentiated into two main groups. The first (46.2% of those analyzed) corresponds to a **set of programming challenges** (e.g., Code.org), in the form of predefined closed levels to solve, usually incorporating new programming structures and increasing the difficulty progressively. The usage sessions can be from a few minutes to a few weeks, where Code.org is making the most remarkable effort to design complete academic trajectories with different levels.

The second group (42.3%) proposes a **visual programming language** in itself (e.g., Scratch), with varying degrees of amplitude, with which the learner can develop his own programs, in principle in a much more open way, which can easily be embedded in a dynamic of project-based learning. Most (27.9%) languages are aimed at programming a 2D game, two are 3D, one is for 3D modeling, and another for mobile device programming. The game component in this group is not really given by the language but by the intention: you can make games but also animations or interactive stories, and really any computer application that the creativity of the user allows (limited by the language primitives, which are not general purpose).

It seems logical to think that with the languages we could define the tools of the first group: that is, with Scratch we could define a programming challenge (or thousands). However, the programming structures themselves are usually not included among the language primitives (i.e., in Scratch, you cannot program a game that raises a programming challenge except with a lot of effort and personalization). In addition, platforms that propose challenges can automatically detect the improvement in each level, give feedback in case of error, and offer the user navigation to the next. In the programming languages, challenges can be proposed, but evaluation and sequencing are foreign to the system. Therefore, there are two different types of tools, although it seems logical that the technologies will continue to approach the possibility of integrating both (as Code.org and Tynker do in a similar way).

At the moment, there are two tools among those analyzed (MakeWorld and Robozzle, 7.7%) that allow users to do both things: users can solve challenges already posed and can also create new coding challenges and publish them for other users to solve. We could then talk about a third set of tools for **creating and solving programming challenges**.

A fourth and last category, represented by Minecraft (3.8%), is that of a **videogame incorporating visual programming in its mechanics**. The main objective of the game is not visual programming (in fact in Minecraft, this feature has appeared after years in which interaction was only possible with text-based languages), but it does incorporate it and allows aspects of CT to work.

3.2. General characteristics

In **Table 1**, we can observe the general characteristics of the 26 analyzed tools. *Type* refers to the classification already mentioned. The country of creation, year of release, and number of languages are indicated. The number of users (in millions) has been indicated, in cases where a reasonably trustworthy approximation has been found.

The hegemony of the USA in this type of tools is prominent. Almost three-quarters (73.1%) of the platforms have been developed there, consistent with the US dominance in Internet services in general, and it may also be a response to an important campaign for interest in basic computing learning at school levels that the USA has been leading for a decade (we can note that in the wake Alice and Scratch, other tools have been emerging continuously). Canada follows it with 11.5%, the same as the whole of Europe, and Australia has its own platform with Cargo-Bot.

The oldest tools are Alice and Scratch, which explains their influence and emphasizes the importance of American universities (MIT and Carnegie Mellon) in the field of visual programming. The implantation data indicate the most widespread: Code.org, Tynker (although it is only in English), and Scratch, although we have not found data on the number of users of some

Game	Type	Ctry	Year	Lang#	User#	Technology						
						Web	Win	Mac	Linux	Andr	iOS	ChrOS
Alice	LANG	USA	1998	23		—	X	X	X	—	—	—
App Inventor	LANG	USA	2010	11	7	X	—	—	—	—	—	—
Bee-Bot	CHAL	USA	2012	1	0.3	—	—	—	—	—	X	—
Beetle Blocks	LANG	USA	2014	39		X	—	—	—	—	—	—
Blockly Games	CHAL	USA	2012	49		X	—	—	—	—	—	—
Cargo-Bot	CHAL	AUS	2012	1	1	—	—	—	—	—	X	—
Code.org - Courses	CHAL	USA	2011	51	430	X	—	—	—	—	—	—
Code.org - Code St	LANG	USA	2014	51	20	X	—	—	—	—	—	—
Daisy the Dinosaur	CHAL	USA	2013	1		—	—	—	—	—	X	—
Kodable	CHAL	USA	2012	1	>1	X	—	—	—	—	X	—
Kodetu	CHAL	ESP	2014	3	0.01	X	—	—	—	—	—	—
Kodu Game Lab	LANG	USA	2009	22	2.5	—	X	—	—	—	—	—
Hopscotch	LANG	USA	2012	3		—	—	—	—	—	X	—
Lightbot	CHAL	CAN	2008	28	7	X*	X	X	—	X	X	—
Made with Code	CHAL	USA	2014	1		X	—	—	—	—	—	—
MakeWorld	CREA	ESP	2016	6	0.002	X	—	—	—	—	—	—
Minecraft	GAME	SWE	2011	11	130	—	X	X	—	X**	X**	—
Robozzle	CREA	USA	2009	1	0.13	X*	—	—	—	X	X	—
Scratch	LANG	USA	2002	72	20	X*	X	X	X	—	—	—
ScratchJr	LANG	USA	2014	7	2	—	—	—	—	X	X	X
Snap!	LANG	USA	2011	39		X	—	—	—	—	—	—
SpriteBox	CHAL	CAN	2016	2		X*	—	—	—	X	X	—
The Foos	CHAL	USA	2014	17	4	X	—	—	—	X	X	—
Tynker	LANG	USA	2013	1	50	X	—	—	—	X	X	—
Tynker - Activities	CHAL	USA	2013	1	50	X	—	—	—	X	X	—
Waterbear	LANG	CAN	2011	1		X	—	—	—	—	—	—

*Browser needs flash plugin, silverlight in case of Robozzle.
**Minecraft has commercial apps for Android and iOS.

Table 1. General characteristics.

significant tools like Alice, ScratchJr, or Blockly. On the other hand, we have the widespread use of Minecraft as a construction game, with no specific data on how many people are using its visual programming possibilities. Availability on the web is clearly a key to massive use, leaving systems that only work on tablets to be more focused on commercial paid licenses, with the iPad holding a predominant place due to its implantation in schools in some countries (like the USA).

For the social data shown in **Table 2**, we have organized the platforms by type, because as you can see, the social options are strongly correlated with the approach of the tool. For those that pose programming challenges, there are no social options, except for Code.org, Blockly Games, and the Foos, which allow users to upload the creations made to the Internet at some levels, which coincide with those that offer a "free mode" (which works in fact as an exception to the rest of the levels, where the challenge has a solution that is either achieved or not.) On the contrary, in the visual programming languages, it is habitual to incorporate an additional community to the language (69% do this), that at least allows users to upload their projects and share them ("share") and, in some cases, more social options such as "like" other users' programs, "report" inappropriate programs, "fav" to bookmark, "follow" another user, or "comm" to comment with free text on the shared creation. In this sense, the two tools of creation and solution work in the same way as the visual languages, with the exception of Robozzle, which is the only one that incorporates "dislike," and the possibility of evaluating other users' puzzles from 1 to 5.

3.3. Learning aspects

Below we consider information relating to the use of these tools in class. First of all, the target age is fundamental, which is shown in **Table 3** where the recommended ages for the different platforms appear, marked according to the indications of the companies themselves, the opinions of the educational community, and the characteristics of the tools. On the one hand, we see that there are various tools for all ages, which is a good news for the educational community. On the other hand, if we consider them by type, as might have been expected, the platforms of challenges are focused on the lowest ages (average age 8.1); the creation and solution of challenges is higher (9.8); and higher still are languages to define games (12.4). This pattern corresponds to the stages that would be desirable if we want to design a longitudinal educational process with these tools: starting with a platform of challenges with the objectives and the path marked, continuing with a creation of challenges based on proposals made by the teacher in a structured and guided way, and ending with a more general-purpose visual language, in a learning environment based on projects and with freedom of personal choice on behalf of the learner to define and carry out the projects.

Table 4 shows aspects of simplicity of installation and use (valued from 0 to 3 according to a defined rubric), richness of interaction (also from 0 to 3), ranges of estimated time dedicated (based on available material and complexity and depth permitted for each system), and material available for teachers (A-D).

You can see the breadth of the range of time dedicated, which in the case of general programming tools such as Scratch or Tynker can vary from a few days to some years (many schools use these tools throughout several years, although not usually continuously). It can also be seen that the challenge systems have a much less ambitious temporal approach, except in the most highly developed levels such as Tynker or Code.org.

Type	Game	Community	Upload allowed	Social options	Remix
Challenges	Bee-Bot	–	–	–	–
	Blockly Games	limited	X*	share*	limited
	Cargo-Bot	–	–	–	–
	Code.org - Courses	–	X*	share*	–
	Daisy the Dinosaur	–	–	–	–
	Kodable	–	–	–	–
	Kodetu	–	–	–	–
	Lightbot	–	–	–	–
	Made with Code	–	–	–	–
	SpriteBox	–	–	–	–
	The Foos	–	X*	like, share*	–
	Tynker - Activities	–	–	–	–
Visual Programming Languages	Alice	–	–	–	exp
	App Inventor	X	–	–	exp
	Beetle Blocks	X	X	fav	X
	Code.org - Code Studio	X	X	share	X
	Hopscotch	X	X	like / share	X
	Kodu Game Lab	X	X	like / share / report	X
	Scratch	X	X	fav / like / report / comm / follow	X
	ScratchJr	–	–	–	–
	Snap!	–	X	–	X
	Tynker	X	X	like / report / share	X
	Waterbear	–	–	–	exp
Creation and playing	MakeWorld	X	X	like / follow / share / comm	X
	Robozzle	X	X	like / dislike / evaluate	–
Game	Minecraft	X	–	–	X

*Only in some levels, exp. = remix from file exported.

Table 2. Social characteristics.

Type	Game	Recommended ages for playing							
		<5	6–7	8–9	10–11	12–13	14–15	16–17	>18
CHAL	Bee-Bot	X	–						
	Blockly Games			X	X	X	X	–	–
	Cargo-Bot	–	X	X	X	–			
	Code.org - Courses		X	X	X	X	–	–	–
	Daisy the Dinosaur	X	X	–					
	Kodable	X	X	X	–	–	–		
	Kodetu			X	X	X	X	–	–
	Lightbot	X	X	X	X	–			
	Made with Code	–	X	X	X	X	X	–	
	SpriteBox	X	X	X	X	–			
	The Foos	X	X	–	–				
	Tynker - Activities			X	X	X	X	–	–
CREA	MakeWorld	–	X	X	X	X	X	–	
	Robozzle		X	X	X	X	–	–	–
LANG	Alice				–	–	X	X	X
	App Inventor						–	X	X
	Beetle Blocks					X	X	X	–
	Code.org - Code Studio				X	X	X	–	–
	Hopscotch			X	X	X	–	–	
	Kodu Game Lab	–	X	X	X	X	–	–	
	Scratch			X	X	X	X	–	–
	ScratchJr	X	X	–	–				
	Snap!			X	X	X	X	X	X
	Tynker			X	X	X	X	–	–
	Waterbear				–	X	X	X	–
GAME	Minecraft						–	X	X

X = recommended, – = viable, space = not recommended.

Table 3. Recommended ages of platforms.

3.4. Engagement

There are no unique or universal expressions of the fun or engagement that a digital activity is capable of producing in a user. Each person has his or her tastes, preferences, and learning; in addition, in the school environment, the way in which an activity is proposed greatly influences its reception. It is not the same for a child to freely choose a game that s/he wants to

Type	Game	Inst [1]	Personal data requested	Us [2]	Int [3]	Apprentice dedication time range	Teacher preparation time range	Av Mat [4]
CHAL	Bee-Bot	0	No	0	0	1 h–10 h	1 h–5 h	B
	Blockly Games	0	No	0	0	1 h-15d	5 h–20 h	C
	Cargo-Bot	0	No	1	1	1 h-5d	1 h–10 h	A
	Code.org - Courses	0	Email (opt.)	0	1	1 h-2 m	5 h–50 h	D
	Daisy the Dinosaur	0	No	0	1	1 h–4 h	1 h–5 h	B
	Kodable	0	No	0	1	1 h-2 m	5 h–50 h	D
	Kodetu	0	Sex, age, school, survey	0	0	1 h–5 h	1 h–5 h	A
	Lightbot	2	No	0	1	1 h–3 h	1 h–5 h	C
	Made with Code	0	No	0	1	1 h–20 h	1 h–20 h	C
	SpriteBox	0	No	0	1	1 h–3 h	1 h–5 h	C
	The Foos	2	Email	0	1	1 h-30d	5 h–30 h	C
	Tynker - Activities	0	Email (opt.)	0	1	1 h-1y	2 h–10 h	C
CREA	MakeWorld	1	Sex, country, age, email	1	2	1 h-2y	5 h–40 h	D
	Robozzle	0	Email (opt.)	1	1	1 h-5d	2 h–10 h	B
LANG	Alice	2	No	3	3	3d-4y	20 h–50 h	D
	App Inventor	3	Google account	3	3	3d-4y	20 h–80 h	D
	Beetle Blocks	0	No	1	2	2d-1y	5 h–40 h	B
	Code.org - Code St	0	Email, age, sex (opt.)	0	2	5d-2y	20 h–50 h	D
	Hopscotch	0	Email (opt.)	2	2	5d-2y	20 h–50 h	C
	Kodu Game Lab	2	No	2	3	5d-2y	10 h–50 h	C
	Scratch	1	Birth date, sex, country, email	2	2	5d-2y	20 h–50 h	D
	ScratchJr	2	No	2	1	1d-2 m	5 h–10 h	D
	Snap!	0	Birth date, email	2	2	5d-2y	20 h–50 h	C
	Tynker	0	Email	1	2	5d-2y	5 h–50 h	C
	Waterbear	0	No	0	2	5d-2y	20 h–50 h	A
GAME	Minecraft	3	Email	3	3	5d-2y	20 h–80 h	D

Inst = Installation simplicity. Us = Usability. Int = Interaction richness. [1–3] evaluated in a range 0–3, where 0 is the simplest and 3 most complex. Av Mat = Available material for teachers [4] is ranged A-D, from no material available (A) to very rich content in many languages (D).

Table 4. Other learning aspects. Installation simplicity.

play when s/he wants, as to be asked to do so by the teacher, more or less obligatorily, within a class. This is a factor that has influenced all educational games from the start. But in any case, we have done the exercise of trying to objectify the "fun" potentially offered by each of our 26 tools, differentiating some of the classic dimensions that influence the experience of the user when it comes to video games and evaluating each of them from 0 (minimum) to 3 (maximum). This gives us an average measure of engagement that is displayed in descending order in **Table 5**.

Game	Type	Sen	Fan	Nar	Cha	Fel	Dis	Exp	Sub	Sto	Engagement
Minecraft	GAME	3	3	3	3	3	3	3	3	2	**2.89**
Code.org - Code Studio	LANG	2	3	2	3	2	2	3	3	3	**2.56**
Tynker	LANG	2	3	2	3	2	2	3	3	3	**2.56**
Scratch	LANG	3	3	2	3	0	2	3	3	3	**2.44**
Hopscotch	LANG	2	3	1	3	2	2	3	3	3	**2.44**
Alice	LANG	2	3	1	3	2	2	3	3	3	**2.44**
Snap!	LANG	2	3	1	3	2	2	3	3	3	**2.44**
MakeWorld	CREA	2	3	2	3	2	2	2	2	3	**2.33**
Kodu Game Lab	LANG	2	3	2	3	0	2	3	3	2	**2.22**
Code.org - Courses	CHAL	2	2	2	3	1	2	2	3	2	**2.11**
ScratchJr	LANG	2	3	1	3	0	1	2	3	2	**1.89**
The Foos	CHAL	2	2	2	3	1	2	1	2	1	**1.78**
Blockly Games	CHAL	1	1	1	3	1	2	2	2	2	**1.67**
Made with Code	CHAL	2	1	1	2	1	2	2	2	2	**1.67**
Tynker - Activities	CHAL	2	2	2	3	1	1	1	2	1	**1.67**
Kodable	CHAL	1	1	2	3	0	2	2	2	1	**1.56**
Beetle Blocks	LANG	1	0	0	3	1	2	2	2	1	**1.33**
Waterbear	LANG	1	0	0	3	0	1	2	2	3	**1.33**
App Inventor	LANG	1	0	0	3	0	2	3	2	0	**1.22**
Cargo-Bot	CHAL	1	1	1	2	1	1	1	2	0	**1.11**
Lightbot	CHAL	1	1	1	3	0	1	1	2	0	**1.11**
Robozzle	CREA	0	0	1	3	2	1	1	2	0	**1.11**
SpriteBox	CHAL	1	1	1	3	0	1	1	1	0	**1.00**
Bee-Bot	CHAL	1	1	1	2	0	1	0	2	0	**0.89**
Kodetu	CHAL	0	1	1	2	1	1	1	1	0	**0.89**
Daisy the Dinosaur	CHAL	1	1	1	1	0	1	1	1	0	**0.78**

Sen = Sensation, Fan = Fantasy, Nar = Narrative, Cha = Challenge, Fel = Fellowship, Dis = Discovery, Exp = Expression, Sub = Submission, Sto = Storytelling.

Table 5. Engagement expressed depending on different dimensions of fun (from 0-min- to 3-max each).

We note that this confirms the logical relationship between the most widespread and the most attractive games (Minecraft, Code.org, Tynker, Scratch). In addition, in general, the languages that allow free creative development and longer periods of engagement are more attractive than those games of challenges whose attraction basically ends when the challenges end. As expected, we see in the lower part the tools that allow shorter periods of engagement and others (like App Inventor) whose complexity and low level coding make the effort invested disproportionate to the attractiveness of the result achieved, from a gaming point of view.

3.5. Computational thinking

It is a fundamental aspect for our analysis to review which of the specific characteristics that are employed in CT are included in the tools analyzed. **Table 6** shows the aspects that each tool includes, or not, along with some significant data such as the number of different blocks that can be used to program (calculated counting all the different blocks that the system allows to be used) or whether the equivalent textual code can be seen in parallel to the visual program that is being developed.

We have not included sequences in the table, which all the tools analyzed have (we cannot imagine a visual programming tool without sequences). We have also seen that flowcharts, a visual tool widely used in programming and in learning programming at the conceptual level, are not used in any of these tools. On the other hand, recursion is used in two different ways: in those tools that do not support loops, (virtually infinite) repeating is performed using recursive calls (this is the case of Cargo-Bot, LightBot, MakeWorld, and Robozzle).

The languages generally support more features and use many more basic blocks to allow greater expressiveness of programming (all have more than 100 constructions, except Hopscotch that limits them due to its orientation to tablets, and ScratchJr that is aimed at the youngest age groups). Conversely, the systems of challenges have much less expressiveness except the four most developed ones which support a large number of levels and greatly diversify the constructions that can be used in each challenge: Code.org, Blockly, Tynker, and Made with Code.

It is also significant that all the languages support events, which speaks of the importance of event-oriented programming in current computing and also shows that the concept of an event that provokes an action has a very natural meaning for learners. Most languages allow multithreading, albeit in a way that is transparent to the learner, who probably does not need to understand the concept to use it implicitly. Only some of the languages (but no challenge tools) allow message passing, object-orientation, 3D, and connection with physical systems. Only one tool (Alice) incorporates the explicit construction of parallel sequences (to launch several blocks in parallel in the same temporal space).

3.6. Design aspects

The last dimension analyzed has been some design considerations of the tools, from the point of view of the approach to the interface, the sequencing of user interaction, and the options available for professors and researchers (see **Table 7**).

Type	Game	Loo	Alt	Deb	Mod	Var	Exp	Blo#	Evn	Thr	Rec	Mes	OO	3D	Txt	Langs	Out
CHAL	Bee-Bot							4									
	Blockly Games	X	X	X	X	X	X	136							X	Js	
	Cargo-Bot		X	X	X			6			X						
	Code.org	X	X	X	X	X	X	>200	X	X					X	Js	
	Daisy	X		X				9	X								
	Kodable	X	X	X	X			7									
	Kodetu			X				9							X	Js	
	Lightbot			X	X			7			X						
	Made w/Code	X	X	X			X	>200									
	SpriteBox	X		X				7							X	Js, Sw	
	The Foos	X	X	X			X	20	X	X							
	Tynker - Act	X	X	X			X	>200	X	X							
CREA	MakeWorld			X	X			17	X	X	X						
	Robozzle		X	X	X			10			X						
LANG	Alice	X	X	X	X	X	X	>200	X	X	X	X	X	X	X	Java	
	App Inventor	X	X		X	X	X	>200	X	X	X	X	X			Java	X
	Beetle Blocks	X	X	X	X	X	X	120	X	X				X			
	Code Studio	X	X	X	X	X	X	>200	X	X	X	X	X		X	Js	
	Hopscotch	X	X		X	X	X	86	X	X	X						
	Kodu						X	>200	X	X				X			
	Scratch	X	X		X	X	X	130	X	X	X	X					X
	ScratchJr	X		X				26	X	X		X					
	Snap!	X	X	X	X	X	X	150	X	X	X	X					X
	Tynker	X	X	X	X	X	X	>200	X	X	X	X			X	Js, Py	X
	Waterbear	X	X			X	X	>200	X			X	X				
GAME	Minecraft	X	X	X		X	X	150	X	X				X	X	Js	

Loo = Loops, Alt = Alternatives, Deb = Visual debugging in execution, Mod = Modules (subprograms), Var = Variables, Exp = Expressions, Blo# = # of code constructs (expressiveness of language), Evn = Events, Thr = Multithreading, Rec = Recursion, Mes = Message passing, OO = OO, 3D = 3D, Txt = Text language equivalent, Langs = Language, Out = Output to physical world (possible connection with robots, sensors, arduino, etc.).

Table 6. Some CT aspects.

In addition to the data given in the table, we have also reviewed the adaptability of the tools but we have not found any. That is, the software always behaves the same regardless of the characteristics of the user (age, gender, educational level, functional diversity, etc) or their behavior (whether the program is wrong or right, better or worse, the game does not change

http://dx.doi.org/10.5772/intechopen.71339

Type	Game	Prog. Interface	Tut	Help	Free	Reg	Grp	Feed	Dash	Use	Res
CHAL	Bee-Bot	Icons*			X						
	Blockly Games	Ver - blocks	X	X	X						
	Cargo-Bot	Hor - icons	X	X	X						
	Code.org	Ver - blocks	X	X	X	X	X	X	3		
	Daisy	Ver - blocks									
	Kodable	Hor - icons	X	X		X	X	X	3		
	Kodetu	Ver - blocks	X				X	X	2		X
	Lightbot	Hor - icons	X	X							
	Made w/Code	Ver - blocks	X	X							
	SpriteBox	Ver - icons	X	X							
	The Foos	Hor - blocks	X	X		opt	X	X	1		
	Tynker - Act	Ver - blocks	X	X		opt	X	X	3		
CREA	MakeWorld	Ver - icons	X		X	X					
	Robozzle	Hor - icons	X		X	opt				X	
LANG	Alice	Ver - blocks	X	X	X						
	App Inventor	Ver - blocks		X	X	X					
	Beetle Blocks	Ver - blocks	X	X	X	opt					
	Code Studio	Ver - blocks	X	X	X	X				X	
	Hopscotch	Ver - blocks	X	X	X	X					
	Kodu	Graph - icons		X	X						
	Scratch	Ver - blocks		X	X	opt		X		X	
	ScratchJr	Hor - blocks		X	X						
	Snap!	Ver - blocks		X	X	opt					
	Tynker	Ver - blocks	X	X	X	X	X	X	2		
	Waterbear	Ver - blocks			X						
GAME	Minecraft	Ver - blocks	X	X	X	X	X	X	2		

Tut = Integrated tutorial, Help = Integrated help, Free = Free navigation, Reg = User registration needed, Grp = Group creation possible (for teachers), Feed = Feedback for teacher of user's behavior, Dash = Teacher's dashboard (0-no to 3-complete), Use = Public access to users' data, Res = Public research access to user data.

Table 7. Design considerations.

the subsequent levels nor does it provide different information or tutorials.) The only thing that approaches adaptability is the score, which we discuss in the following table.

Reviewing the type of interface that is proposed for the metaphor of "code" (the panel to which you can drag the pieces to develop the program), we see that the most common option is vertical (69.2%), which represents the sequence from top to bottom, and rather less common is horizontal (23.1%) which represents the sequence from left to right (in a few cases with local adaptation to the languages that are written from right to left). There are two special tools that do not fit into these two schemes: Kodu that proposes a creative graphic interface in a circle where the options are carried out by levels, and each level shows the available options with icons, joined in a circle; and Bee-Bot, which has no explicit code space: each learner has to remember by heart the program sequence that s/he "loads" in the bee (just as happens with the bee-bot physical device).

The preference in vertical interfaces is for blocks (only MakeWorld and SpriteBox, aimed at lower age bands, propose vertical icons), and in horizontal interfaces, icons (except for the Foos and ScratchJr which develop graphically elaborated blocks to represent the repetitive structures mounted on repeating icons). The tendency is to use horizontal structures with younger age groups and vertical ones with older age groups. The blocks usually have the visual form of a puzzle, colored to differentiate the types of construction visually. In some cases like Alice, App Inventor, or Waterbear, the blocks represent concepts that are very close to the corresponding low-level text-based code.

In the table, you can also see the tools provided for the teachers. Those that provide information to the teacher and allow him/her to manage groups of students, often also have an online dashboard in which the teacher, through the web, can consult information on the actions of his/her group. This is fairly complete in the case of Code.org and Kodable (progress by topic, lessons completed), and especially detailed in Tynker (also including the skills worked and the level).

Type	Game	Pre-level	Error	Success	Progress	Progress info accessible
CHAL	Bee-Bot	X		X	X	Stars, points
	Blockly Games	X		X	X	Levels passed
	Cargo-Bot	X	X	X	X	Stars, levels passed
	Code.org	X	X	X	X	Levels passed, Code length
	Daisy	X		X		
	Kodable	X	X	X	X	Levels passed, points
	Kodetu	X		X		
	Lightbot			X		
	Made w/Code	X	X	X		
	SpriteBox			X	X	Levels passed, points
	The Foos	X	X	X	X	Levels passed, stars
	Tynker - Act	X	X	X	X	Levels p., stars, prizes, certifs, concepts
CREA	MakeWorld			X		
	Robozzle			X	X	Levels passed, solution length

Pre-level = Feedback before each level, Error = Feedback after levels failed, Success = Feedback after levels passed, Progress = Explicit info on user's progress in game.

Table 8. Feedback to user.

Public access to data is not common; very few tools show general use data and even less allow access to information for research.

Finally, in **Table 8**, we can see information about the feedback that is given to the user as the system progresses. We only consider challenge games, these being the ones that can guide the learner through an expected series of actions.

4. Conclusions

Throughout this chapter, we have seen that there are a growing number of options to lead a learner through CT. An interesting learning path can be to start with some of the challenge games for a few days and move on from there to a visual programming language that can involve weeks or months of activity. The fun is assured, and there are multiple options, in addition to a diversity of motifs that make use of well-known themes of films or video games to reinforce the experience.

However, there are still some limitations to be considered for the next generation of CT games. There is excessive use of action primitives that have to do with movement and orthogonal rotation (influenced perhaps, as we are all, by Logo and its historical importance); instead of other auditory, rhythmic, or visual options, that also allow for developing algorithmic thought and exploring abilities other than spatial vision: in this sense, we note some of the most recent activities incorporated by Code.org and Made w/Code with multimedia elements. We also find the predominance of blocks; tools like Kodu using flowcharts open possibilities to design new CT tools combining both and other visual expressions, beyond the only visual abstraction of nested blocks. Another widespread lack is that in this nascent field, it is especially important to investigate how users behave and how systems facilitate their learning, so it would be desirable for original digital tools to facilitate the use of open-access information for learning analytics, to allow improvement and provide quantum leaps in the design of new levels and tools. A final important gap is the lack of adaptive learning; practically, all the tools behave always the same, regardless of age, prior knowledge, or the skill shown by the user. It is important that tools begin to use passed user activity to adapt and significantly improve the educational experience, something that should also be especially feasible in this type of fully digital systems.

A key issue in learning is assessment. In the games (which pose a quantifiable, measurable and observable challenge), an adequate assessment is more feasible. In fact, it is already being considered in some platforms: code size—number of blocks—in Code.org, stars for time or level objectives in the Foos and others, and so on. Assessment should be improved to include more key indicators in CT skills, such as program efficiency (number of execution steps) and user behavior in the process, not just the result (number of errors, number of code changes, type of development to the right result, etc). In programming languages, assessment is much more complicated. In the same way that a programming teacher working with a text-based language (e.g., Python or Java) has a complex task to evaluate his students, even more so for a primary or secondary teacher who is not necessarily a computing expert and is not looking for the same things. Therefore, though remixing can be used to reinforce the skills included in CT [13], the tools still lack the automatic possibilities or even of capacities for teachers to carry out a progressive monitoring of the learner experience in open environments: new mechanisms of analysis and evaluation are needed so that we can verify that students go beyond solving a problem, and study how they solve it and how they progress. Probably, subsystems of the type proposed in Dr. Scratch [14] will be incorporated to facilitate indicators that enrich the process for both learners and teachers. There is also an important need for common criteria to know CT skills so as to develop and evaluate them. In this respect, easily digitized tools such as the CTtest proposed by Román-González [15] can be a great complement for assessment in medium-term training processes, using both games and languages.

Observing only the category of games based on programming challenges, we review the importance of generating more engagement after the challenges are over, incorporating techniques of gamification known as punctuation, classifications, proposals for improvement, and the incorporation of creative levels in which the challenge is not limited by simple quantifiable objectives; a line in which the entities with more resources, such as Code.org and Tynker, are already working. Another key issue in these systems is the scaffolding. In addition to the obvious effort of level design (a need shared by both games and education), guided by the experience of designers, it is a challenge to systematize the process to ensure the good development of learning and progression of motivation, seeking the flow that so many games achieve; it is also necessary to investigate the guidelines for the automatic generation of levels/challenges, in the line already known in many procedural generation video games. It will also be important to consider how to set out the introductions and tutorials to maximize the learning objective and identify the type of thinking that the learner is applying to solve each progressive challenge, as discussed using Kodu in [16]. Another final gap in challenge games is that few systems allow the creation of new challenges for learners or their teachers, limiting the experience and prematurely closing and limiting the learning cycle. Tools like MakeWorld or Robozzle, which not only allow you to play but also to edit new worlds, will be in the next generation of games to increase the personalization of challenges through modification or creative contribution to different challenges, in a characteristic type of remix.

Regarding the programming languages category, there are intrinsic limitations to block-based visual environments compared to text-based languages. This is more noticeable in large programming projects due to limitations on the visibility of the code, code navigation difficulty, or lack of control in source modifications [7]. Bidirectional conversion between visual and text programming language is available in an increasing number of platforms such as Code.org App Lab. This feature allows learners to choose the most useful view depending on the complexity of the project. We also note that game-oriented platforms are also including teachers' dashboards (Code.org, Kodable, Tynker) but are still very limited or nonexistent in the programming languages category, reflecting the lack of assessment tools already mentioned.

Finally, we have included, in our analysis, a small category of videogames that allow using visual programming in their mechanics. In this regard, Minecraft is an interesting example

http://dx.doi.org/10.5772/intechopen.71339

for game designers. Good videogames can also be designed taking into account specific CT mechanics. We believe this is one of the challenges for the following years in game design, not only for construction games but also for graphic adventures, RPGs, FPS, and many other types of videogames.

Author details

Andoni Eguíluz*, Pablo Garaizar and Mariluz Guenaga

*Address all correspondence to: andoni.eguiluz@deusto.es

Faculty of Engineering, Universidad de Deusto, Bilbao, Spain

References

[1] Wing JM. Computational thinking. Communications of the ACM. 2006;**49**(2):33-35. DOI: 10.1145/1118178.1118215

[2] Buitrago Flórez F, Casallas R, Hernández M, Reyes A, Restrepo S, Danies G. Changing a generation's way of thinking: Teaching computational thinking through programming. Review of Educational Research. 2017. DOI: 10.3102/0034654317710096

[3] Wing JM, Stanzione D. Progress in computational thinking, and expanding the HPC community. Communications of the ACM. 2016;**59**(7):10-11. DOI: 10.1145/2933410

[4] Tedre M, Denning PJ. The long quest for computational thinking. In: Proceedings of the 16th Koli Calling International Conference on Computing Education Research (Koli Calling '16); New York, NY, USA. ACM; 2016. p. 120-129. DOI: 10.1145/2999541.2999542

[5] Denning PJ. Remaining trouble spots with computational thinking. Communications of the ACM. 2017;**60**(6):33-39. DOI: 10.1145/2998438

[6] Kazimogl C, Kiernan M, Bacon L, MacKinnon L. Learning programming at the computational thinking level via digital game-play. Procedia Computer Science. 2012;**9**:522-531. DOI: 10.1016/j.procs.2012.04.056

[7] Bau D, Gray J, Kelleher C, Sheldon J, Turbak F. Learnable programming: Blocks and beyond. Communications of the ACM. 2017;**60**(6):72-80. DOI: 10.1145/3015455

[8] Powers K, Gross P, Cooper S, Mcnally M, Goldman K, Proulx V, Carlisle M. Tools for teaching introductory programming: What works? ACM SIGCSE Bulletin. 2006;**38**(1):560. DOI: 10.1145/1124706.1121514

[9] García-PeñalvoFJ,HughesJ,ReesA,JormanainenI,ToivonenT,ReimannD,TuulM,VirnesM. Evaluation of existing resources (study/analysis). Belgium: TACCLE3 Consortium. 2016; DOI: 10.5281/zenodo.163112

[10] Sandoval-Reyes S, Galicia-Galicia P, Gutierrez-Sanchez I. Visual learning environments for computer programming. In: Electronics, Robotics and Automotive Mechanics Conference (CERMA); IEEE; 2011. p. 439-444. DOI: 10.1109/CERMA.2011.76

[11] Daly T. Using introductory programming tools to teach programming concepts: A literature review. The Journal for Computing Teachers. 2009;Fall:1-6

[12] Panitz M, Sung K, Rosenberg R. Game programming in CS0: A scaffolded approach. Journal of Computing Sciences in Colleges. 2010;**26**(1):126-132

[13] Dasgupta S, Hale W, Monroy-Hernández A, Hill BM. Remixing as a pathway to computational thinking. In: Proceedings of the 19th ACM Conference on Computer-Supported Cooperative Work & Social Computing (CSCW '16); New York, NY, USA: ACM; 2016. p. 1438-1449. DOI: 10.1145/2818048.2819984

[14] Moreno-León J, Robles G. Dr. Scratch: A Web Tool to Automatically Evaluate Scratch Projects. In: Proceedings of the Workshop in Primary and Secondary Computing Education (WiPSCE '15); New York, NY, USA. ACM; 2015. p. 132-133. DOI: 10.1145/2818314.2818338

[15] Román-González M, Pérez-González JC, JiménezFernandez C. Which cognitive abilities underlie computational thinking? Criterion validity of the Computational Thinking Test. Computers in Human Behavior. 2016:1-14

[16] Touretzky DS, Gardner-McCune C, Aggarwal A. Semantic reasoning in young programmers. In: Proceedings of the 2017 ACM SIGCSE Technical Symposium on Computer Science Education (SIGCSE '17); New York, NY, USA: ACM; 2017. p. 585-590. DOI: 10.1145/3017680.3017787

Chapter 10

Artificial Intelligence: Are You Sure? Beware of What You Wish!

Hugo Miguel da Luz dos Santos

Additional information is available at the end of the chapter

http://dx.doi.org/10.5772/intechopen.71143

Abstract

Looming in the purview of gaming leisure industry is the utmost importance of artificial intelligence (AI). Its burgeoning preponderance can be straightforwardly depicted by the following conundrum: imagine you walk through into a dazzling casino in Macau aiming to play "Baccarat." As soon as you sit down in order to initiate your gambling journey, you actually realize that the casino table dealer has been replaced by a cutting-edge robot fully equipped to enhance even further casino's house advantage (that in the realm of "Baccarat" is very narrow). What would be your immediate thought? Should you proceed with your gambling endeavors? Should you refrain yourself from initiating your gambling endeavors? Or has your self-confidence just been boosted by this unexpected challenge? Nonetheless, if you scratch deep enough, underpinning these nonrhetorical questions is a rather twisted question: what if the casino patron or high roller (player) decides himself to foster his gambling skills through AI aiming to curb or even override casino's "house advantage?" In any event, should not we take AI on the scope of gaming leisure industry very seriously in order to avoid disrepute or moral hazard of casino gaming leisure industry as a whole in light of its corporate social responsibility? This chapter will provide an overview about the current prominence of AI or simulation-based AI in gaming leisure industry, mainly for research purposes in the context of problem gambling and of forecasting online casino patron's churn behavior. Finally, this chapter will carve out the foundations of candent challenges gaming leisure industry will face in the forthcoming future about the "moral hazard" deeply enshrined in the breadth of AI, especially if robots are due to replace humans as casino table dealers in the realm of table games.

Keywords: artificial intelligence, simulation, gaming leisure industry, corporate social responsibility, moral hazard, fiduciary duties, fiduciary norms, problem gaming, responsible gaming, baccarat, poker, predicting churn behavior, Turing test, electronic gambling machines, harm minimization strategies, intelligent ambient, big data, data mining, empiric research gathered through AI-based technology

1. Introduction

Artificial intelligence plays a pivotal role in the realm of gaming leisure industry. Its prominence stretches from the cradle of the biggest breakthroughs in gaming leisure industry (enabled by the research-based approach) to the scope of the table games. This very statement poses a sizable challenge to the gaming leisure industry altogether. The thriving of artificial intelligence in this profitable industry – namely in table games – is deeply intertwined with corporate social responsibility and with moral hazard of gaming leisure industry. More artificial intelligence in table games could bring along disrepute and opaqueness to this business activity. In the long run, artificial intelligence in table games could spark an outbreak of gambling-related crimes over the control of this cutting-edge technology, wreaking havoc in gaming leisure industry.

Future, as you may know, is not up for grabs. Even though, one does not need to have a capacious imagination to foresee that artificial intelligence is definitely a "game changer" in gambling leisure industry, as it tends to increasingly replace "human intelligence" in the ambit of "simulation" and "gaming," concretely for research purposes, but not all. Just imagine the possibility of a robot taking over the place of humans as casino table dealers in the context of table games, namely Baccarat. Inextricably linked with this anecdotal possibility, just imagine if a human (casino patron or high roller) decides to use AI to enhance his ability to thwart casino's house advantage. In these grounds, one should foresee that a "moral hazard" is intertwined with this issue. In this axiom, lies the importance of moral boundaries that ought to be swiftly set out for the sake of long-term stability of gaming leisure industry.

2. Artificial intelligence: definition

Definitions of artificial intelligence may vary according to recent textbooks. These definitions vary along two main dimensions. The ones on top are concerned with *thought processes* and *reasoning,* whereas the ones on the bottom address *behavior.* Also, other definitions measure success in terms of *human* performance, whereas another range of definitions measure success against an *ideal* concept of intelligence, which we will call **rationality**. System is rational if it does the right thing. This gives us four possible goals to pursue in **artificial intelligence** [1].

Historically, all four approaches have been followed. As one might expect, a tension exists between approaches centered around humans and approaches centered around rationality. A human-centered approach must be an empirical science, involving hypothesis and experimental.

How can one know if a robot playing the role of a human casino table dealer acts like one? One shall use the Turing test, whose feasibility has sound importance in regards of AI in table games.

The Turing test has been proposed by Alan Turing. It lies in a simple functioning criterion: how can one provide a definition of intelligent behavior? Turing carved out the definition of intelligent behavior as the ability to achieve human-level performance in all cognitive tasks, sufficient to fool an interrogator. Turing test aims to evaluate intelligent behavior. To proficiently evaluate intelligent behavior, the computer should be interrogated by a human via a teletype, and passes the test if the interrogator cannot tell if there is a computer or a human at the other end. The framework of Turing test lies in the following and successive phases: the computer would need to possess the following capabilities: **0 natural language processing** to enable it to communicate successfully in English (or some other human language); moreover, <C> **knowledge representation** to store information provided before or during the interrogation; furthermore, <) **automated reasoning** to use the stored information to answer questions and to draw new conclusions; and another feature needed is <) **machine learning** to adapt to new circumstances and to detect and extrapolate patterns. Finally, to pass the total Turing test, the computer will need computer vision <) **computer vision** to perceive objects and robotics (> **robotics** to move them about [1].

As for gaming leisure industry, the issue of acting like a human comes up primarily when AI programs (robots) have to interact with people (casino patrons or high rollers) in a regular casino in Macau or elsewhere. To ascertain robot's intelligent behavior, Turing's test should be a reference. To pass Turing's test, robots (or AI programs) must behave according to certain normal conventions of human interaction in order to make themselves understand [1]. Again, aforementioned underlying representation should be tested in light of **Turing test** as to whether an AI robot can perform human duties such as casino table dealer and act accordingly.

2.1. Background: main importance of artificial intelligence (AI) and simulation in gaming leisure industry in present days: the empirical research related in electronic gambling machines (EGMs) and problem gambling context

The acute significance of AI speaks for itself as it not only dates back centuries as likewise depicts a perennial human aspiration to acquire transcendent intelligence (AI). The evolution of research-based approach in the realm of problem gambling portrays, in a certain way, the prominence of artificial intelligence and simulation.

Electronic gambling machines (EGMs) represent a large part of the gaming leisure industry. AI and simulation-based AI play a pivotal role for gathering empiric evidence related with EGM's and problem gambling.

EGMs are the core of gambling leisure industry, except in the casinos of Macau, where the table games, namely the *Baccarat*, heavily outweigh EGMs. Knowledge creators' focus has been driven toward the empirical evidence for the differential impact of gambling outcome on behavior in electronic gambling. Research undertaken in this specific field has achieved a major breakthrough: EGM's are the realm of addictive patterns of gambling behavior as they enhance the illusion of control of the players about the outcome of the game.

Furthermore, EGM's are markedly the domain of the loss-chasing behavior, the core characteristic of problem gambling, which can be thoroughly explained because approximately 13% of EGM gamblers meet diagnostic criteria for problem gambling (PG), which is one of the highest rates of among all other forms of gambling. EGMs can be found everywhere. They are interactive, computerized gambling platforms that operate indistinctively across this boundless and globalized data-driven world. Licensed betting offices, casinos, and other leisure facilities, of course, are no exception.

What is the role of EGMs as for bolstering problem gambling? What is more, do EGMs enhance player's illusion of control as for the outcome of game or bet? EGMs reinforce addictive patterns of gambling behavior. It is really an empiric axiom: EGMs have been shown to instill and maintain irrational and superstitious beliefs, as well as distort concepts of randomness and probability that can contribute to illusions of control. Such features may act to maintain or indeed contribute to the onset of PG behaviors.

This empiric axiom (EGMs contribute to instill and maintain addictive patterns of gambling behavior) is inextricably linked with sizable prize sizes: EGMs offer high maximum stake and prize sizes and the fact that accessibility of EGMs are abundant on the high street brings along another simmering danger: even inexperienced and leisure gamblers are at risk of increased rate and volume of loss, irrespective of whether they would be classed as PG or not. A rapid speed of play provided by EGMs offers fewer opportunities between bets to break trancelike dissociative states gamblers experience, as well as less time to consider one's decisions in an informed and controlled manner.

Furthermore, EGM play also allows for a high rate and volume of loss, which is allowed to further exacerbate if one engages in *loss-chasing behavior* – as stated above, a core characteristic of PG. Loss chasing may not however, be limited to PGs, and there is a potential for the fast-paced characteristic of EGM play to negatively impact on [2].

In this regard, a recent research (simulation) has investigated how these EGM characteristics interact with winning and losing outcomes and the resulting gambling behavior, as there is wide body of evidence outside of gambling research that suggests gains and losses have an asymmetrical impact on affect and arousal, as well as cognitive capacity and decision making – essential components to be controlled and rational gambling decisions [2].

Conversely, losses compared to wins, have a larger effect on physiological arousal. Hochman and Yechiam reported significantly larger pupil diameter and increased heart beat in response to losses compared to equivalent-sized wins [2].

AI research-based approach has had a pivotal role as for ascertaining that losses lead to a greater increase in psychological arousal, this may result in the gambler's optimal level of arousal being surpassed, which may be detrimental to rational decision making and lead to a loss of control during gambling, where the fast-paced and high stakes features of EGM play may exacerbate the harm caused by a loss of control [2].

Having this body of evidence very firmly in mind, it is very important to implement strategies that enable a gambler to remain in control during the gambling session so that gambling-related decisions are made in a rational manner. The implementation of that assortment of measures embodies the deemed harm minimization strategies that have been put in motion pursuant empiric evidence gathered through computerized simulation (and AI). In this axiom lies the uttermost relevance of simulation-based AI as this body of evidence would never surface in gaming leisure industry's horizon if it were not its invaluable contribution.

2.2. Background: the importance of artificial intelligence and simulation in the scope of gambling leisure industry: empirical evidence in the context of electronic gambling machines (EGMs) and the harm minimization strategies: the pop-up messages and the personalized feedback

If wins and losses do indeed result in an asymmetrical impact on a gambler's behavior during EGM gambling, it is important to implement harm minimization strategies in a timely manner before harmful behavior augment or escalate.

Nonetheless, prior to the implementation of any harm minimization strategies whatsoever, there is a major paradigm shift yet to be undertaken: the problem gambling should be approached in a proactive manner rather than a purely reactive one.

That very statement emphasizes the major importance of AI or simulation-based AI in the context of problem gambling in present days, as the bulk of empirical evidence gathered contributes for the creation of healthy gambling environments, in a timely manner.

A striking example of this is the research conducted into cognitive psychology of gambling. This simulation-based AI has shown that irrational gambling-related cognitions and misunderstandings linked to randomness and probabilities represent some of the key components contributing to the initiation and maintenance of problematic gambling in general, and in electronic gambling in particular [3, 4]. Furthermore, it has been shown that problematic gambling behavior can be curtailed pursuant to cognitive-behavioral therapy and similar cognitive interventions gathered through simulation-based AI. As a consequence, some organizations and gaming operators are beginning to offer players information about common gambling myths and erroneous beliefs. Furthermore, players can now access general advice on healthy and responsible gambling [3, 4].

A small body of empirical research gathered through simulation-based AI has shown that educational programs about erroneous beliefs can successfully help change the targeted cognitions. Take the example of the simulation-based AI conducted by Wohl et al. He has developed an animation-based educational video regarding the function of slot machines, their results depicted that the animation was indeed effective in promoting responsible gaming as demonstrated by those viewing the video staying within their pre-set limits. The aforementioned survey also demonstrated that animated educational information on slot machines (EGMs) can be an effective to enhance user adherence to pre-set limits [3, 4].

Simulations based on AI have also shown that the way the information is presented is significant. Several studies and simulations based on AI have investigated the effects of interactive pop-up messages during gambling sessions. Static messages do not appear to be as effective, whereas interactive pop-up messages and animated information can change both irrational beliefs and behavior [3, 4]. Stewart and Wohl reported that participants (in simulation-based AI) who received a monetary limit pop-up reminder were significantly more likely to adhere to monetary limits than participants who did not [3, 4].

Increasingly arising on the horizon of the gambling field is the personalized feedback, developed for responsible gambling purposes through simulation-based AI.

Personalized feedback is a behavioral tracking tool, for responsible gambling purposes. There are several programs that constitute a striking example of it, such as *Playscan, Mentor, Bet Buddy.*

Scholars emphasize that players receiving tailored feedback about their online gambling behavior are more likely to change their gambling behavior (as measured by the amount of time and money spent) compared to those who do not receive a tailored feedback [3, 4].

A recent simulation-based AI analyzed the behavioral change in vast array online gamblers (279, to be accurate) that received personalized feedback after they had signed up to a voluntary service (i.e., mentor or any other responsible gaming feature) at a European online gaming website. Those signing up to use the personalized feedback system were compared with 65, 423 have managed to match controls. The precursory results of that study demonstrated that personalized behavioral feedback within a motivational framework appears to be both an effective and accurate path of changing gambling behavior in a positive way (i.e., players notably curbed the amount of time and/or money they spent gambling after receiving personalized feedback). For example, if a player remarkably augments the amount of money they have deposited over a certain time frame (for instance, half year time period), they received the following message: "Over the last 6 months the amount of money deposited into your account has increased. Are you spending more money than you intended? You can check the amount you have spent gambling on your account page and use our helpful tools to set a daily/weekly/monthly limit" [3, 4].

Overall, the personalization approaches carved out above intend to overhaul a person's behavior through behavioral feedback. Such approaches are supported on both the "Stages of Change" model and motivational interviewing. He et al. specifically emphasized the importance of tailored information. They have managed to synthesized a vast array of motivational psychology literature to develop a motivational framework based on the transtheoretical (i.e., states of behavior change), which asserts that individuals making efforts to overhaul their behavior in a certain way experience a series of stages (i.e., pre-contemplation, contemplation, preparation, action, maintenance, and relapse). For each stage, they asserted the motivational aim (s) and recommendation (s) as to how technologies (simulation-based AI, to be precise) can boost sustainable energy usage behaviors by people [3, 4].

In sum, behavioral feedback systems enable an optimistic approach of responsible gambling, as they achieve the targeted goal of helping the players sensibly limit the amount of time and money spent gambling.

Again, that could never be achieved without the inestimable guidance of simulation-based AI that has enabled all stakeholders of gaming leisure industry to be cognizant of exciting pieces of research gathered through empiric evidence.

2.3. Background: the importance of artificial intelligence and simulation in the scope of gaming leisure industry: empirical evidence to predict *online casino patron's churn behavior*

Both in professional and everyday life, people have to interact with and reason about a large number of computerized systems. Artificial intelligence (AI) based on computer simulations can be used to construct interactive environments by means of which people can develop knowledge about the behavior of these systems. The steadfast increase in computing power has in fact given simulation a solid position within the area of gaming leisure industry. However, quite a few studies have shown that simulation-based AI is only effective when proper and sound guidance is duly provided. Automating certain tutoring and training functions aiming to provide such guidance requires the simulation-based AI model to be *articulate* and fully functional. Two other requirements follow from this. Firstly, a given simulation model ought to portray all the behavioral features of the 'real' system as far as those are important to the educational objectives. Secondly, a simulation model must have the appropriate *handles*, by means of which these features are indexed, to enable a knowledgeable communication with the learner about the model contents. Qualitative and reliable simulators, such as QPE and GARP, provide a ground for generating articulate simulation models [5]. They are crucially important in gaming leisure industry.

Empirical evidence gathered purposefully to predict online casino patron's churn behavior constitutes a striking example of prominence of artificial intelligence (AI) based on computer simulations.

Recent research has focused on customer retention in the online gaming industry by predicting player churn propensity (the likelihood to leave or stop playing at an online casino) at the individual player level. More specifically, that empirical research examined whether a **data mining algorithm** can be an effective method to predict customer churn based on online players' historical and tracked gaming data. Furthermore, it identifies the important churn predictors and predicts online players' churn behavior by incorporating an individual player's visitation and play pattern in the churn prediction model. The methodological approach advanced herein introduces a data-drive method to predict which customers are likely to churn based on individual player's gaming and demographic data. The application of this approach can help casino managers identify potential churners more precisely at the earliest possible point and eventually develop more targeted retention programs geared toward the customers at high risk of churn. This in turn will not only help them proactively prevent customer attrition but also optimize their marketing campaign and spend based on insights gained by analyzing customer behavioral data. Furthermore, the targeted retention strategy will help casino managers lower their direct marketing costs and save substantial amount of marketing dollars [6].

In the prediction of customer churn behavior, researchers have employed various **data mining algorithms**. In the gaming literature, decision tree algorithms were employed in several studies. Braverman et al. applied Chi-squared Automatic Interaction Detector (CHAID) to individual players' transaction data at an online betting website to identify high-risk players. Coussement and De Bock and Suh and Alhaery also utilized decision tree approach, classification and regression trees (CART) and exhaustive CHAID (E-CHAID), respectively, to predict player attrition behavior. Decision tree analysis methods are best known for mining large data sets. A decision tree divides any given population into subgroups based on the strongest predictors that provide the greatest degree of separation of one group from another in relation to the target variable. Additionally, **gaming data** is rather skewed with a large concentration of players having very little play [6].

Overall, the application of the predictive churn model advanced by these renowned researchers can help casino managers identify potential churners before they churn. Once the potential churners are identified, a more effective retention program and targeted marketing messages can be created and deployed to intervene and prevent customer attrition. If a customer appears to have churned, casino managers can prioritize their reactivation efforts according to the customer's churn propensity scores. Those customers with low propensity scores could be relatively easy to convert into active players in comparison to those with high churn propensity scores. It may not be worth spending the time and marketing dollars to convert some of the players with high churn propensity scores and low gaming values to the casino [6].

In these grounds lies the importance of simulation-based AI that keeps gaming leisure industry abreast with the newest developments of empiric research aimed to accelerate the benefits of global innovation.

2.4. The importance of *artificial intelligence* (*AI*) and its brotherhood with *intelligent ambient* (*IAm*) in gaming leisure industry

Evidence presented throughout this chapter is overwhelming: AI is everywhere. It spans through every aspects of our daily life, even tiny and apparently insignificant ones. As for gaming leisure industry, one cannot forsake or disregard the utmost importance of *intelligent ambient* (*IAm*), which is closely linked to the very concept of *artificial intelligence* (*AI*). Both concepts are deeply intertwined with privacy issues (*big data*) of casino patrons. Currently, this is a major concern to the gaming leisure industry as a whole.

The concept of *intelligent ambient* or *IAm* [7] (From the English *ambient intelligence*) [8–10] represents a digital and pervasive ambient created by the convergence of the technologies of radio transmission and broadcasting (as an identification by radiofrequency (*RFID*)) [11], agents of software, sensor networks, processing of data by personal mobile devices, which provides, in cyberspace, the integration and the interaction of the devices named as "*intelligent*" [12]. This new reality in gaming leisure industry depicts an *ambient* (*intelligent*) in which the casino patrons or high rollers are surrounded by intuitive interfaces embedded in every corner (even the most uncongenial and unexpected ones) of the casino [13].

Conversely, casinos have a remarkable apparatus of objects (enshrining the taxonomy of digital ambient) embodying one capacity of analysis of context and of adjustment (standardization) to the needs of the casino patrons and high rollers of the casinos [14, 15].

Those intuitive interfaces capture, collect and store, in real time, the high rollers personal data (or quite simply gamblers). Those intuitive interfaces ultimately intend to shape and standardize their real necessities, habits, and attitudes. Therefore, those intuitive interfaces allow casinos to maximize and optimize the intelligent ambient in which those intuitive interfaces were primarily created. This is only achievable due to AI proficiency and accuracy that precedes *IAm*.

Having that specific goal in mind, systems of *IAm* of the casinos have to collect and process large amounts of *personal data* and outline (or carve out) the casino patrons or high rollers profiles. These personal data are commonly collected and processed without any notification of the casino patrons or high rollers [16] through devices and techniques, which carry out a

http://dx.doi.org/10.5772/intechopen.71143

silent and continuous tracking of players' private habits [17, 18], violating, at least in theory, one of its primary requirements – the indispensable existence of consent of the holder of the personal data [12, 19]: the casino patron or high roller.

In the realm of intelligent ambient of the casinos (or overachingly, gaming leisure industry), systems of surveillance (constituted by *artificial intelligence* and *ambient intelligent*) entails the risk of an undue processing unsolicited of personal data of casino patrons or high rollers [12, 20, 21].

The aforementioned brings along an imperilment: in the cases of use of personal data for spurious purposes (*e.g.*, blackmail), there is an unreachable core of casino patron's privacy that is violated: the *thematic privacy* and *spatial privacy* of the casino patrons.

What is *thematic privacy* and *spatial privacy*? According to the German Constitutional Court (*Bundesverfassungsgericht – BVerfGE*), one can define the thematic privacy by universe of factual constellations covered by *privacy in a material sense*, refers to those personal data or realities that the holder (casino patron or high roller) of the fundamental right intend to subtract to the curiosity and to the public discussions, such as sexuality, deviant behaviors, and diseases.

This approach brings up the first caveat regarding *AI* and *IAm*: cutting-edge technology is a great leap forward for gaming leisure industry but moral boundaries should be set out, especially when it comes to handle adroitly the risk of an undue processing and unsolicited of personal data of casino patrons.

One can outrightly foresee the grounds for these enmeshed concerns: there is an *unreachable core of privacy* that is deeply intertwined with universe of personal data of the casino patrons or high rollers that involves, and identifies with – the universe of things, facts, events, experiences, emotions, places, meaning that they are a core of irreducible subjectivity, individuality, and personhood the casino patron or high roller understandably intends to keep to himself and for a scarce number of "others"; therefore being that a *space of guardianship of privacy*, converted into a place of fulfillment of private life of casino patrons or high rollers (thus, unreachable core of thematic privacy and spatial privacy, we have been referring to throughout this chapter) [22, 23].

In this light, the use of personal data of casino patrons or high rollers for strange purposes (e.g., blackmail) to the services trade and of functionalities given by the casinos comprises a "*big profligate*" (*grosser Lauschangriff*) [24, 25]. In sum, mischievous use of casino patron's personal data for purposes other than casino functionalities or marketing should be fiercely forbidden. In these grounds, one can foresee the moral boundaries that we have been insistently referring to throughout this chapter. Moral boundaries regarding this specific topic (apposite use of casino patron's personal data) are to be set out or reputational damages may occur in the realm of gaming leisure industry.

2.5. Discussion: *artificial intelligence* (*AI*) and gaming: what lies ahead?

I came across AI a few years ago through insightful thoughts of Stefen J. Karoul that reportedly was working with a group of scientists who have developed a very effective new AI model for Poker. Back then, he told me that AI opens up many creative new thoughts and opportunities going in different directions ranging from educational to just learning how to become a better

Poker player or a more skilled gambler. He wondered how long it will be before they begin to focus on other casino games such as Baccarat, Blackjack, or Roulette? That will in effect change the face of legal casino gaming again. How will gaming management react to AI? Will it be viewed in the same vein as card counting? How will surveillance detect and monitor AI on the casino floor? However, most importantly, how will players or consumers react to AI? Will they view it as something positive and try to learn more about it, how it works, the benefits, and or the risks? Or will players view AI as something negative that will now put them in an unfair position when they visit legal casinos both land-based and online to gamble? Will they think that casinos can afford to develop and exploit AI to help guarantee that they will win more money from players? What else will change in the future that will impact casinos as we know them today?

The aforementioned array of remarkable thoughts poses a far more intriguing question: will gaming leisure industry ever be the same when (and if) robots or AI-computerized humans replace casino table dealers in table games, such as Baccarat?

Gaming leisure industry landscape ought to be drastically overhauled if that replacement is to be undertaken. Foundations of our concerns can be summarized as follows: firstly, if robots or AI-computerized robots who can perform human tasks according to the **Turing test** (see point 2) are to replace casino table dealers most likely ought to deepen imbalance between casinos and players as for house advantage in table games; secondly, AI will give rise to "black market commercial trades" regarding the purchase and sale of AI cutting-edge technology, as common sense dictates everyone will feel confident enough as for tentatively embarking in a winning streak that allegedly will bring casinos "to its knees" – it is an assertion that rests upon on an exquisite alignment between common sense and cavernous knowledge about human nature; thirdly and inherently, surreptitious trades related with AI will grow exponentially giving rise to "system-sided disputes" between criminal factions over the control of AI businesses-related; fourthly, AI ought to enhance player's erroneous beliefs that house advantage can be outright overturned through an "artificial intelligence" at arm's length; fifthly, being AI at player's arm's length will reinforce distortions about the so-called illusion of control of players about the outcome of game or bet, bringing back "old phantoms" that science-based approach is so keenly and effortlessly tearing apart; sixthly, an atmosphere of unbearable suspicion will overshadow gaming leisure industry as whole, as antagonism between players and casinos over the control of outcomes of table games will dramatically rise; seventhly, an outbreak of "cheating sprees" will surely be a murky reality in gaming leisure industry, as players and casinos will effortlessly try to quash each other's odds, regardless if that is to be achieved in a honest way; eighthly, gloomy as it seems, AI ought to cause massive labor contract terminations, as human casino table dealers will be no longer needed in table games; ninthly, AI in the realm of table games will surely thwart the effectiveness of deemed *corporate social responsibility* of gaming leisure industry as casinos and player's will spare no efforts to maximize their winning streaks, regardless of putative and harmful side-effects; tenthly, AI at arm's length to casino patrons or high rollers ought to be a "nightmare" for casino's surveillance as IAm underpinning surveillance systems is absolutely clueless of whether a casino patron or high roller is using AI cutting-edge technology to enhance his gambling skills or the casino patron or high roller is just a very skilled player who happens to be in a "skill-based winning streak" – this uncertainty entails suspicion in gaming leisure industry that is not to be welcomed.

In this chapter's abstract, a hazy gaming leisure scenario has been depicted in the event of replacement of casino table dealers by robots or AI-computerized robots that can perform human tasks according to the **Turing test.** Those concerns are to be maintained, if not heightened, should moral boundaries are forsaken in this specific topic. Aiming to carve out those moral boundaries that ought to refrain everyone's appetite for AI (at least in regards of replacing casino table dealers in table games, such as Baccarat), this chapter will lay the foundations for those moral limits that ought to pervade gaming leisure industry as whole.

2.6. Discussion: *artificial intelligence* (*AI*) and gaming: corporate social responsibility of gaming leisure industry is not a chimera and should be taken seriously or reputational damages may otherwise occur: beware of what you wish!

Moral boundaries regarding AI are to be set out for the sake of the long-term stability of gaming leisure. This very statement does not jeopardize the cardinal importance of AI and simulation in the context of empiric research, but quite the opposite, as abundantly shown in **Sections 2.1.–2.5.**, AI and simulation play a pivotal role as for shedding light about the relevance of a much-needed science-based approach in gaming leisure industry. Problem gambling is a fine example of the overruling importance of AI and simulation for research purposes. Having this assertion very firmly in mind, AI and simulation role in gaming leisure industry should not be tarnished by spurious intentions of replacing the **human element** (casino table dealer in table games) that ensure experience in a casino as fun for all. Can you imagine playing against a robot that would outright quash your gambling skills in table games (namely in Baccarat)? What's the fun in that after all? Apart from that, will not such a replacement comprise a professed whim to blowing casino's corporate social responsibility to pieces? I avowedly emphasize that such a replacement is the very obliteration of corporate social responsibility that is deeply embedded in casino's activities, and overarchingly, gaming leisure industry.

Fiduciary duties and especially corporate social responsibility of gaming leisure industry are not a grotesque product of imagination. They actually exist. If they are to be disregarded by the very guardian that ought to hold them dear (casinos) reputational damages may occur. Conversely, moral hazard of gaming leisure industry shall not fall far behind.

How can one outline corporate social responsibility (CSR) [26–28]? CSR has been a trendy issue for many years now. Corporate social responsibility sprout (or quite simply, germinate) of the community's and social groups' expectations [29] that enterprises should not only care about short-term profits. Instead, enterprises must take appropriate actions to foster the well-being of the community in which they operate and make business with. Because most companies operate within the boundaries of human communities, they should also have social responsibilities that they are duty-bound or even compelled to fulfill [30, 31] – to make the world a worthier place to live in. Enterprises should perpend the impacts of their business activities on all stakeholders including their customers (casino patrons or high rollers), trade partners, employees, investors, and community at large. Needless to say, a vast array of enterprises view CSR as a way of surrender some prosperity to the community in which gaming leisure operates. Oftentimes, corporate social responsibility is ordinarily viewed as public relations. However, these conventional and long-established views of CSR are too narrowly outlined. While there is diffuse adoption of the concept due to societal pressure, many enterprises and people still erroneously lucubrate that CSR does not make good business sense. The fact is: CSR encompass much more than just the mere meaning of good business – it can be an apposite path to achieve a sustainable competitive advantage [32] for gaming leisure industry [33]. A long-term imperishable competitive advantage (to be accurate: business sustainability) of the gaming leisure industry. To be clear-cut: a long-term stability of the gaming leisure industry in the forthcoming future. In this light, corporate social responsibility is inextricably linked not only to business sustainability but likewise with long-term stability of the gaming leisure industry in the forthcoming future.

Finding a balance between corporate resources, profit objectives, and social expectations is a key factor in CSR concept [34]. It is not just about social responsibility; it is about socially integrating the operator's values with societal values [35] – a delicate balance of values. Operators must realize that in operating a casino in Macau or elsewhere, they should find common values between themselves and the society.

These values become essential for business sustainability [36] – again, the aforementioned positive play and the creation of a healthy gambling environment, which means that gaming industry's efforts to curb AI in table games should not be spared. Social responsibility of casino industry encompasses the economic, legal, ethical, and discretionary expectations that society has of organizations at a given point in time [37–39]. The CSR firm, for instance gaming industry, should strive to make a profit, obey the law, be ethical, and be a good corporate citizen [40].

Should gaming leisure industry fails to comply with their corporate social responsibility by replacing the human element (casino table dealer in table games such as Baccarat) aiming to boost house advantage, reputational damages may occur. What does reputational damage mean?

It means damages to the social image of the gaming leisure industry [41, 42] – these are "indirect patrimonial damages" [43, 44], as its occurrence may cause an effective downturn on casino's revenues.

Reference to the indirect patrimonial damages means also reputational damages [45] of gaming industry [46] essentially relates to their reputation [47] – a precious asset when it comes to a long-term business sustainability. In these grounds, one can find plausibility of corporate social responsibility (CSR) [48] of gaming leisure that, if obliterated, might just give rise to a turmoil. Furthermore, ought to create "moral hazard" for gaming leisure industry.

In this scope, take the example of Canada. It is assertable that Ontario, *Ontario Lottery, and Gaming Corporation* (*OLGC*), and gaming leisure industry are bound to a positive *duty of care* to aid the problem gambler in given circumstances. It is an axiom that casinos have a wide range of *electronic and intelligent tools* with which to monitor the gambling habits and losses of their casino patrons or high rollers (enabled by the aforementioned tandem between *artificial intelligence, ambient intelligence,* and *surveillance* that allows casinos to proficiently track gambler's addictive patterns arisen from problem gambling). In this regard, it has been asserted that gaming leisure industry is bound to a general duty to operate in "the public interest and in accordance with the principles of honesty and integrity". Lastly, casinos and problem gamblers are bound to a contractual relationship in which, like the *tavern keeper,* the casino has an "abnormal" inducement to heighten gambling activity and casino patron's losses; in this scope, on 26-10-2006, the decision of Madam Justice Sachs in *Edmonds v. Laplante,* following the *legal reasoning* stated in *Cooper v. Hobart,* asserted that, according to *Anns test,* the *Ontario Lottery and Gaming Corporation* (*OLGC*) owe a *duty of care* to assist the problem gamblers [48]. In this light, one should foresee the utmost importance of corporate social responsibility in gaming leisure industry.

2.7. Discussion: *artificial intelligence* (*AI*) and gaming: gaming leisure industry ought to uphold/comply with fiduciary norms or bear the costs of "*moral hazard*"

AI architecture in gaming leisure industry has already been put in motion. One can straightforwardly confirm that in the ambit of Poker. AI and Poker make an exquisite alignment (or shall we say combination?) but it is also to some extent a new testing ground for intricate AI research. While producing computer agents that are apposite and prone (thus, able) to play poker, scientists face many appealing and perplexing problems, which need to be thoughtfully addressed and tested. One Russian software company has created a vast number of new artificial intelligences to play poker at a professional level. The Poker games include both *No Limit Texas Holdem* (2–10 players) and *Fixed Limit Texas Holdem* (2–10 players). This concrete Russian company now promotes that they have developed professional level AI poker players or Bots (robots) and that this uncommon know how can now be used in a cutting-edge training system. Presently, their lab is working on a new poker training service, which will enable people (regular casino patrons) to enhance their poker skills with visually demonstrated deviation from optimal play along with recommended strategy adjustments in real time. They have further asserted that this is not only a standalone product but a product that could also be seamlessly integrated into any gambling portal or online poker room. With further detailed research one can also find an American software company offering a wide range of professionally produced tutorials that are also partially based upon AI to help train members to become sharpened poker players. They have produced over 200 educational videos ranging in skill level from beginner to intermediate to advanced [49].

It is now crystal-clear that an unrelenting drive to excellence, aiming to bolster player's skills in Poker, has already begun. An immediate question emerges: how long until this drive broadens its horizons to Baccarat or any other table games? Should not this unanticipated spree or race to capitalize benefits of cutting-edge technology such as AI be as equivalent as opening a Pandora Box in gaming leisure industry? Our assessment on this is adamant and very clear: should gaming leisure industry fail to take this issue seriously and accordingly take appropriate actions to prevent proliferation of AI in table games its moral hazard might surface as an outbreak of gambling-related criminality will darken this lucrative industry. Gaming leisure industry ought to step up and lead the way against proliferation of AI in table games. In order to achieve that gaming leisure industry ought to uphold fiduciary norms that are deeply ingrained in its corporate social responsibility.

Gaming leisure industry ought to abide to fiduciary norms deeply intertwined with their corporate social responsibility. Fiduciary norms are apposite to gaming leisure industry as its three main features bear striking resemblance with norms of contract, tort, and criminal law that are intrinsically connected with gaming leisure industry activity as a whole. Fiduciary norms are sharply linked to corporate social responsibility as gaming leisure industry ought to drive its focus to do no harm to the social community in which operates. One can forthrightly understand the grounds for this linkage. First, fiduciary norms impose deliberative requirements: they make specific types of demands on an agent's deliberation in addition to her behavior. Second, complying with fiduciary norms requires a special conscientiousness, a corporate social responsibility consciousness. Living up to a fiduciary obligation depends not only on how gaming leisure industry behaves and deliberates, but also on whether she does so for the right reasons such as performing adroitly their corporate social responsibility for the sake of the long-term stability of gaming leisure industry. Third, fiduciary norms impose "robust" demands, which require the fiduciary to seek out and respond appropriately to new information about the interests of her beneficiaries (the whole community in which gaming leisure operates). As a result, our thesis is that fiduciary principles can be fruitfully applied to many domains of public law such as gaming law. A note in our use of the terms "fiduciary norms" and "fiduciary principles": according to a definition of norms that we find appealing, every norm has both a normative element (that is, it is constituted by "normative principles") and a *socio-empirical element* (in that it operates over and is "somehow *accepted* in" the particular domain over which it applies) [50]. On our usage, fiduciary norms are constituted by fiduciary principles (which are usually, but not necessarily, stated in the form of requirements applicable to the fiduciary) that operate over and are accepted within the domains (generally those in private law) over which fiduciary laws apply [51]. Thus, fiduciary duties are established and entailed by fiduciary norms and principles [52–57, 59].

Failing to perform adroitly those fiduciary duties (that enshrines fiduciary norms and principles, as seen above), and foremost, its corporate social responsibility, as for preventing proliferation of AI in table games, originates gaming leisure industry's moral hazard.

Moral hazard in the realm of gaming leisure industry lies in a simple question: what obligations do gaming leisure gaming have to perform in order to prevent or alleviate the suffering of others or to eschew disrepute to this lucrative business altogether?

When it comes to corporate social responsibility, the concept of "moral hazard" is one of the most prominent, and least well understood, of the cogent tools applied to these and other social responsibility questions. Whether the issue is related to products liability law, workers' compensation, welfare, health care, banking regulation, bankruptcy law, takings law, or business law, moral hazard is a cardinal part of the law. From a law and economics standpoint, moral hazard sheds light about how things are and came to be as they are. Moral hazard is punctiliously related with moral boundaries that ingrain corporate social responsibility. The tandem between corporate social responsibility and moral hazard explains why moral boundaries ought to be outlined in the ambit of AI in table games: the long-term sustainability and stability of gaming leisure industry depends on whether this lucrative industry abides to its fiduciary duties to curb AI in table games.

The best way to portray the ubiquity of the moral hazard lens on corporate social responsibility in gaming leisure industry is to quote a well-known writer that described the "lesson of moral hazard" as follows: what moral hazard means is that, if you cushion the consequences of bad behavior, then you encourage that bad behavior [58].

Moral hazard encompasses a simple lesson: less is more. As for gaming leisure industry, less AI in table games is definitively more corporate social responsibility and a bullet-proof hope in the long-term stability of this profitable industry. Should AI door be wide open to table games, requirements for a perfect storm are met and gaming leisure industry might not be able to bounce back from its sequels.

Author details

Hugo Miguel da Luz dos Santos

Address all correspondence to: hugo.miguel.luz@gmail.com

Research Group about Gaming Law, Macau, China

References

[1] Russell SJ, Norvig P. Artificial Intelligence: A Modern Approach. Prentice-Hall, Inc. A Simon & Schuster Company: Prentice-Hall; 1995

[2] Harris A, Parke A. Empirical evidence for the differential impact of gambling outcome on behaviour in electronic gambling: Implications for harm-minimization strategies. Responsible Gaming Review. 2015;**1**(2):10-11 April 2015

[3] Auer M, Griffths MD. Personalized feedback in the promotion of responsible gambling: A brief overview. Responsible Gaming Review. 2014;**1**(1):28 January 2014

[4] Auer M, Litler A, Griffiths MD. Legal aspects of responsible gaming pre-commitment and personal feedback initiatives. Gaming Law Review and Economics (GLRE). 2015;**19**(6): 444-456

[5] De Koning K, Bredeweg B, Breuker J, Wielinga B. Artificial intelligence: Model-based reasoning about learner behaviour. Artificial Intelligence. 2000;**117**:25-35

[6] Suh E, Alhaery M. Customer retention: Reducing online casino player churn through the application of predictive modelling. UNLV Gaming Research and Review Journal. 2016;**20**(2):1-22 Las Vegas, United States of America

[7] Santos HLD. A brave new world of ambient intelligence in the casinos of Macau: Reality or fiction? UNLV Gaming Research and Review Journal. 2015;**19**(2):1-4 Las Vegas, United States of America

[8] Rabinovich-Einy O, Katsch E. Lessons from online dispute resolution for dispute systems design. In: Online Dispute Resolution Theory and Practice. Hague, Netherlands: Eleven International Publishing; 2013. p. 39-40

[9] Friedewald M, Vildjiouane E, Punie Y, Wright D. The brave new world of ambient intelligence: An analysis of scenarios regarding security, security and privacy issues. In: Security in Persuasive Computing. Proceedings of the Third International Conference. New York: Springer; 2006. p. 3934

[10] Thiessen A, Looder E. The role of artificial intelligence in online dispute resolution. In: Workshop on Online Dispute Resolution at the International Conference on Artificial Intelligence and Law. Edinburgh, United Kingdom, 2003. pp. 4-5

[11] Yelshyna A, Andrade F, Novais P. Um ambiente inteligente de resolução de litígios – Repercussões jurídicas na privacidade e protecção de dados. Scientia Ivridica (SI), Revista de Direito Comparado Português e Brasileiro. 2015;**LXIV**(337):113-123. Janeiro/Abril 2015, Braga, p. 113 and following

[12] Arts E, Roovers R. Embedded system design issues in ambient intelligence. In: Ambient Intelligence: Impact on Embedded System Design. Norwell: Kluwer Academic Publishers; 2003. p. 11-29

[13] Friedwald M, Vildjiounaite E, Punie Y, Wright D. The brave new world of ambient intelligence: An analysis of scenarios regarding privacy, identity and security issues. In: Security in Pervasive Computing. Proceedings of the Third International Conference. New York: Springer; 2006. p. 119

[14] Punie Y. The future of ambient intelligence in Europe: The need for more everyday ife. In: Communications and Strategies. Seville; 2005. p. 142. https://www.researchgate.net/publication/250729794 (Accessed: July 27, 2017)

[15] Novais P, Costa R, Carneiro D, Neves J. Inter-organization cooperation for ambient assisted living. Journal of Ambient Intelligence and Smart Environments (IOS Press). 2010;**2**:179-195

[16] Solove D. Introduction: Privacy self-management and the consent dilemma. Harvard Law Review. 2012;**126**:1888-1889

[17] Balkin JM, The constitution in the National Surveillance State, In: Yale Law School Legal Scholarship Repository, Faculty Scholarship Series, Paper 225; 2008. p. 13

[18] Solove D. The Digital Person: Technology and Privacy in the Information Age. New York: New York University Press; 2004. p. 42-49

[19] Castro CSE. Direito da Informática. Almedina, Coimbra: Privacidade e Dados Pessoais; 2005. p. 206

[20] Gabel JD. CSI Las Vegas: Privacy, policing, and profiteering in casino structured intelligence. UNLV Gaming Law Journal. 2012;**3**Nevada, Reno:41

[21] Andrade MDC. Domicílio, intimidade e Constituição. Revista de Legislação e Jurisprudência (RLJ). 2008;**138**(3953); (Novembro-Dezembro de 2008 Coimbra Editora, Coimbra):110

[22] Böckenforde. Die Methoden der Verfassungsinterpretation. Juristichen Zeitung (JZ). 2008;**1**:926

[23] Engels S, Jürgens U. Auswirkungen der EGMR-Rechts-prechung zum Privatsphärenschutz. Möglichkeiten und Grenzen der Umsetzung des "Caroline" – Urteis in deutschen Recht. Neue Juristichen Wochenschrift (NJW). 2007;**2**:2520

[24] Serra C. A responsabilidade social das empresas – Sinais de um Instituto Jurídico Iminente? In: Estudos em Homenagem ao Prof. Doutor Manuel Henrique Mesquita, Stvdia Ivridica 96, Ad Honorem – 4, Boletim da Faculdade de Direito da Universidade de Coimbra (BFDUC). Vol. II. Coimbra: Coimbra Editora; 2009. p. 836-867

[25] Nogueira Serens M. Corporate social responsability: Vinho velho em odres novos. Direito das Sociedades em Revista (DSR). 2013;**10**(5):75-96 Outubro 2013; Almedina, Coimbra

[26] Oliveira MPD. Direito de voto nas sociedades cotadas: da admissibilidade de categorias de ações com direito de voto plural às L-shares. Revista de Direito das Sociedades em Revista (DSR). 2015, 2016;**VII**(2):436 Almedina, Coimbra

[27] McGuire JW. Business and Society. New York: McGraw-Hill; 1963

[28] Carrol AB. Corporate social responsibility – Evolution of a definitional construct. In: Business and Society. New York: McGraw-Hill; 1953. p. 6

[29] Zhao J. Corporate Social Responsibility in Contemporary China. Edward Elgar, Cheltenham. Massachusetts; 2014

[30] D Lam. Corporate Social Integration in Macao. Available from: urbino.net [Accessed: August 2, 2017]

[31] Gustafson AB. Book review – challenging corporate social responsibility: Lessons for public relations from the casino industry. UNLV Gaming Research & Review Journal. 2017;**21**(1):1-4

[32] Bowen HR. Social Responsibilities of the Businessman. New York: McGraw-Hill; 1953

[33] Caroll AC. A three-dimensional conceptual model of corporate social performance. Academy of Management Review (AMR). 1979;**4**(4). pp. 497-e ff

[34] Caroll AC. Business and Society: Managing Corporate Social Performance. 1981

[35] Caroll AC. Social issues in management research: Experts' views, analysis and commentary. In: Business and Society, McGraw-Hill. 1994 pp. 5 ff

[36] Caroll AC. The pyramid of corporate social responsibility: Toward the moral Management of organizational stakeholders. In: Business Horizons, McGraw-Hill. 1991 pp. 39 e ff

[37] Mcclure K. Tip-pooling at Nevada casinos – The case at the Wynn and why the Nevada state gaming commission should set strict regulations on tip-pooling to protect the rights of dealers, casinos, and the reputation of the Nevada gaming industry. UNLV Gaming Law Journal. 2014;**5**(81):96 Spring 2014

[38] Ricouer P. Le Conflits des Interprétations. In: Essais d' Herméneutique. Paris: Dalloz; 1969

[39] Grunsky W. Aktuell probleme zum begriff des vermogensschadens. Beck, München, 2: Auflage; 2008

[40] Cortina A. Ética de la razón cordial: educar en la ciudadania en el siglo XXI. Oviedo: Nobel; 2007

[41] Mertens K. Kommentar zum Aktiengesetz, 2/1, 3, Auflage; Carl Heymanns, 2010. pp 76-94

[42] Scognamiglio R. Il dano morale. Contributo alla teoria del danno extracontrattuale. In: Rivista de Diritto Civile. Padova: Cedam; 1957. p. 283-285

[43] Massaro T, Stryker R. Political discourse, civility, and harm: Freedom of speech, liberal democracy, and emerging evidence on civility and effective democratic engagement. Arizona Law Review. 2012;**54**:374

[44] Sasso WV, Kalajdzic J. Do Ontario and its gaming venues owe a duty of care to problem gamblers? Gaming Law Review and Economics (GLR&E). 2006;**10**(6):552-567

[45] Karoul SJ. Artificial Intelligence. Poker: Poker Bots and Wining; 2013. p. 1

[46] Brennan G et al. Explaining Norms. Oxford University Press; 2013. p. 2-3

[47] Lieb EJ, Galoub SR. Fiduciary political theory: A critique. Yale Law Journal (YLJ). 2016;**125**:1820

[48] Criddle EJ. Fiduciary administration: Rethinking popular representation in agency rulemaking. Texas Law Review. 2010;**88**:441

[49] Criddle EJ. Fiduciary foundations of administrative law. UCLA Law Review. 2006;**54**:117

[50] Criddle EJ. Mending holes in the rule of (administrative) law. Northwestern University Law Review. 2010;**104**:1271

[51] Criddle EJ. When delegation begets domination: Due process of administrative lawmaking. Georgia Law Review. 2011;**46**:117

[52] Fox-Decent E, Criddle EJ. The fiduciary constitution of human rights. Legal Theory. 2009;**15**:301

[53] Waldron J. Are sovereigns entitled to the benefit of the international rule of law? European Journal of International Law. 2011;**22**:315

[54] Nagy DM. Insider trading, congressional officials, and duties of entrustment. Boston University Law Review Journal. 2011;**91**:1105

[55] Perino MA. A scandalous perversion of trust: Modern lessons from the early history of congressional insider trading. Rutgers University Law Review. 2015;**67**:335

[56] Glassman JK. Drop budget fight, shift to welfare. St. Louis Post-Dispatch, Feb. ll, 1996, at B3. http://www.umsl.edu/~libweb/universityarchives/campusorganizations/universitysenate/Senate,%201999.pdf (Accessed: July 15, 2017)

[57] Richard A. Epstein, products liability as an insurance market. The Journal of Legal Studies. 1985;**14**:645-666

[58] Baker T. On the genealogy of moral hazard. University of Pennsylvania Law School Penn Law: Legal Scholarship Repository: 1-59. http://scholarship.law.upenn.edu/faculty_scholarship/872/ (Accessed: July 18, 2017)

[59] Ben-Sahar O, Logue KD. Outsourcing Regulation: how Insurance Reduces Moral Hazard. University of Chicago Law School Chicago Unbound; 2012. p. 198-245

Chapter 11

War-Gaming Applications for Achieving Optimum Acquisition of Future Space Systems

Tien M. Nguyen, Andy T. Guillen,
Sumner S. Matsunaga, Hien T. Tran and Tung X. Bui

Additional information is available at the end of the chapter

http://dx.doi.org/10.5772/intechopen.71044

Abstract

This chapter describes an innovative modeling and simulation approach using newly proposed Advanced Game-based Mathematical Framework (AGMF), Unified Game-based Acquisition Framework (UGAF) and a set of War-Gaming Engines (WGEs) to address future space systems acquisition challenges. Its objective is to assist the DoD Acquisition Authority (DAA) to understand the contractor's perspective and to seek optimum Program-and-Technical-Baseline (PTB) solution and corresponding acquisition strategy under both the perspectives of the government and the contractors. The proposed approach calls for an interdisciplinary research that involves game theory, probability and statistics, and non-linear programming. The goal of this chapter is to apply the proposed war-gaming frameworks to develop and evaluate PTB solutions and associated acquisition strategies in the context of acquisition of future space systems. Our simulation results suggest that our optimization problem for the acquisition of future space systems meets the affordability and innovative requirements with minimum acquisition risk.

Keywords: game theory, probability and statistics, non-linear programming, mathematical modeling, simulation, Program and Technical Baseline, acquisition strategy, space systems

1. Introduction

The U.S. Department of Defense (DoD) has recently released the Defense Innovation Initiative (DII) with the goal to "reinvigorate war-gaming" and to make DoD (best) practices more innovative [1]. In addition, DoD and U.S. Air Force have generated new acquisition regulations and initiatives to promote "Owning the Technical Baseline" (OTB) and "modular open system approach (MOSA)" as enablers for affordability [2, 3]. The Aerospace Corporation has been investigating and developing war-gaming techniques to improve the DoD acquisition efficiency and productivity by using AGMF-UGAF to generate optimum PTB solutions and associated optimum acquisition strategies for future space systems [4–9]. The goal is to provide a set of decision support tools that can be used by the DoD Acquisition Authority (DAA) to make joined acquisition-and-programmatic decisions that will avoid acquiring the "mission area stovepipe" space systems in the future. Although the focus of this chapter is on the future space systems, but the models presented in this chapter can be adapted and used for general civil and commercial systems with minor modifications.

The UGAF-AGMF [4, 7] describes two levels of War-Gaming Engines (WGEs) or game models, namely, one representing the government's "Acquisition" perspective, and the other representing the contractor's "Bidding" perspective. The multivariate optimization involves the government objective to maximize performance and minimize cost for "affordability," and the contractor objective to maximize performance and maximize profits. The framework establishes government models (DAA-WGE) and contractor models (KTR-WGE). Each of these WGEs is further subdivided into PTB (P) solution models and corresponding Acquisition (A)/Bidding (B) strategy models; government models are abbreviated as DAA-PWGE and DAA-AWGE; contractor models are KTR-PWGE and KTR-BWGE. These proposed frameworks and associated game models address technical baseline, contract type, associated incentives, source selection criteria described in Sections L & M of a Request for Proposal (RFP) [10].

The chapter discusses AGMF that utilizes static and dynamic games and associated WGEs that employ Bayesian cooperative and non-cooperative games with both complete and incomplete information scenarios, and the use of UGAF for employing appropriate WGEs and solving conflicting system and acquisition requirements. In addition, this chapter also presents and discusses simulation results obtained from the proposed DAA-PWGE, DAA-AWGE, KTR-PWGE and KTR-BWGE. The Chapter is organized as follow:

- Section 2 presents the "Acquisition War-Gaming Concept" and discusses the "Art versus Science" for the development of the AGMF and UGAF frameworks;
- Section 3 provides a detailed description of AGMF; Section 4 discusses the UGAF;
- Section 5 describes the PTB-WGEs or PWGEs including DAA-PWGE and KTR-PWGE;
- Section 6 describes and discusses the government "Acquisition" DAA-AWGEs and contractor "Bidding" KTR-AWGE for commonly used contract types, including Firmed-Fixed Price (FFP), Fixed Price Incentive Firm (FPIF), and Cost Plus Incentive Firm (CPIF);
- Section 7 presents the MATLAB models[1] and simulation results obtained from the DAA-PWGE, DAA-AWGE, KTR-PWGE and KTR-BWGE models for commonly used contract types discussed above.
- Section 8 provides a brief discussion on the integration of PWGEs and AWGEs. Note that the optimum PTB solution will be selected by integrating the DAA-PWGE and KTR-PWGE,

[1]The MATLAB models presented in this chapter were implemented by a Nationally-Diverse Student Team (NDST) under the support of the National Science Foundation (NSF), Grant Number DMS-1461148, through the NCSU Industrial and Applied Mathematics Research Experience for Undergraduates (REU) Project. Note that the NDST is also referred to as the REU team.

while the optimum acquisition strategy is selected by integrating the DAA-AWGE and KTR-AWGE.

- Finally, Section 9 presents the conclusion and discusses way-forward.

2. Acquisition War-Gaming Concept: Art versus Science

Our proposed "Acquisition War-Gaming" frameworks leverage existing war-gaming concept, which is defined as a step-by-step process of action, reaction, and counteraction for visualizing the execution of each friendly Course-Of-Action (COA) in relation to an enemy's COA and reactions. In the war-gaming process, planners determine how to apply combat multipliers to the COA to improve the possibility of mission success and minimize risks to soldiers. "Acquisition War-Gaming" employs "Game Theory" in the "war-gaming" concept to optimize (i) the Program and Technical Baseline (PTB) solution for a set of warfighter requirements, and (ii) associated acquisition strategy and contract incentives for acquiring the "PTB solution." The optimization games require "Payoff and Cost Functions" or PCFs and associated "Objective Function." The readers can find detailed description of PTB and its components in Refs. [4–6].

As discussed in Ref. [7], we envision two categories of War-Gaming Engines (WGE[2]), namely, DAA War-Gaming Engine (DAA-WGE) and Contractor-WGE (KTR-WGE). **Figure 1** depicts our vision for the two categories of war-gaming applications [7]. DAA-WGE is to be played by DAA and its stakeholders (see **Figure 1(a)**). KTR-WGE is to be played by potential contractors (or organizations posing as contractors), with game rules dictated by DAA and its stakeholders (see **Figure 1(b)**). The DAA-WGE and KTR-WGE will be developed and integrated such that DAA and its stakeholders can use them for the development and generation of optimum PTB solutions and associated acquisition strategy, respectively. Note that the optimum acquisition strategy addresses contract type, associated incentives, and RFP and source selection criteria. To achieve this goal, we define and develop the following four types of game models:

- DAA-PWGE: government plays the game to select optimum PTB solutions. Past acquisition data and market survey data are used to characterize each contractor's bidding behavior. A PTB solution is selected based on minimum program execution risk and cost.
- DAA-AWGE: government plays the game to select an optimum acquisition strategy associated with a PTB solution. Past acquisition data and market survey data are used to characterize each contractor's bidding behavior. An acquisition strategy is selected based on minimum program execution risk and cost.
- KTR-PWGE: in this game, we simulate the contractors as players and the goal is to select optimum contractors' PTB solutions. Past acquisition data and market survey data are used to characterize each contractor's bidding behavior. A PTB solution is selected for each contractor based on minimum program execution risk and maximum contractor profit.

---

[2]WGE is defined a set of Algorithms, characterizing the Program and Technical Baseline (PTB), technology enablers, architectural solutions, contracting parameters, and industry bidding position, implemented in MATLAB statistical optimization models.

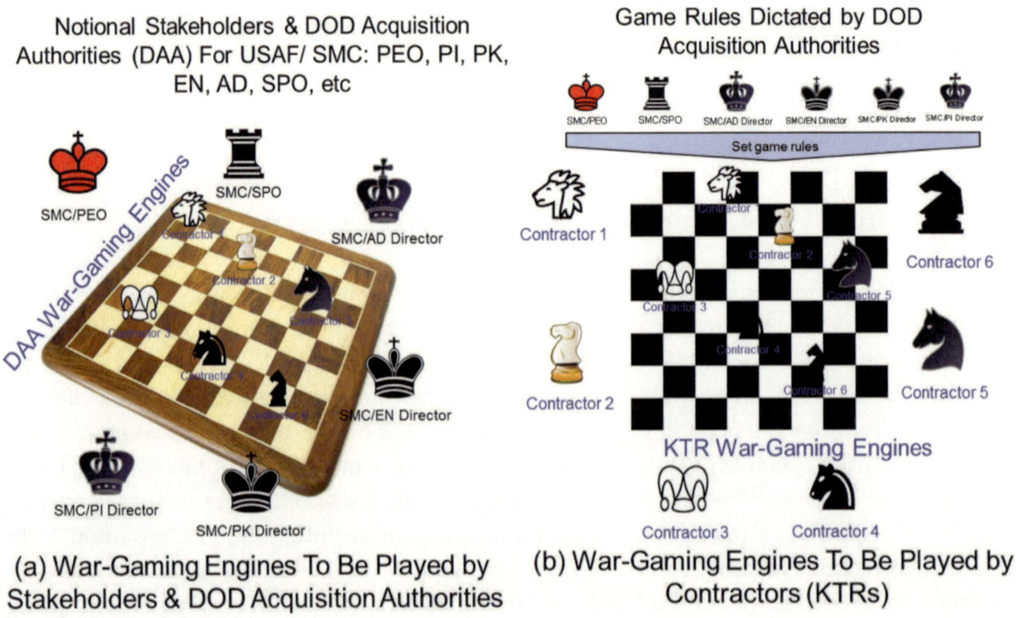

Figure 1. Our vision for war-gaming applications [7].

- KTR-BWGE: this game also is referred to as KTR-AWGE because the contractor's bidding strategy will be derived based on the acquisition strategy specified by the government or DAA-AWGE. The KTR-AWGE game simulates the contractors as players and the goal is to select the optimum bidding strategy associated with each contractor's selected PTB solution. Past acquisition data and market survey data are used to characterize each contractor's bidding behavior. A bidding strategy is selected based on minimum program execution risk and maximum contractor profit.

To integrate these War-Gaming Engines together, we need a unified framework that can achieve the vision shown in **Figure 1**. The proposed unified framework described in Ref. [7] consists of two frameworks, namely, AGMF and UGAF. The development of AGMF framework to apply war-gaming concept for "Acquisition" is a "Science." The AGMF is a framework for selecting optimum game structure and game type depending on the information available for PTB Action Space (PAS) and Acquisition Action Space (AAS). On the other hand, the development of UGAF for "Exercising" AGMF is an "Art." UGAF is used for the exercising of the AGMF to generate optimum PTB solutions and optimum acquisition strategies. The overview of these unified frameworks will be provided in the following sections.

3. Advanced Game-based Mathematical Framework (AGMF)

Figure 2 describes the framework where it captures the Bayesian game structures and seven game types (game selection from #1 through #7) for DAA-PWGE, DAA-AWGE, KTR-PWGE

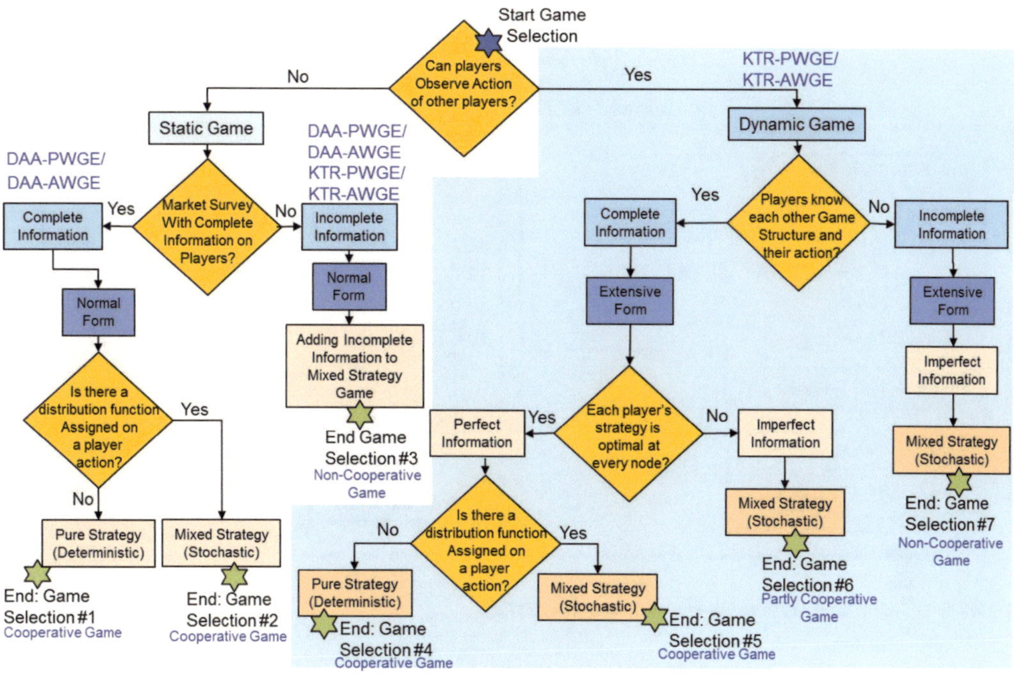

Figure 2. AGMF: selection of optimum war-gaming structure and type [7].

and KTR-AWGE depending on the information available for PAS and AAS [7]. As shown in **Figure 2**, the framework starts the game selection by answering a question concerning the player's ability to observe other player action. As depicted in **Figure 2**, the DAA-PWGE and DAA-AWGE always have the static game structure since all the games will be played by the DAA and its stakeholders, with contractors as players in each game. On the other hand, the KTR-PWGE and KTR-AWGE can have either static game or dynamic game structure. The KTR-PWGE and KTR-AWGE can have a dynamic game structure when the DAA and its stakeholders assume that the one contractor can observe other contractor's action when the games are played. For dynamic game structure, the players make move based on the information released from the RFP and the players' ability (or contractor's ability) to observe other players' action through the "intelligent" information gathered on the competitors. A detailed discussion of AGMF is provided in Ref. [7].

4. Unified Game-based Acquisition Framework (UGAF)

The goal for UAGF is two-fold, namely, (i) play games to determine optimum PTB solution for a specified set of warfighter needs, and (ii) play games to determine the corresponding optimum acquisition strategy for a specified optimum PTB solution [7]. The optimum PTB solution

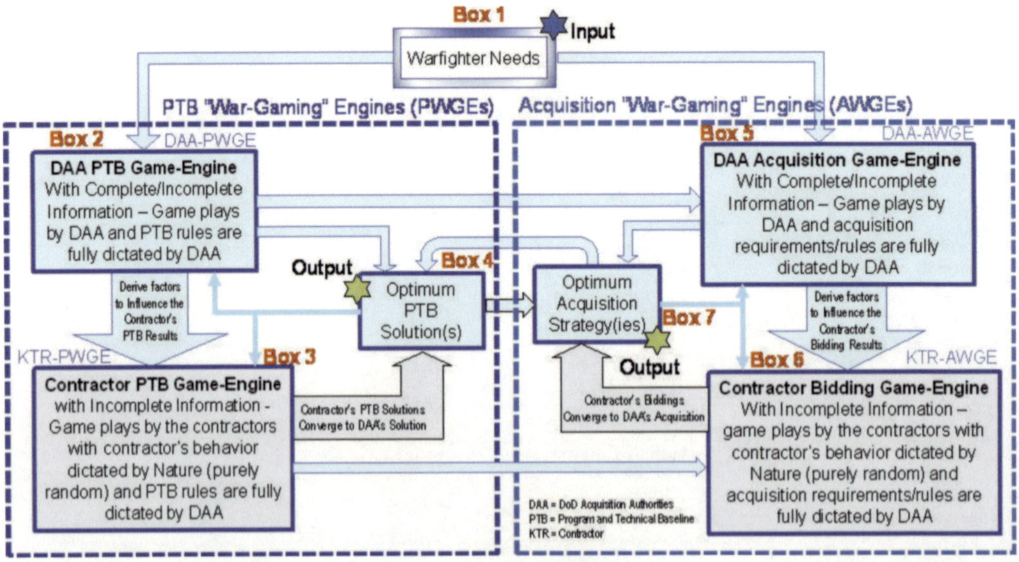

Figure 3. UGAF: a unified approach for exercising AGMF [7].

is defined as the "Architecture Solution[3]" (ARCS) for the required warfighter needs that meets the affordability and innovative requirements with minimum acquisition risk. **Figure 3** describes our proposed unified framework to exercise the AGMF. It describes the processing flow for the DAA-PWGE, DAA-AWGE, KTR-PWGE and KTR-AWGE to generate optimum PTB solutions and associated optimum acquisition strategies. **Figure 3** also shows seven processing boxes, in the order of execution. Detailed descriptions of Boxes #1 through #7 are described in Ref. [7].

5. PTB War-Gaming Engines (PWGEs)

This section provides an overview of DAA-PWGE and KTR-PWGE models. The approach presented in this section follows [8]. It focuses on static Bayesian game models with "Pure" and "Mixed" games depending on the outcomes of the market survey results. For a pure game with complete and perfect information, the contractors are "surer" of their risk assessments on the selected TEs. The risk is either "Good" or "Bad" with probability of 1 and the "Belief" and/or "Weighting" functions for this game type are not needed. For mixed games with complete and imperfect information, the contractors are "more uncertain" of their risk assessments on TEs and the "Belief" and/or "Weighting" functions are needed for assessing TE risks. In this case, the TEs are weighted based on their priorities and using a probability density function with either uniform or triangular distribution depending on the TE's uncertainty.

[3] Architecture solution or ARCS is descried in terms of a set of selected "Technology Enablers" (TEs) that can provide the required system capabilities, which meet the warfighter needs. TE is a specific technology solution that meets a "capability" alone or in combination with other TEs, e.g. a telemetry communications system.

The TE's uncertainties are expressed in terms technology and market uncertainties. The definition for the system requirement types and associated PTB solution framework for classifying a PTB Solution are described in **Figure 4** [8]. As an example, a Type 1 Requirement is mapped into a "Less Innovative & Conservative PTB Solution" where the "Market Uncertainty" and "Technology Uncertainty" are "Low" and "Low," respectively. Since each "Requirement Type" is associated with specific measure of technology and market uncertainties, the proposed PTB solution framework allows us to select the appropriate acquisition strategy for each "Requirement Type" and assess the technology and cost risk for each "PTB Solution Type." **Figure 5** provides a PTB mapping framework to identify the "Acquisition Strategy" and risks associated with each "Requirement Type" and "PTB Solution."

A detailed description of PTB System Engineering (SE) frameworks, the analytical and simulation modeling approaches for developing optimum PTB solutions can be found in Ref. [8].

5.1. Analytical and simulation modeling approach for government PTB games

This section provides an overview description of the analytical and simulation modeling approaches for PTB cooperative Bayesian games for complete information with pure and mixed strategies [8].

5.1.1. DAA-PWGE cooperative Bayesian games set-up for complete information with pure and mixed strategies

The DAA plays static Bayesian cooperative games with either complete and perfect information (pure game) or complete and imperfect information (mixed game) using normal-form

System Requirements Type

Requirement Type	Requirement Type Description
Type 1	Firmed and fixed requirements with known Technology Enablers and known market
Type 2	Well-defined requirements with some uncertainties on technology enabler and market. Note that firm Requirements with unknown market is classified as this Type 2
Type 3	Requirements are somewhat known with some market uncertainty but can not identify the exact technology enablers
Type 4	Requirements are somewhat known with some technology uncertainty but can not identify the exact company (or companies) to provide the technology enabler
Type 5	Unknown Requirements with unkhown technology enable and market

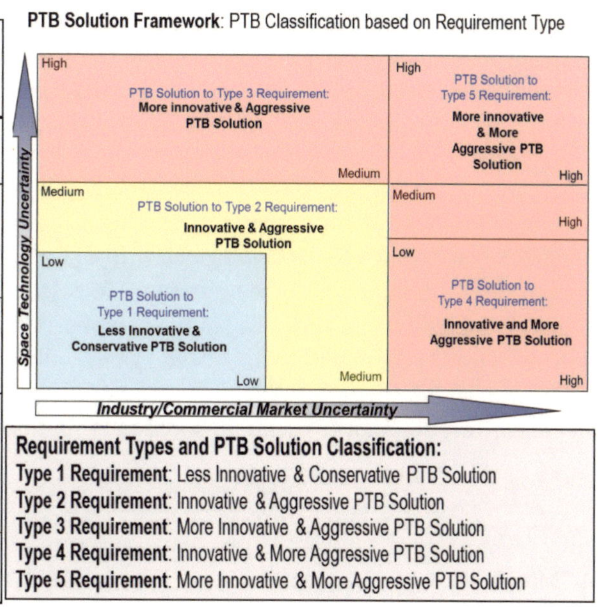

Figure 4. PTB framework for classifying PTB solution according to requirement uncertainties.

Requirements Classifications, Advanced Acquisition Strategy Mapping, PTB Solution Classification and PTB Risk Assessment							
Requirement Type	Requirement Type Description	Market Uncertainty	Technology Uncertainty	Advanced Acquisition Strategy Mapping	PTB Solution Type Classification	PTB Risk Assessment	
						Technical & Performance Risks	Cost & Schedule Risks
Type 1	Firmed and fixed requirements with known Technology Enablers	Low	Low	Enhancement Launch: FFP, FPEPA	PTB Type 1 Solution: Conservative	Low	Low
Type 2	Well-defined requirements with some uncertainties on technology enabler and market	Low	Medium	Platform Launch: FPIF, FPAF	PTB Type 2 Solution: Innovative	Low	Medium
		Medium	Low			Medium	Low
		Medium	Medium			Medium	Medium
Type 3	Requirements are somewhat known with some market uncertainty but can not identify the exact technology enablers	Medium	High	Positioning Option: CPIF	PTB Type 3 Solution: More Innovative	High	Medium
Type 4	Requirements are somewhat known with some technology uncertainty but can not identify the exact company (or companies) to provide the technology enabler	High	Medium	Scouting Option: CPAF, CPIF	PTB Type 4 Solution: Less Conservative	Medium	High
Type 5	Unknown Requirements with unkhown technology enable and market	High	High	Stepping Stone Option: CPAF, CPFF	PTB Type 5 Solution: Most Innovative	High	High

Figure 5. PTB mapping framework: requirement type-acquisition strategy mapping [7].

representation of the Bayesian games [8]. Our game models assume "N" suppliers (or contractors (KTRs)) participating in the bidding games and the availability of market survey data for which Government's "request for information" (RFI) is used to collect the required data from each contractor for assessing potential TEs identified by DAA. The contractor set is defined mathematically as

$$KTR = \{KTR_n, n = 1, 2, \ldots, N\} \tag{1}$$

The DAA defines PTB strategies involving potential architecture solutions and make them available to each supplier through RFI. The DAA estimates payoff received by each supplier for each combination of PTB strategies that could be chosen by the suppliers. The potential "I" architecture solutions set or ARCS is defined mathematically as

$$ARCS = \{ARCS_i, n = 1, 2, \ldots, I\} \tag{2}$$

The DAA plays complete-Bayesian game with a "Pure" or "Mixed" strategy, depending on the market survey data, to select the optimum PTB solution that can achieve "Nash" equilibrium. "Pure" game will be played if the market survey data show "complete and perfect information" for TEs. On the other hand, "Mixed" game will be played when the data show "complete and imperfect information." A "Pure" strategy, $\boldsymbol{S_{Pure}}$, is a strategy for a contractor "k" to map an architecture solution "i" to a PTB solution "j" defined as

$$S_{Pure} = \left\{S_{i,j}^{k} : ARCS_{i}^{k} \rightarrow PTB_{j}^{k}; i = 1, 2, \ldots I; j = 1, 2, 3, 4, 5; k = 1, 2, \ldots, N\right\} \tag{3}$$

A "Mixed" strategy, $\boldsymbol{S_{Mixed}}$, is a strategy for a contractor "k" to map an architecture solution "i" to a PTB solution "j" with a "Belief" function $\boldsymbol{P_{i,j}^{k}}$ defined as

$$S_{Mixed} = \left\{ \boldsymbol{S}^k_{i,j} : \boldsymbol{ARCS}^k_i \overset{P^k_{i,j}}{\rightarrow} \boldsymbol{PTB}^k_j ; \boldsymbol{i} = 1, 2, \ldots \boldsymbol{I}; \boldsymbol{j} = 1, 2, 3, 4, 5; \boldsymbol{k} = 1, 2, \ldots, \boldsymbol{N} \right\} \tag{4}$$

The "Belief" function set or "Conditional" probability set P is defined as "the probability of selecting a PTB solution type "*j*" given an architecture solution "*i*""

$$P = \left\{ P^k_{i,j}; i = 1, 2, \ldots I; j = 1, 2, 3, 4, 5; k = 1, 2, \ldots, N \right\} \tag{5}$$

The "Belief" function $\boldsymbol{P^k_{i,j}}$ must satisfy the following conditions

$$0 \le P^k_{i,j} \le 1 \text{ and } \sum\nolimits_{i=1}^{I} P^k_{i,j} = 1 \tag{6}$$

Note that the ARCS-PTB mapping rules are based on the "Requirement Type" that is given in **Figure 5**. The PTB "Utility" set for a "Pure Strategy," U_{Pure}, is defined as the Payoff and Cost Function (PCF) for selecting a pure strategy $S^k_{i,}$ for each contractor "*k*," which can be expressed mathematically as:

$$U_{Pure} = \left\{ U^k_{i,j} : S^k_{i,j} \rightarrow PCF^k_{i,j}; i = 1, 2, \ldots I; j = 1, 2, 3, 4, 5; k = 1, 2, \ldots, N \right\} \tag{7}$$

Similarly, the PTB "Utility" set for a "Mixed" strategy, U_{Mixed}, is defined as the PCF for selecting a mixed strategy $S^k_{i,j}$ for each contractor "*k*" with a "Belief" function $P^k_{i,j}$ is defined as follow:

$$U_{Mixed} = \left\{ U^k_{i,j} : S^k_{i,j} \overset{P^k_{i,j}}{\rightarrow} PCF^k_{i,j}; i = 1, 2, \ldots I; j = 1, 2, 3, 4, 5; k = 1, 2, \ldots, N \right\} \tag{8}$$

A notional description of PCF, $PCF^k_{i,j}$, and PCF scoring[4] approach are provided in Ref. [8].

5.1.2. DAA-PWGE cooperative game with complete information and pure strategy

DAA plays the DAA-PWGE "**Pure Strategy**" games to "**Minimize**" the **Cost** and "**Maximize**" the **Payoff** (e.g., performance) for the selected optimum strategy, S_{Opt}. Mathematically, DAA plays the following DAA-PTB "**Pure**" strategy Bayesian games

[4]Ref. [9] describes the PCF scoring approach based on seven DOD initiatives including Initiative (i): "Proposed Technical Requirements and Associated TEs Incorporated Industry's Input"; Initiative (ii): "Should Cost Data Available for Each TE"; Initiative (iii): "Should Cost Data Available for Overall System"; Initiative (iv): "Leverage DOD IRAD to Lower Cost"; Initiative (v): "Leverage Contractor's IRAD to Lower Cost"; Initiative (vi): "Provide Incentives to Allow Contractor to Make IRAD an Allowable Cost"; and Initiative (vii): "Leverage MOSA for Architecture Design Solution." The higher the PCF score, the better PTB solution is.

$$Optimum\ PTB\ Solution \equiv S_{Opt} = \underset{\forall i,j,k}{MinMax} \left\{ U_{i,j}^{k} : S_{i,j}^{k} \rightarrow PCF_{i,j}^{k} \right\} \tag{9}$$

Where $S_{i,j}^{k}$ is defined as in Eq. (3) and $U_{i,j}^{k}$ is given by Eq. (7). This is the "MinMax" optimization problem to search for S_{Opt} such that, assuming that the $ARCS_i$ is the optimum solution with PTB Type 1 solution:

$$S_{Opt} = \left\{ U_{i,1}^{k} > U_{i,2}^{k} > U_{i,3}^{k} > U_{i,4}^{k} > U_{i,5}^{k}, for\ \forall i\ and\ \forall k \right\} \tag{10}$$

The above optimum solution is said to achieve the Nash equilibrium, which is a stable solution to this game theoretic problem in which no individual contractor can improve their payoff by a unilateral change in his bidding behavior. The DAA-PWGE pure game algorithm is shown in **Figure 6** with details provided in Ref. [8].

5.1.3. DAA-PWGE cooperative game with complete information and mixed strategy

Similar to the "Pure" strategy, DAA plays the DAA-PWGE "Mixed Strategy" games to "Minimize" the Cost and "Maximize" the Payoff. Mathematically, DAA plays the following DAA-PTB "Mixed" Strategy Bayesian games:

$$Optimum\ PTB\ Solution \equiv S_{Opt_{Mixed}} = \underset{\forall i,j,k}{MinMax} \left\{ U_{i,j}^{k} : S_{i,j}^{k} \xrightarrow{P_{i,j}^{k}} PCF_{i,j}^{k}; i = 1,..,I; j = 1,..5; k = 1,..,N \right\} \tag{11}$$

Where $S_{i,j}^{k}$ is defined as in Eq. (4), $U_{i,j}^{k}$ is given by Eq. (8) and the "Belief" function $P_{i,j}^{k}$ is given by Eq. (5). Again, this is the "MinMax" optimization problem that reaches the "Nash equilibrium"

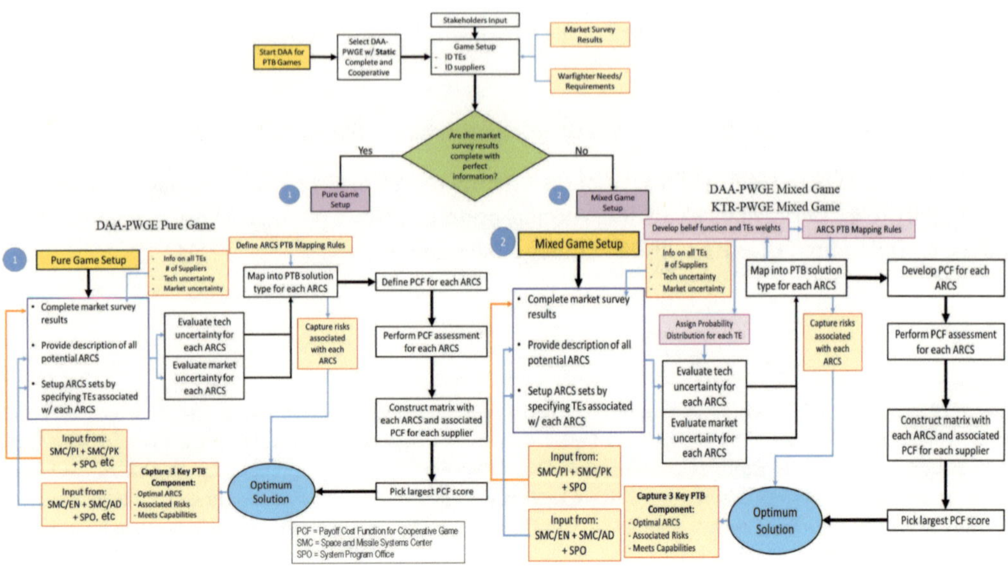

Figure 6. Description of DAA-PWGE and KTR-PWGE algorithms.

when $S_{Opt_{Mixed}}$ satisfies the following condition, assuming that $ARCS_i$ is the optimum solution with PTB Type 1 solution:

$$S_{Opt_{Mixed}} = \left\{U_{i,1}^k > U_{i,2}^k > U_{i,3}^k > U_{i,4}^k > U_{i,5}^k, for\ \forall i\ and\ \forall k\right\} \tag{12}$$

The DAA Plays the DAA-PTB "Mixed Strategy" games to maximize the payoff for the selected optimum strategy $S_{Opt_{Mixed}}$ resulting from the optimally mapping an ARCS to a PTB Solution for a given set of "Belief Function $P_{i,j}^k$" defined in Eq. (5). The conditional probability that the kth supplier/contractor (KTR) selects the lth TE with a weighting factor of W_l for the ith architecture solution, $ARCS_i$, given that the $ARCS_i$ is mapped to PTB Type "j" is defined as:

$$\Pr_{i,j,l}^k = W_l.PrTE_{i,j,l}^k \tag{13}$$

where

$$PrTE_{i,j,l}^k = \Pr\left\{KTR\text{"}k\text{" } Selects\ TE_l^k\ forARCS_i / KTR\text{"}k\text{" } maps\ ARCS_i\ to\ PTB\ Type\text{"}j\text{"}\right\} \tag{14}$$

The "Belief Function" set "P" for all architecture solutions, $i = 1, 2,\ldots, I$, can be calculated using the following equation:

$$P_{i,j}^k = \sum_{l=1}^{L} W_l.PrTE_{i,j,l}^k \tag{15}$$

Note that our team[5] has recently found that the above equation provides a better mathematical model than the one described in Ref. [8] for the belief function. Since each TE will have its own "Technology Risk" and "Market Risk",[6] Eq. (15) becomes:

$$P_{1,j}^{k\_Tech} = \sum_{l=1}^{L} W_l.PrTE_{i,j,l}^{k\_Tech} \tag{16}$$

$$P_{1,j}^{k\_Market} = \sum_{l=1}^{L} W_l.PrTE_{i,j,l}^{k\_Market} \tag{17}$$

$P_{i,j}^{k\_Tech}$ and $P_{i,j}^{k\_Market}$ must satisfy the following conditions:

$$0 \le P_{i,j}^{k\_Tech} \le 1 \text{ and } \sum\nolimits_{i=1}^{6} P_{i,j}^{k\_Tech} = 1, \text{ for } \forall k \tag{18}$$

$$0 \le P_{i,j}^{k\_Market} \le 1 \text{ and } \sum\nolimits_{i=1}^{6} P_{i,j}^{k_{Market}} = 1, \text{ for } \forall k \tag{19}$$

[5]Our team for the FY 2017 includes the REU team funded by NSF with the following selected undergraduate students: Brittany Dyer, Claire Goldhammer, Daniel Chertock and Scott Mahan. The 2017 REU team also includes Amanda Coons, a graduate assistant, and Prof. Hien Tran, a NCSU faculty advisor.

[6]Note that the terms "Technology Risk/Market Risk" and "Technology Uncertainty/Market Uncertainty" are used interchangeably in this chapter.

A detailed description of the calculation approach for the belief function is provided in Ref. [8]. The DAA-PWGE mixed game algorithm is shown in **Figure 6** with the details provided in Ref. [8]. The calculation approach described in Ref. [8] should be modified as shown in Eq. (15). The PTB tracking tool described in Ref. [6] will be used to capture the PTB solution captured by the DAA-PWGE.

5.2. Analytical and simulation modeling approach for contractor PTB games

For KTR-PWGE model, the DAA plays game on behalf of the contractors [8]. Similar to DAA-PWGE, the KTR, actually played by DAA, plays the static Bayesian "Non-Cooperative" (NC) games with complete and imperfect information or mixed game using normal-form representation of the game. The game is NC because it is assumed that the contractors do not share their bidding information. The KTR plays game to select optimum PTB solution that can maximize profits and reduce execution risks. The KTR is assumed to play games to search for an optimum PTB solution that can achieve the "Nash" equilibrium. The KTR game is set-up as follows:

- Step 1: contractor set: assume to have N contractors to play the game (see Eq. (1)).
- Step 2: contractor identifies a set of potential "*I*" architecture solution $ARCS_{NC}$ based on the requirements described in the release of RFI or RFP from a government agency:

$$ARCS_{NC} = \{ARCS_{NC\_i}, n = 1, 2, ..., I\} \tag{20}$$

- Step 3: each architecture solution selected by a KTR will be mapped into a unique PTB solution type defined by DAA.
- Step 4: the Non-Cooperative (NC) game with mixed strategy and incomplete information: The strategy for the kth contractor to map the ith architecture solution to the jth PTB solution type is performed using the following mathematical expression:

$$S_{Mixed\_Non\_Coop} = \left\{ S^k_{NC\_i,j} : ARCS^k_{NC\_i} \overset{P^k_{NC\_i,j}}{\rightarrow} PTB^k_{NC\_j}; i = 1, 2, ...I; j = 1, 2, 3, 4, 5; k = 1, 2, ..., N \right\} \tag{21}$$

- Step 5: The "Belief Function" set or conditional probability set "P" for NC games: For each contractor "k", the belief function "$P_{Non-Coop}$" is defined as the probability of selecting a PTB solution type "*j*" given the ith architecture solution:

$$P_{Non-Coop} = \left\{ P^k_{NC_i,j}; i = 1, 2, ...I; j = 1, 2, 3, 4, 5; k = 1, 2, ..., N \right\} \tag{22}$$

where $P^k_{NC_i,j}$ is defined as:

$$P^k_{NC_i,j} = \sum_{l=1}^{L} W_{NC_l}.PrTE^k_{NC_i,j,l} = \left\{ \begin{aligned} P^{k_{Tech}}_{NC_i,j} &= \sum_{l=1}^{L} W_{NC_l}.PrTE^{k_{Tech}}_{NC_i,j,l} \\ P^{k_{Market}}_{NC_i,j} &= \sum_{l=1}^{L} W_{NC_l}.PrTE^{k_{Market}}_{NC_i,j,l} \end{aligned} \right\} \tag{23}$$

Similar to the DAA games, the above equation provides a better mathematical model than the one described in Ref. [8] for contractor games, and Eq. (22) must also satisfy the following condition:

$$0 \le P^k_{NC_i,j} \le 1 \text{ and } \sum_{i=1}^{I} P^k_{NC_i,j} = 1 \tag{24}$$

- Step 6: PTB Utility Set for a "NC Mixed Strategy" is defined as $U_{Mixed\_Non\_Coop}$. This is the PCF_{NC} for selecting a mixed strategy $S^k_{i,j}$ for the kth contractor. Mathematical, it is given by the following equation:

$$U_{Mixed\_Non\_Coop} = \left\{ U^k_{NC\_i,j} : S^k_{NC\_i,j} \overset{P^k_{NC\_i,j}}{\rightarrow} PCF^k_{NC\_i,j}; i = 1, 2, \ldots I; j = 1, 2, 3, 4, 5; k = 1, 2, \ldots, N \right\} \tag{25}$$

- Step 7: The KTR plays the following mixed game to select the optimum PTB solution:

$$KTR\ Optimum\ PTB\ Solution = S_{Opt\_KTR} = \underset{\forall i, j, k}{\text{Max}} \left\{ U^k_{NC\_i,j} : S^k_{NC\_i,j} \overset{P^k_{NC\_i,j}}{\rightarrow} PCF^k_{NC\_i,j} \right\} \tag{26}$$

Similar to DAA-PWGE, the contractor plays KTR-PWGE to maximize his payoff or "Profit" for the selected optimum strategy $S_{Opt_{KTR}}$ resulting from optimally mapping an ARCS to a PTB Solution for a given set of belief function "$P_{Non-Coop}$." The detailed KTR-PWGE mixed game algorithm is shown in **Figure 6** with details provided in Ref. [8]. The PTB tracking tool described in Ref. [6] will be used to capture the PTB solution captured by the KTR-PWGE.

6. Acquisition-bidding War-Gaming Engines (AWGEs)

The approach for the development of Acquisition-bidding WGEs presented in this section follows Ref. [9]. An overview description of the government "Acquisition" DAA-AWGEs and contractor "Bidding" KTR-AWGE will be presented in this section for commonly used contract types, including Firmed-Fixed Price (FFP[7]) and Cost Plus Incentive Firm (CPIF). The Fixed Price Incentive Firm (FPIF) contract type can be found in Ref. [9].

6.1. Acquisition-bidding WGE set-up

The acquisition-bidding game model assumes that there are N contractors participating in the bidding of the space system with the contractor set given by Eq. (1). The following subsections describe the game setup from the government and contractor perspectives, namely, DAA-AWGE and KTR-AWGE, respectively.

[7]FFP is also referred to Fixed Price Seal Bid (FPSB).

6.1.1. DAA-AWGE game set-up

The KTRDAA-AWGE model simulates the government's acquisition games from the government perspective based on the "Contract Type" selected based on the PTB solution obtained from DAA-PWGE models described in Section 5. The DAA-AWGE strategy is to map the optimum "Type i^{th} PTB Solution" (PTB_i), obtained from DAA-PWGE and KTR-PWGE games described in Section 5 above, to the optimum "Acquisition Strategy" and the associated "Type i^{th} Contract" (CT_i). Denote the government strategy as S_{DAA}, mathematically S_{DAA} for Bayesian games with complete and imperfect information can be written as:

$$S_{DAA} = \left\{ S_{DAA_i} : PTB_i \overset{p_i^{DAA}}{\rightarrow} CT_i; i = 1, 2, \ldots N \right\} \tag{27}$$

where p_i^{DAA} is the government "Belief Function" describing the probability that the DAA will map PTB_i to CT_i. It is defined as follows:

$$\mathrm{P_{DAA}} = \{\mathrm{p_i^{DAA}}; \mathrm{i} = 1, 2, \ldots \mathrm{N}\} \tag{28}$$

Each p_i^{DAA} must satisfy the following conditions:

$$0 \le \mathrm{p_i^{DAA}} \le 1 \text{ and } \sum_{i=1}^{N} \mathrm{p_i^{DAA}} = 1 \tag{29}$$

The DAA utility function U_{DAA} is defined as:

$$\mathrm{U_{DAA}} = \left\{ \mathrm{U_{DAA\_i}} : \mathrm{S_{DAA_i}} \overset{\mathrm{p_i^{DAA}}}{\rightarrow} \mathrm{PCF_{DAA_i}}; \mathrm{i} = 1, 2, \ldots \mathrm{N} \right\} \tag{30}$$

where PCF_{DAA_i} is the government "Payoff and Cost Function" (PCF) associated with the selection of the ith strategy S_{DAA_i}. If PCF is the government estimated "contractor cost" associated with the space system being acquired ($\mathrm{PCF}_{DAA\_KTR_i}$), the "Nash strategy" dictates that the optimum strategy for selecting the contract parameters is to minimize the PCF according to:

$$\mathrm{S_{DAA_{Opt}}} = \underset{\forall \mathrm{i}}{\mathrm{Min}} \{PCF_{DAA\_KTR_i}\} = \underset{\forall \mathrm{i}}{\mathrm{Min}} \left\{ \mathrm{S_{DAA_i}} \overset{\mathrm{p_i^{DAA}}}{\rightarrow} \mathrm{PCF}_{DAA\_KTR_i}; \mathrm{i} = 1, 2, \ldots \mathrm{N} \right\} \tag{31}$$

If the government utility function $U_{DAA_{i=1}}$ represents the optimum government saving strategy expressed in Eq. (30), $S_{DAA_{Opt}}$, the following condition must be true according to Nash:

$$\mathrm{U_{DAA\_KTR_{i=1}}} = \left\{ \mathrm{S_{DAA_1}} \overset{\mathrm{p_1^{DAA}}}{\rightarrow} \mathrm{PCF_{DAA\_KTR_{i=1}}} \right\} < \mathrm{U_{DAA\_KTR_{i=2}}} < \mathrm{U_{DAA\_KTR_{i=3}}} < \ldots < \mathrm{U_{DAA\_KTR_{i=N}}} \tag{32}$$

If PCF is the government saving associated with the space system being acquired ($\mathrm{PCF_{DAA\_Saving_i}}$), "Nash strategy" dictates that the optimum contract parameters can be selected by maximizing the saving or PCF according to:

$$\mathrm{S}_{\mathrm{DAA}_{Opt}} = \underset{\forall \mathrm{i}}{\mathrm{Min}} \left\{ PCF_{DAA\_Saving_i} \right\} = \underset{\forall \mathrm{i}}{\mathrm{Max}} \left\{ \mathrm{S}_{\mathrm{DAA}_i} \overset{\mathrm{P}_\mathrm{i}^{\mathrm{DAA}}}{\rightarrow} \mathrm{PCF}_{\mathrm{DAA}\_Saving_i}; \mathrm{i} = 1, 2, \ldots \mathrm{N} \right\} \tag{33}$$

If the government utility function $U_{DAA_{i=1}}$ represents the optimum government saving strategy expressed in Eq. (32), $S_{DAA_{Opt}}$, the following condition must be true according to Nash strategy:

$$\mathrm{U}_{\mathrm{DAA}\_Saving_{i=1}} = \left\{ \mathrm{S}_{\mathrm{DAA}_1} \overset{\mathrm{P}_1^{\mathrm{DAA}}}{\rightarrow} \mathrm{PCF}_{\mathrm{DAA}\_Saving_1} \right\} > \mathrm{U}_{\mathrm{DAA}\_Saving_{i=2}} > \ldots > \mathrm{U}_{\mathrm{DAA}\_Saving_{i=N}} \tag{34}$$

The DAA can play non-cooperative or cooperative games depending on the "Contract Type." For example, for the FFP contract type, the DAA plays non-cooperative games if the DAA provides a clear direction on the FFP contract that the lowest bidder will be selected and there is no negotiation between the government and the selected contractor. On the contrary, the FPIF contract type requires the cooperation between DAA and the selected contractor to agree on a set of sharing ratios, and perhaps on the Point of Total Assumption (PTA) [12] as well.

6.1.2. KTR-AWGE game set-up

The KTR-AWGE model simulates the contractor's bidding games from the contractor perspective based on the "Contract Type" and the associated contract parameters generated from the DAA-AWGE games. Let b_i be the bidding strategy for the ith contractor, the contractor strategy set for Bayesian game with complete and imperfect information, S_{KTR}, is defined as:

$$S_{KTR} = \left\{ S_{KTR_i} : KTR_i \overset{p_i^{KTR}}{\rightarrow} b_i; i = 1, 2, \ldots N \right\} \tag{35}$$

where p_i^{KTR} is the conditional probability that the ith contractor selects the ith bidding strategy given by:

$$P_{KTR} = \left\{ p_i^{KTR}; i = 1, 2, \ldots n \right\} \tag{36}$$

$$\sum_{i=1}^{n} p_i^{KTR} = 1 \tag{37}$$

The contractor utility function U_{KTR} is defined as:

$$U_{KTR} = \left\{ U_{KTR_i} : S_{KTR_i} \overset{p_i^{KTR}}{\rightarrow} PCF_{KTR_i}; i = 1, 2, \ldots N \right\} \tag{38}$$

where PCF_{KTR_i} is the contractor "Payoff and Cost Function" associated with the ith contractor, KTR_i, who selects the ith bidding strategy S_{DAA_i}. Since the PCF_{KTR_i} is the contractor cost associated with the space system being acquired ($PCF_{DAA\_KTR_i}$), "Nash strategy" dictates that the optimum bidding parameters are selected by maximizing the contractor cost function according to:

$$S_{KTR_{Opt}} = \underset{\forall i}{Max} \{PCF_{KTR_i}\} = \underset{\forall i}{Max} \left\{ S_{KTR_i} \overset{p_i^{KTR}}{\rightarrow} PCF_{KTR_i}; i = 1, 2, \ldots N \right\} \tag{39}$$

If the contractor utility function $U_{KTR_{i=1}}$ represents the optimum contractor profit strategy expressed in Eq. (38), $S_{KTR_{Opt}}$, the following condition must be true according to Nash strategy:

$$U_{KTR_{i=1}} = \left\{ S_{KTR_1} \overset{p_1^{KTR}}{\rightarrow} PCF_{KTR_1} \right\} > U_{KTR_{i=2}} > U_{KTR_{i=3}} > \ldots > U_{KTR_{i=N}} \tag{40}$$

Note that the KTR-AWGE models always assume non-cooperative games since the contractors do not share their bidding strategies among themselves.

6.2. Analytical and simulation modeling approach for government acquisition games: DAA-AWGE

6.2.1. DAA-AWGE for FFP contract type

The DAA-AWGE game for FFP assumes that the PTB solution obtained from the DAA-PWGE game model described in Section 5 is the "Type 1 PTB Solution" and the corresponding optimum "Contract Type" is FFP (see **Figure 5**). The FFP game assumes that the contractor actual costs are unknown with a cost ranges of $[C_{min}, C_{max}]$, and the actual cost has either an uniform distribution or a triangular distribution. For this game, from the government's perspective, the higher is the contractor's bid, the lower is the probability of winning the contract. For optimum acquisition strategy, the contractor needs to use the "Nash strategy" to maximize the expected profit taking into consideration both his bid and other contractors' 'expected bids. For non-optimum strategy, the contractor profit is selected by a random percentage over the target cost. The DAA strategy is to minimize contractor profits by searching for a bidding solution that will increase the number of bidders to at least two bidders for increased competition at the minimum possible price. To simplify the modeling effort, the government and the contractors are assumed to have the same risk.

For FFP, the DAA-AWGE game seeks the optimum contract parameters, including the optimum fixed price $P_{C_{opt}}$. Thus, for FFP, the ith contractor's profit function $\mathrm{PF}_{\mathrm{KTR}_i}$ is defined as:

$$\mathrm{PF}_{\mathrm{KTR}_i} = \{\mathrm{P_c} - \mathrm{c_i}, \mathrm{i} = 1, 2, \ldots, \mathrm{N}\} \tag{41}$$

where P_C is the fixed price and c_i is the actual production cost of the ith contractor. The government payment is the fixed price P_C. The DAA-AWGE game is to minimize P_C. This section provides a war-gaming model for deriving the optimum fixed price $P_{C_{opt\_Gov}}$ from the government perspective. From Section 5, the optimum strategy for selecting the FFP contract parameters is defined as:

$$\mathrm{S}_{\mathrm{DAA}_{Opt}} = \underset{\forall \mathrm{i}}{Min} \{PCF_{DAA\_KTR_i} = \mathrm{PF}_{\mathrm{KTR}_n}\} = \underset{\forall \mathrm{i}}{Min} \left\{ \mathrm{S}_{\mathrm{DAA}_i} \overset{\mathrm{P_i^{DAA}}}{\rightarrow} (\mathrm{P_c} - \mathrm{c_i}); \mathrm{i} = 1, 2, \ldots \mathrm{N} \right\} \tag{42}$$

From Eq. (17), the optimum government fixed price, $P_{C_{opt\_Gov}}$, can be found by solving the following optimization problem:

http://dx.doi.org/10.5772/intechopen.71044

$$P_{C_{opt\_Gov}} = \underset{\forall i}{\text{Min}} \{(PF_{KTR_i}\} + c_i = \underset{\forall i}{\text{Min}} \{b_i - c_i\} + c_i \text{ for } b_i \geq c_i \text{ and } i = 1, 2, \ldots N \quad (43)$$

Note the actual production cost c_i for the ith contractor cannot be minimized. And $b(c_i)$ is the ith contractor bidding function given by [11]

$$b(c_i) = \left\{ \begin{matrix} b_i, \text{ for } b_i \geq c_i \\ 0, \text{ for } b_i < c_i \end{matrix} \right\} \quad (44)$$

Using calculus of variation approach, the optimum fixed price from the government perspective for uniform distribution can be shown to have the following form [9]:

$$P_{C_{opt\_Gov}} = \underset{\forall i}{\text{Min}} \left\{ \frac{C_{max} - c_i}{N}, \right\} + c_i, \text{ for } c_i \in [C_{min}, C_{max}], \text{ and } i = 1, 2, \ldots N \quad (45)$$

The expected contractor cost c_i or the "Target Cost" T_C can be determined from the cost analysis using the cost "S-Curve" or using the expected value of the cost distribution. For uniform case, the target cost is found to be [9]:

$$E\{c_i\} = T_c = T_{c\_Uni} = {}^{(C_{Max}+C_{Min})}/_{2} \quad (46)$$

The optimum fixed price from when the production cost c_i has the triangular distributed over $[C_{min}, m, C_{max}]$ with m as the mode, can be shown to have the following form [9]:

$$P_{C_{opt\_Gov}} = \left\{ \begin{matrix} \underset{\forall i}{\text{Min}} \left\{ \frac{A + [B + 2C]^{0.5}}{(2N - 1)} \right\} + c_i, \text{for } C_{min} < c_i < m, \text{and } i = 1, 2, \ldots N \\ \underset{\forall i}{\text{Min}} \left\{ \frac{C_{max} - c_j}{(2N - 1)} \right\} + c_i, \text{for } m < c_i < C_{max}, \text{and } i = 1, 2, \ldots N \end{matrix} \right\} \quad (47)$$

where:

$$\left\{ \begin{matrix} A = N.C_{min} - (N + 1).c_i \\ B = (N.c_{min} + (N - 1).c_i)^2 \\ C = ((N - 1) + 0.5).(\rho - c_{min}^2 - 2(N - 1).c_i.c_{min}) \\ \rho = (C_{max} - C_{min}).(m - C_{min}) \end{matrix} \right\} \quad (48)$$

As point out in Ref. [9], the "Nash strategy" indicates that the optimum contractor profit is determined by the maximum expected cost C_{max}, contractor actual production cost c_i, and the number of contractors "N" participating in the bidding. Using the optimum "Nash strategy," an optimum bidder can make a smaller profit compared to the non-optimum bidders on a specific bid; however, in the long run, the optimum bidder is expected to make more profit than the non-optimum bidders since he wins more bids. The DAA-AWGE algorithm for FFP Contract Type is shown in **Figure 7**.

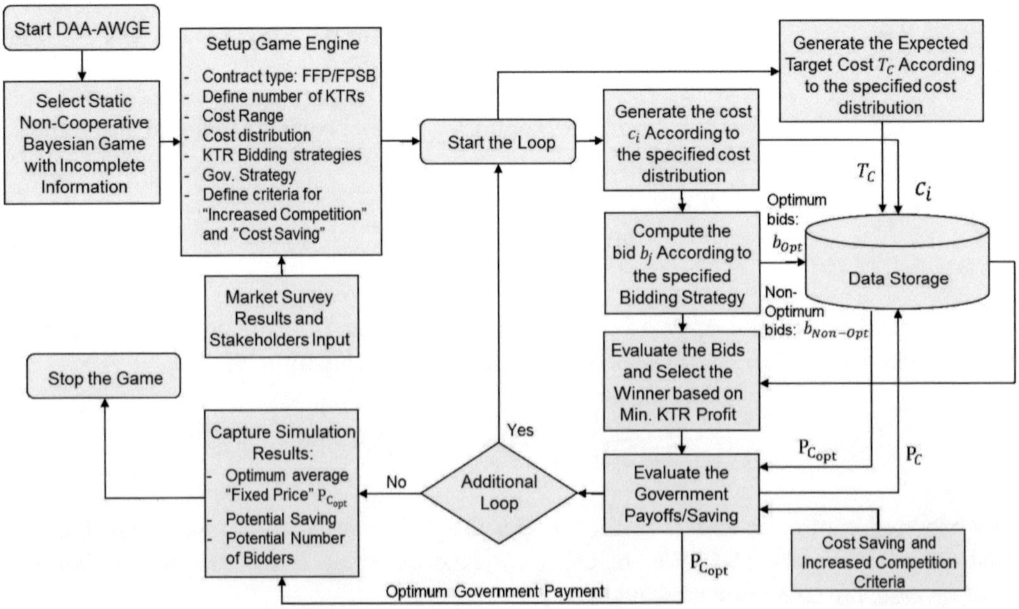

Figure 7. DAA-AWGE modeling and simulation approach for FFP contract type [9].

6.2.2. DAA-AWGE for CPIF contract type

This game assumes that the PTB solution obtained from the DAA-PWGE model described in Section 5 above is the "Type 3 PTB Solution" and the corresponding optimum "Contract Type" is CPIF (see **Figure 5**). The modeling development approach for the DAA-AWGE CPIF contract type is identical to FPIF approach described in Ref. [9]. The model assumes that both the government and the contractor will cooperate to maximize their minimum saving/profit. Therefore, their bargaining objective will be the maximization of the minimum outcome of the saving/profit, i.e., the "maximum" value of the saving/profit. Let PCF_{Gov} and PCF_{KTR_i} be the final compromised saving/profit points, and PCF^0_{Gov} and $PCF^0_{KTR_i}$ be the benchmark saving/profit points for the negotiation between the government and the ith contractor, respectively. The optimum CPIF contract parameters can be obtained by solving the following optimization problem [9]:

$$\underset{\forall i}{\text{Max}}\left\{F_i : F_i = \left(PCF_{Gov} - PCF^0_{Gov}\right).\left(PCF_{KTR_i} - PCF^0_{KTR_i}\right); i = 1, 2, \ldots N\right\} \tag{49}$$

Note that PCF_{Gov} and PCF_{KTR_i} are also defined as the government's "Cost Saving" and the ith contractor profit, respectively, and they are given by [9]:

$$PCF_{Gov} = C_p + SR_{G_i}(T_c - A_{C_i}) - (A_{C_i} + PCF_{KTR_i}); i = 1, 2, \ldots N \tag{50}$$

$$PCF_{KTR_i} = \left(T_{P_i} - T_c\right) + SR_{C_i}.(T_c - A_{C_i}); i = 1, 2, \ldots N \tag{51}$$

where SR_{G_i} is the government sharing ratio and A_{c_i} is the actual production cost for the ith contractor, which is unknown and as before, it is assumed to be either uniformly distributed over $[O_c, P_c]$, or triangularly distributed over $[O_c, P_c]$ with mode "m." Substituting PCF_{KTR_i} into PCF_{Gov}, the government's "Cost Saving" in terms of the contract parameters can be obtained as:

$$PCF_{Gov} = C_p + 2.(1 - SR_{C_i}).(T_c - A_{C_i}) - T_{p_i}; i = 1, 2, \ldots N \tag{52}$$

Substituting Eq. (52) into Eq. (49), and using the calculus of variation approach, the optimization problem can be solved by searching for the Sharing Ratios (SRs) that can maximize F_i and then search for the optimum target price T_P that can maximize F_i. For both DAA and KTR games, we first maximize the cost function F_i with respect to the contractor sharing ratio, SR_C, by solving the following equation:

$$\frac{\partial \mathrm{F_i}}{\partial \mathrm{SR_{C_i}}} = 0, \mathrm{i} = 1, 2, \ldots \mathrm{N} \tag{53}$$

Note that the contractor sharing ratio ranges from 0 to 1 and the government sharing ratio for the ith contractor, SR_{Gi}, is defined as:

$$\mathrm{SR_{G_i}} = 1 - \mathrm{SR_{C_i}} \tag{54}$$

For DAA-AWGE game from the DAA perspective, the optimization occurs with the following partial differential equation with respect to the contractor:

$$\frac{\partial \mathrm{F_i}}{\partial \mathrm{PCF_{KTR_i}}} = 0, \mathrm{i} = 1, 2, \ldots \mathrm{N} \tag{55}$$

Note that for KTR-AWGE game from the contractor perspective, Eq. (52) becomes:

$$\frac{\partial \mathrm{F_i}}{\partial \mathrm{PCF_{Gov}}} = 0 \tag{56}$$

Solving Eq. (50) and Eq. (52), the optimum win-win sharing ratio, SR_{C_Opt}, and optimum win-win target price, $T_{P_{Opt_i}}$, from the DAA perspective are found as follow [9]:

$$SR_{C\_Opt_i} = \frac{2\ PCF^0_{KTR_i} - PCF^0_{Gov} - (3T_p - 4T_C) + (C_p - 2A_{C_i})}{4.(T_c - A_{C_i})}, i = 1, 2, \ldots N \tag{57}$$

$$T_{P_{Opt_i}} = (2A_{C_i} - C_P) + \left[PCF^0_{Gov} + 2PCF^0_{KTR_i}\right]; i = 1, 2, \ldots N \tag{58}$$

For CPIF, the optimum contract parameters depend on whether the contract is the under-run or over-run case. The under-run case occurs when the actual cost of the ith contractor is less than or equal to target cost, i.e., $A_{C_i} \leq T_c$. The over-run case occurs when $A_{C_i} > T_c$.

- **Case 1**: Under-run case: $A_{C_i} \leq T_c$

For this case, the benchmark saving/profit points for the negotiation between the government and the ith contractor become:

$$PCF^0_{Gov} = \propto (T_c - A_{C_i}); i = 1, 2, \ldots n \tag{59}$$

$$PCF^0_{KTR_i} = (C_p - T_c) \tag{60}$$

Substituting Eqs. (59) and (60) into Eqs. (57) and (57), we obtain the optimum target price,[8] $T_{P_{UOpti}}$, and the optimum win-win contractor sharing ratio, $SR_{C_{UOpti}}$, for the under-run case:

$$T_{P_{UOpt_i}} = C_P - 1.5SR_{CU_i}.(T_c - A_{C_i}); i = 1, 2, \ldots, n \tag{61}$$

$$SR_{C_{UOpt_i}} = \frac{2(2 - \alpha)}{3}, (1/2) \le \alpha \le 2, \forall i \tag{62}$$

Using the optimum $T_{P_{UOpt_i}}$ and $SR_{C_{UOpt_i}}$, the optimum government payment can be calculated from:

$$P_{Gov_{UOpt_{CPIF}}} = A_{C_i} + \left(T_{P_{UOpt_i}} - T_c\right) + SR_{C_{UOpt_i}}.(T_c - A_{C_i}); i = 1, 2, \ldots n \tag{63}$$

The parameter α in Eq. (59) will be selected to minimize the government payment.

- **Case 2**: Over-run case: $A_{C_i} > T_c$

For this case, the benchmark saving/profit points for the negotiation between the government and the ith contractor become:

$$PCF^0_{Gov} = 0 \tag{64}$$

$$PCF^0_{KTR_i} = \beta(C_p - A_{C_i}); i = 1, 2, \ldots n \tag{65}$$

Substituting Eqs. (64) and (65) into Eqs. (57) and (58) above, we obtain the optimum target price,[9] $T_{P_{OOpti}}$, and the optimum win-win contractor sharing ratio, $SR_{C_{OOpt_i}}$ for the over-run case:

$$T_{P_{OOpt_i}} = C_P - 1.5.(1 - SR_{CO_i}).(A_{C_i} - T_c); i = 1, 2, \ldots, n \tag{66}$$

$$SR_{C_{OOpt_i}} = 1 - \frac{4}{3}\frac{(1 - \beta)(C_P - A_{C_i})}{(A_{C_i} - T_c)}, \left[1 - \frac{3}{4}\frac{(A_{C_i} - T_c)}{(C_P - A_{C_i})}\right] \le \beta \le 1; i = 1, 2, \ldots n \tag{67}$$

Using the optimum $T_{P_{OOpti}}$ and $SR_{C_{OOpti}}$, the optimum government payment can be calculated from the following equation:

$$P_{Gov_{OOpt_{CPIF}}} = A_{C_i} + \left(T_{P_{OOpt_i}} - T_c\right) + SR_{C_{OOpt_i}}.(T_c - A_{C_i}); i = 1, 2, \ldots n \tag{68}$$

The parameter β in Eq. (65) will be selected to minimize the government payment. The optimum target price depends on the ceiling price, contractor sharing ratio, target cost and

---

[8] Note that the optimum target price expressed in Eq. (47) indicates the optimum target price that is acceptable to Government when the optimum value of α, α_{Opt}, is selected based on the minimum Government payment.

[9] This is the optimum target price that the contractor is seeking by selecting the optimum value of β based on the maximum contractor profit.

actual cost of the ith contractor. **Figure 8** describes the DAA-AWGE-CPIF Monte Carlo simulation approach to determine the optimum target price, sharing ratios, and government payment under government's perspective.

As indicated in **Figure 8**, the output of the DAA-AWGE CPIF model includes the average optimum values of the target fee (F_{T_ave}), minimum fee (F_{min_ave}) and maximum fee (F_{max_ave}), assuming there will be N optimum values for all of the selected contractors by the end of the games. The calculation of these optimum values are derived from Ref. [12] and given by the following formulas:

$$F_{T\_ave} = \sum_{i=1}^{N} \frac{\left(T_{P_{UOpt_i}} - T_C\right)}{N} \tag{69}$$

$$F_{\min\_ave\ i} = \sum_{i=1}^{N} \frac{\left(F_{T\_ave} - SR_{C_{OOpt_i}}(P_c - T_c)\right)}{N} \tag{70}$$

$$F_{\max\_ave} = \sum_{i=1}^{N} \frac{\left(SR_{C_{UOpt_i}}(T_c - O_c) + F_{T\_ave}\right)}{N} \tag{71}$$

where $T_{P_{UOpt_i}}$, $SR_{C_{OOpt_i}}$ and $SR_{C_{UOpt_i}}$ are defined as above. The estimate costs O_c, T_c and P_c are the optimistic cost estimate, target cost estimate and pessimistic cost estimate are given by the cost estimate group from engineering department or finance department or contract department depending on the organization and game rules.

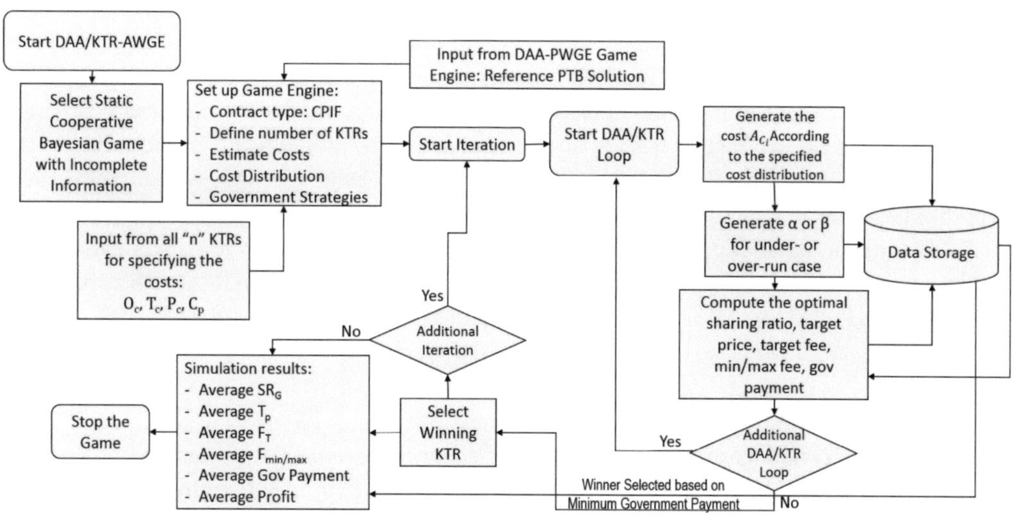

Figure 8. DAA-AWGE modeling and simulation approach for CPIF contract type.

6.3. Analytical and simulation modeling approach for contractor bidding games: KTR-AWGE

6.3.1. KTR-AWGE for FFP contract type

The contractor bidding game, KTR-AWGE, follows the setup described in Section 6.1.2 and [9]. Similar to DAA-AWGE model for FFP, the PTB solution obtained from the KTR-PWGE game model is the "Type 1 Requirement" and the corresponding optimum "Contract Type" is FFP. For FFP, the KTR-AWGE game seeks the optimum contract parameters, including the optimum fixed price $P_{C_{opt}}$, that maximizes the contractor's profit $\mathrm{PCF}_{\mathrm{KTR}_i}$ [9]:

$$S_{KTR_{Opt_i}} = \underset{\forall i}{\mathrm{Max}} \{\mathrm{PCF}_{\mathrm{KTR}_i}\}, \text{for } i = 1, 2, \ldots N \tag{72}$$

where contractor profit function, $\mathrm{PCF}_{\mathrm{KTR}_i}$, is defined as:

$$\mathrm{PCF}_{\mathrm{KTR}_i} = \left\{ \begin{array}{l} b_i(c_i) - c_i, \text{ if } b_i = \min(b_1, \ldots, b_n), \text{ and } b_i > c_i \\ (1/N).[b_i(c_i) - c_i], \text{ if } b_i = b_j, \ldots, b_N, \text{ and } b_i > c_i \\ 0, \text{ if } b_i > \min(b_1, \ldots, b_n) \end{array} \right\} \tag{73}$$

where N, $b_i(c_i)$ and c_i are defined in the above sections as the number of contractors, bidding price and associated actual production cost of the ith contractor, respectively. Using the calculus of variation approach and assuming the cost to be uniformly distributed between [C_{min}, C_{max}], the solution to Eq. (72) is the optimum bidding price, $b_{\mathrm{Unif\_Opt}_i}$, from the contractor perspective has the same form as that from the government perspective, i.e.,

$$b_{\mathrm{Unif\_Opt}_i} = \underset{\forall i}{\mathrm{Max}} \left\{ \frac{C_{max} - c_i}{N}, \right\} + c_i, \text{ for } c_i \in [C_{min}, C_{max}], \text{ and } i = 1, 2, \ldots N \tag{74}$$

For the triangular distribution case, the optimum bidding price from the contractor perspective can be found in Ref. [9]. The KTR-AWGE model shows that, using the "Nash strategy," the optimum contractor bidding price is also dependent on the maximum expected cost C_{max}, the contractor actual production cost, c_i, and the number of contractors "N" participating in the bidding. The model shows that a contractor's bidding strategy is optimum when it maximizes his profit based on the maximum expected cost, the actual cost and the number of bidders. The modeling and simulation approach proposed for the FFP KTR-AWGE is to combine the above analytical models with Monte Carlo simulation. The flow chart for FFP KTR-AWGE approach is very similar to FFP DAA-AWGE and can be found in Ref. [9].

6.3.2. KTR-AWGE for CPIF contract type

The CPIF KTR-AWGE game described in this section follows [9]. It assumes that the PTB solution obtained from the KTR-PWGE game model is "Type 3 Requirement" and the corresponding optimum "Contract Type" is CPIF. The objective of the KTR-AWGE model is to seek the optimum "bidding" target price and the associated contractor sharing ratios for maximum contractor profit, i.e., maximum benefit from the contractor perspective. Rewrite PCF_{KTR_i} (Eq. (50)) as a function of PCF_{Gov} as follow:

$$PCF_{KTR_i} = C_p + SR_{G_i}(T_c - A_{C_i}) - (A_{C_i} + PCF_{Gov}); i = 1, 2, \ldots N \tag{75}$$

The optimization problem shown in Eq. (49) becomes [9]:

$$\underset{\forall i}{Max}\left\{F_i = \left(PCF_{Gov_i} - PCF^0_{Gov_i}\right).\left(C_p + SR_{G_i}\right)(T_c - A_{C_i}) - A_{C_i} - PCF_{Gov_i} - PCF^0_{KTR_i}\right\}, i = 1, 2, \ldots N \tag{76}$$

where PCF_{Gov}, $PCF^0_{Gov_i}$, C_p, SR_G, T_c, A_{C_i} and $PCF^0_{KTR_i}$ are as defined in Section 6.2 above.

Again, using the calculus of variation approach described in Eq. (56), the optimum "bidding" target price, $T_{p_{Opt_i}}$ is found to be [9]:

$$T_{P_{KOpt_i}} = (2A_{C_i} - C_P) + 2\left[PCF^0_{KTR_i} + 0.5PCF^0_{Gov}\right); i = 1, 2, \ldots N \tag{77}$$

Note that for the KTR-AWGE game, the optimum win-win sharing ratio from the contractor perspective, $SR_{C_{Opt_i}}$, is identical to the DAA perspective, which is shown to have the form expressed in Eq. (57). As discussed earlier, the optimum contract parameters depend on the whether the contractor is under-run or over-run. The following paragraphs describe the approach to determine the optimum sharing ratios and the target price from the contractor perspective.

- **Case 1**: Under-run case: $A_{C_i} \leq T_c$

For this case, we set $\alpha = 2$ and the benchmark saving/profit points for the negotiation between the government and the ith contractor become [9]:

$$PCF^0_{Gov} = 2(T_c - A_{C_i}); i = 1, 2, \ldots n \tag{78}$$

$$PCF^0_{KTR_i} = (C_p - T_c) \tag{79}$$

From the contractor's perspective, when $\alpha = 2$ the optimum contractor sharing ratio, $SR_{C_{UKOpt_i}}$, is 0% (see Eq. (62)) and the government takes 100% responsibility to pay off the profit when the contractor is under-run. The optimum bidding target price, $T_{P_{KUOpt_i}}$, for this given by [9]:

$$T_{P_{KUOpt_i}} = C_P; i = 1, 2, \ldots n \tag{80}$$

From the contractor perspective, the optimum price is the ceiling price. Using the optimum bidding target price $T_{P_{KUOpt_i}}$ and sharing ratio $SR_{C_{UKOpt_i}}$, the optimum government payment can be calculated from the following Eq. [9]:

$$P_{Gov_{UOpt_{CPIF}}} = A_{C_i} + (C_P - T_c); i = 1, 2, \ldots n \tag{81}$$

- **Case 2**: Over-run case: $A_{C_i} > T_c$

For this case, we set $\beta = 1$ and the benchmark saving/profit points for the negotiation between the government and the ith contractor become [9]:

$$PCF^0_{Gov} = 0 \tag{82}$$

$$PCF^0_{KTR_i} = (C_p - A_{C_i}); i = 1, 2, \ldots n \tag{83}$$

The optimum bidding target price for the over-run case, $T_{P_{OOpt_i}}$, is found to be [9]:

$$\mathrm{T}_{\mathrm{P_{KOOpt_i}}} = \mathrm{C_P}; \mathrm{i} = 1, 2, \ldots \mathrm{n} \tag{84}$$

Again, from the contractor perspective, the optimum price is the ceiling price. Similarly, the optimum sharing ratio, SR_{C_OKOpt}, for the over-run case is given by [9]:

$$\mathrm{SR}_{C_{OKOpt_i}} = 1, \mathrm{i} = 1, 2, \ldots \mathrm{n} \tag{85}$$

This means the contractor takes 100% responsibility when it is over-run! Using the optimum bidding target price $T_{P_{KOOpt_i}}$ and contractor sharing ratio SR_{C_OKOpt}, the government payment is given by [9]:

$$\mathrm{P}_{\mathrm{Gov}_{OKOpt_{CPIF}}} = \mathrm{C_P}; \mathrm{i} = 1, 2, \ldots \mathrm{n} \tag{86}$$

The modeling and simulation approach for CPIF KTR-AWGE is found to be similar to FPIF KTR-AWGE with the new optimum bidding target prices, $T_{P_{UOpt_i}}$ and $T_{P_{OOpt_i}}$, and contractor sharing ratios, $SR_{C_{UOpt_i}}$ and $SR_{C_{OOpt_i}}$, described above. The flow chart for CPIF KTR-AWGE approach is very similar to CPIF DAA-AWGE and is shown in **Figure 8**.

7. Simulation results for sample PTB solutions and commonly used contract types

Contributors: Brittany Dyer, Claire Goldhammer, Daniel Chertock and Scott Mahan

The models discussed in this chapter to evaluate PTB solutions and associated acquisition strategies for acquiring future space systems were implemented in MATLAB. The simulation results shown in this section were obtained by the 2017 REU team. In particular, we will present simulation results associated with the CPIF model for acquisition strategy. Simulation results associated with FFP contract type can be found in Ref. [13].

7.1. PTB-WGE mixed game model simulation results

The above PTB-WGE models are implemented in MATLAB. The inputs for the PTB-WGE models, which include market survey results and for risk information, potential architecture solutions describing technology combinations, and the PCF information, are manually input into the PTB-WGE program using the input dialog function in MATLAB. The belief function is calculated in a Monte Carlo simulation and aggregates individual technology risk information into a risk assessment for the architecture solution as a whole. The risk and PCF assessments are then combined to form a metric, which is used to select the optimal KTR and contract type using the PTB-ARCS mapping rules shown in **Figure 5**. Examples of the inputs to DAA-PWGE model are shown in **Figures 9–11**.

Notional Payoff-and-Cost Function Template For the Supplier/Contract #1: $PCF_{1,1}^{1}$										
Architecture Assessment for the Architecture Solution #1 and Associated PTB Solution Type 1										
DAA-PWGE Assessment Metric / Yes / No / Plan	Technical Requirements				Affordability Requirements					
	Proposed Tech Reqts and Associated Tech Enablers Incorporated Industry's Input	Align Tech Reqts w/ Warfighter Needs and Tech Enaqblers	Capability Deliveries Meet the Warfighter Needs	Performance Meet Threshold Reqts	Should Cost Data Available for Each Tech Enabler	Should Cost Data Available for Overall System	Leverage DOD IRAD to Lower Cost	Leverage Contractor's IRAD to Lower Cost	Provide Incentives to Allow Contractor to Make IRAD an Allowable Cost	Leverage MOSA for Architecture Design Solution
BBP 3.0 Directive (Weighting factor = 0, 1, 2, 3, and 4)	4	0	0	0	1	2	3	3	3	4
Yes -> Payoff with Weighting factor 1, 2, 3, 4	4	1	3	4	1 (Provide Cost Est)	2 (Provide Cost Est)	3 (Include in Cost Est)	0	3 (Include in RFP)	0
No -> Loss/Cost with weighting factor 0, -1, -2, -3 and -4	0	0	0	0	0	0	0	0	0	0
Plan to do it (Potential Payoff) with weighting factor 0.25, 0.5, 0.75, 1	0	0	0	0	0	0	0	1	0	1
Assessment Score	8	1	3	4	2	4	6	4	6	5
Average Score	4				4.5					
Total Average Score	4.25									

Figure 9. Example of the PCF score for contractor #1 with architecture solution #1 (ARCS #1).

Notional Technology Enabler-Supplier (TE-SP) Matrix			
Warfighter Needs (WN)	Desired Capabilities	Potential Technology Enabler (TE)	Potential Contractor (KTR)
WN #1	Capability A	TE-A-1	KTR #1, KTR #2, KTR #3, KTR #4
		TE-A-2	
		TE-A-3	
WN #2	Capability B	TE-B-1	KTR #1, KTR #2, KTR #3, KTR #4
		TE-B-2	
WN #3	Capability C	TE-C-1	KTR #1, KTR #2, KTR #3, KTR #4
		TE-C-2	
		TE-C-3	
		TE-C-4	

System Architecture Design: Assume ARCS set of Six Potential Architecture Solutions :

$$ARCS = \{ARCS_i, i = 1, 2, \ldots, 6\}$$

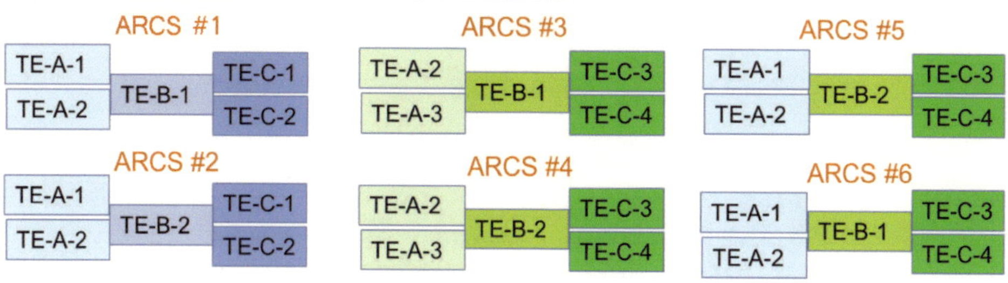

Figure 10. An example of warfighter needs and architecture solution set.

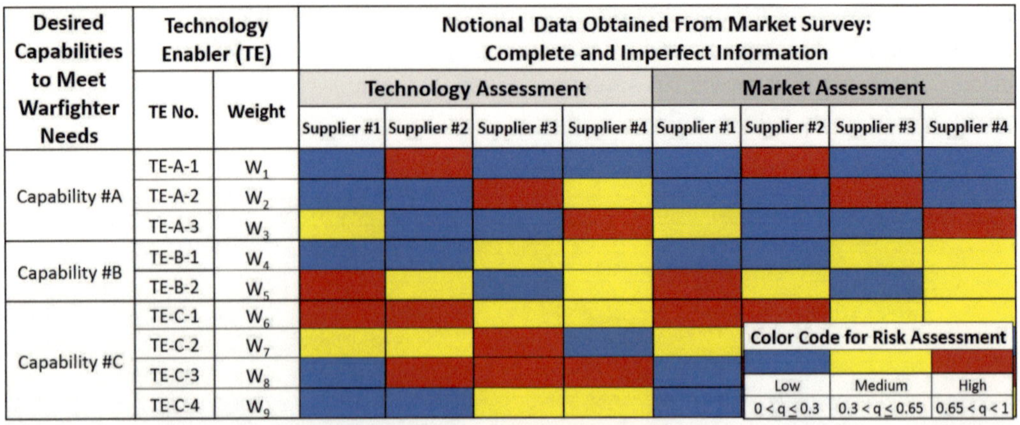

Figure 11. An example of market survey results for DAA-PWGE mixed game model.

Figure 9 shows an example of the PCF score assigned for contractor #1 with ARCS #1. If the architecture solution set consists of 6 architecture solutions (ARCS's) as shown in **Figure 10**, there will be 6 PCF score sheets for each contractor. This example assumes 4 contractors, hence there will be 24-PCF score sheets input to the DAA-PWGE model. **Figure 11** shows an example of the market survey results for four contractors or suppliers.

Example output of the DAA-PWGE program for mixed game model, including the optimum supplier, ARCS, and associated risk, is shown in **Figure 12**.

7.2. DAA-AWGE CPIF model simulation results

To average out the randomness in the optimal solutions, the acquisition and bidding models were iterated several thousand times. The CPIF program outputs the average value for each optimal contract parameter, as well as average government payment, the fee adjustment formula, and average initial conditions PCF_G^0 and $PCF_{K_i}^0$. Here, we present simulation results

```
The following is the optimal solution:

Choose Architectural Solution #4 from Supplier 1.

PTB Solution Composition: {TE-2,TE-3,TE-5,TE-8,TE-9}
Capability 1 is met by TE-2,TE-3.
Capability 2 is met by TE-5.
Capability 3 is met by TE-8,TE-9.


Technical risk is: Low Risk.
Market risk is: Low Risk.
So this is a Type 1 solution.
```

Figure 12. PTB program output example.

http://dx.doi.org/10.5772/intechopen.71044

of four contractors and three optimal bidders. Among the optimal bidders, the limits for the randomly generated control parameters α and β are adjusted to model different bidding behavior. In this simulation, we treat contractor one as the "average" bidder. The limits for contractor two are changed so that this contractor tends to select unfavorable sharing ratios from the DAA perspective; hence, contractor two is "non-cooperative." On the other hand, contractor three tends to select sharing ratios favorable to the DAA and is called the "cooperative" bidder. The precise limits for these control parameters are depicted in **Figure 13**.

Figures 14 and **15** show the Graphical User Interface (GUI) for DAA-AWGE CPIF input parameters and program output, respectively. The simulation results depicting average government payments and savings as well as sharing rations are shown in **Figures 16–18**. Contract three, the "cooperative" bidder, gives the DAA more savings than the other optimal bidders despite receiving more profit (see **Figure 19**). Hence, it can benefit the contractor to select the sharing ratio that benefits the DAA, both in terms of profit per contract and total long-run profit.

Figure 19 shows a stark difference between the profit earned by optimal bidders and that earned by the non-optimal bidder. **Figure 19**(**a**) depicts that contractor four chooses contract

Contractor Number	Behavior	Lower α limit	Upper α limit	Lower β limit	Upper β limit
1	"Average"	1.25	1.25	0.9	0.99
2	"Non-cooperative"	0.7	1.23	0.9	0.978
3	"Cooperative"	1.27	1.8	0.9	1

Figure 13. DAA-AWGE CPIF optimal bidder α and β limits.

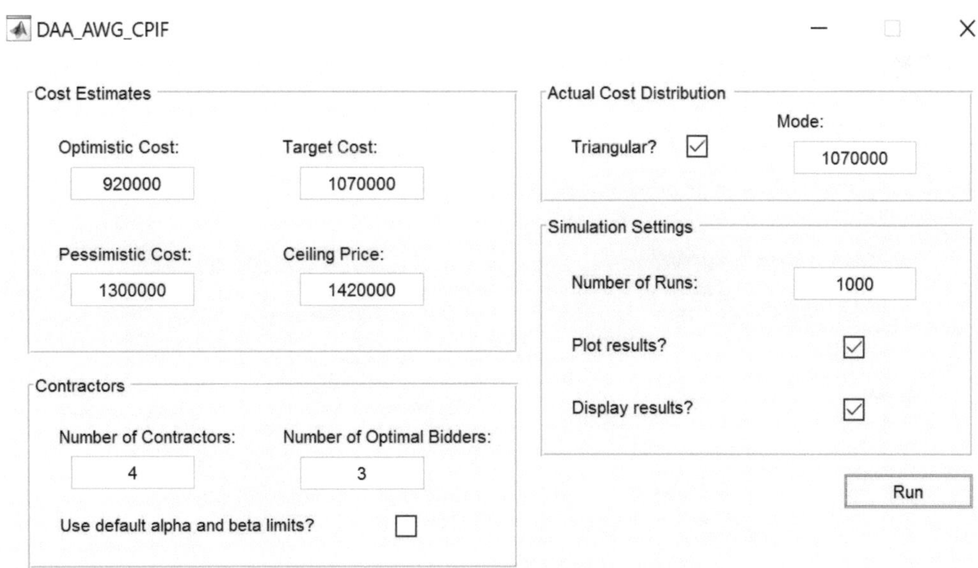

Figure 14. DAA-AWGE CPIF input.

```
The average optimum target price for the under-run case is 1360912.7635.
The average optimum sharing ratio for the under-run case is 0.49353.
The average optimum alpha parameter is 1.2767.
The optimum initial condition for government savings in the under-run case is 106774.4189.
The optimum initial condition for contractor profit in the under-run case is 350000.
The average optimum target fee for the under-run case is 290912.7635.
The average optimum maximum fee is 364941.5759.
The adjustment formula for calculating the optimum fee for the under-run case is F_under = 0.49353*(1070000-Ac) + 290912.7635.
The average government payment for the under-run case is 1318892.4954.
The average government savings for the under-run case is 143127.7726.
The average winning contractor profit for the under-run case is 332525.0907.

The average optimum target price for the over-run case is 1409373.746.
The average optimum sharing ratio for the over-run case is 0.72029.
The average optimum beta parameter is 0.97964.
The optimum initial condition for government savings in the over-run case is 0.
The optimum initial condition for contractor profit in the over-run case is 282138.7333.
The average optimum target fee for the over-run case is 339373.746.
The average optimum minimum fee is 173706.8474.
The adjustment formula for calculating the optimum fee for the over-run case is F_over = 339373.746 - 0.72029*(1300000-Ac).
The average government payment for the over-run case is 1416390.5226.
The average government savings for the over-run case is -3407.2993.
The average winning contractor profit for the over-run case is 284391.5588.
```

Figure 15. DAA-AWGE CPIF output.

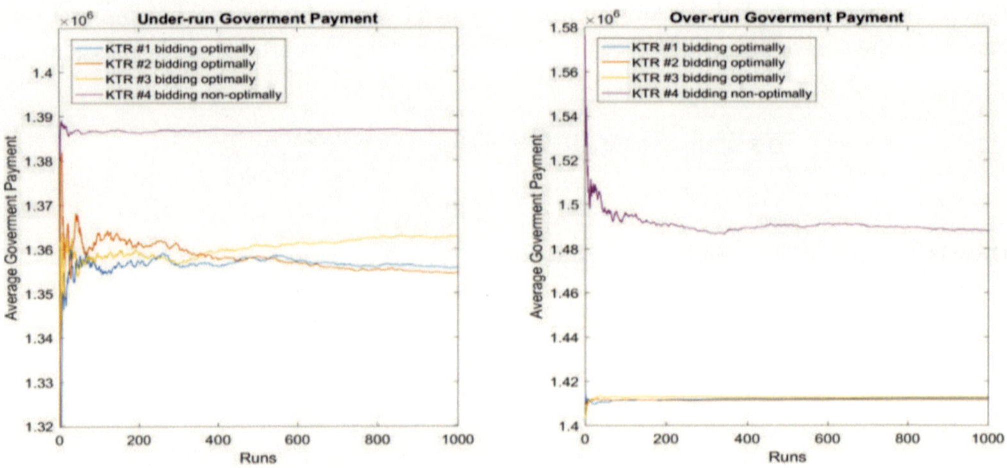

Figure 16. DAA-AWGE CPIF average government payments.

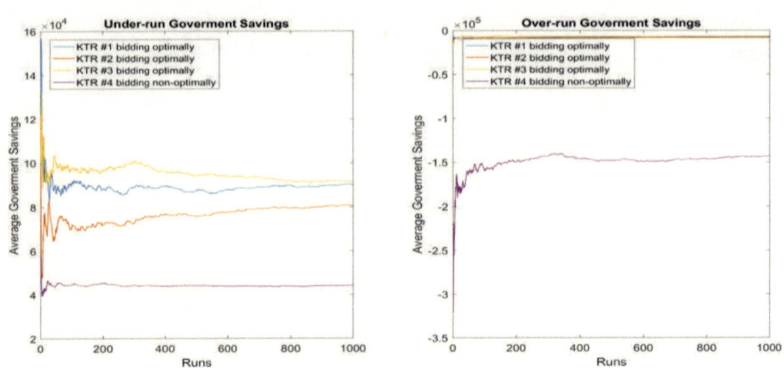

Figure 17. DAA-AWGE CPIF average government savings.

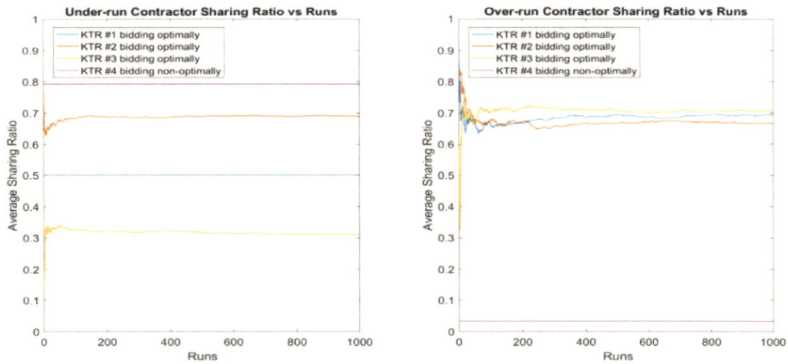

Figure 18. DAA-AWGE CPIF average sharing ratios.

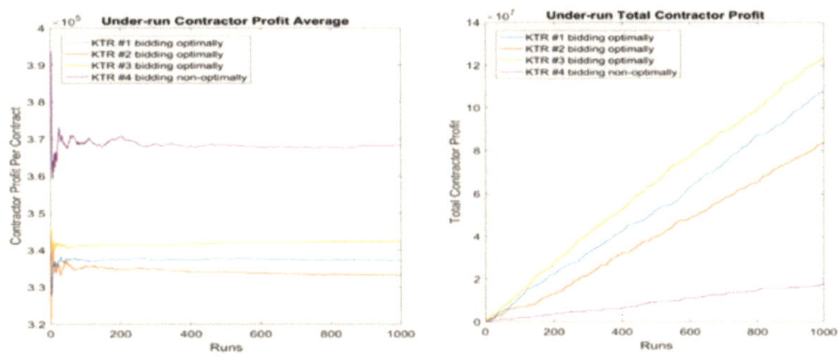

(a) Profit per contract

(b) Total profit

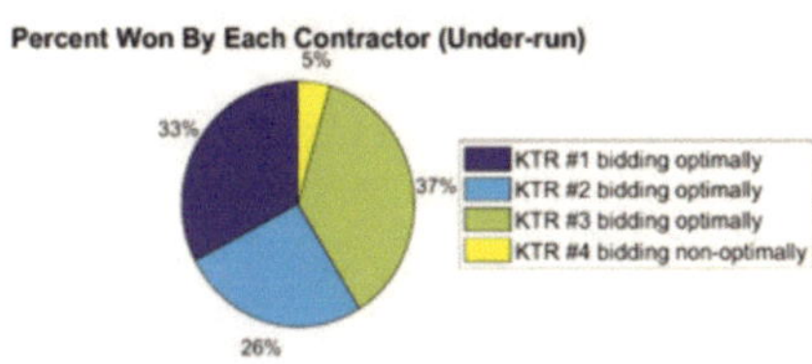

(c) Winning percentages

Figure 19. KTR-AWGE CPIF simulation results. (a) Profit per contract; (b) total profit; and (c) winning percentages.

parameters aggressively; the non-optimal bidding strategy demands more profit per contract but wins far less often, as shown in **Figure 19(c)**. **Figure 19(b)** shows that in the long run, the optimal bidders receive more total profit because of their higher winning percentages. Contractor four, the non-optimal bidder, would benefit from using the Nash equilibrium bidding strategy rather than aiming for a fixed profit rate. Changing the control parameter limits for the optimal bidders also affects long-run profit. Note that the "cooperative" contractor three demand more profit per contract than the other optimal bidders in **Figure 19(a)** but wins more contracts according to **Figure 19(c)**. This result is feasible because the DAA and contractors are not playing a zero-sum game, that is, PCF_G and PCF_{K_i} do not sum to zero.

8. Integration of PWGEs and AWGEs

The objective for the development of DAA-PWGE, DAA-AWGE, KTR-PWGE and KTR-AWGE analytical and simulation models is to assist the DAA to understand the contractor's perspective and to seek optimum PTB solution and corresponding acquisition strategy under both Government's and contractor's perspectives. Thus, the government PTB solution for a given set of "requirements" should be optimized to achieve government saving and at the same time to have more than one contractor bidding the solution. This means that there will be at least two contractors converge to the same Government's PTB solution with similar market and technology risks as predicted by the DAA-PWGE. And, the contract type and associated contract parameters and incentives are derived based on the compromised results obtained from both DAA-AWGE and KTR-AGWE. In another word, the PTB solution will be obtained from the integrated DAA-PWGE and KTR-PWGE. The final acquisition strategy for acquiring the PTB solution obtained from the integrated DAA-PWGE and KTR-PWGE is to be generated from the integrated DAA-AWGE and KTR-AWGE. As presented in the proposed UGAF shown in **Figure 3**, the selection of PTB solution and acquisition strategy is a close-loop process and the PTB solution and associated contract type are converge to a single PTB solution with more than one contractor is willing to bid on it. As mention in Section 5, the PTB solution is selected based on the highest PCF score with an assigned "belief" score (or probability). The integrated DAA-PWGE and KTR-PWGE algorithm searches for the highest PCF score and assigned "belief" score that both DAA and KTR can converge to these scores. It is straight

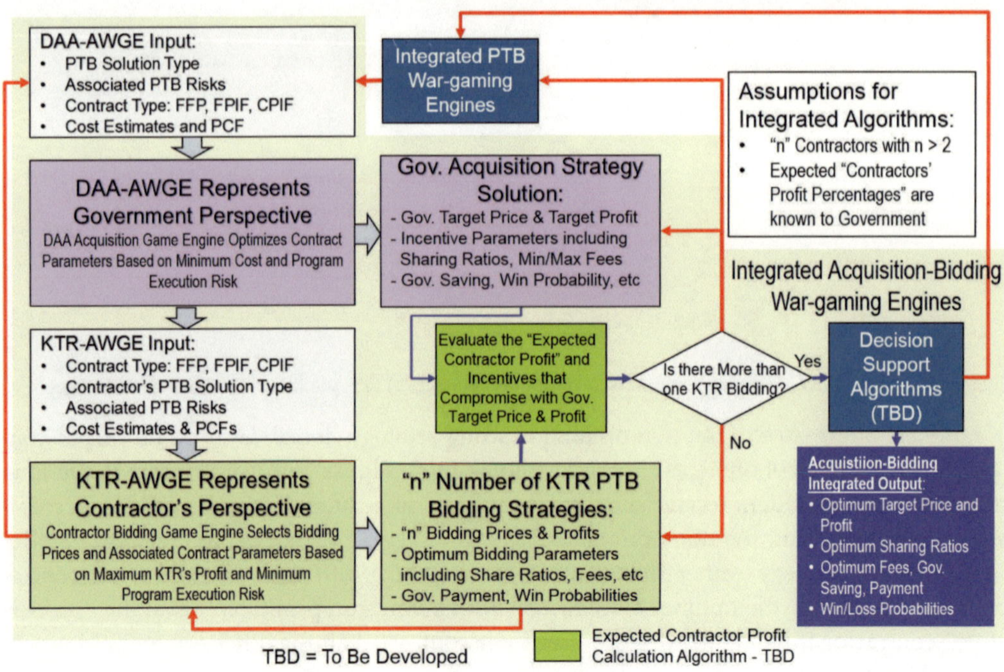

Figure 20. PTB War-Gaming Engines integration algorithm.

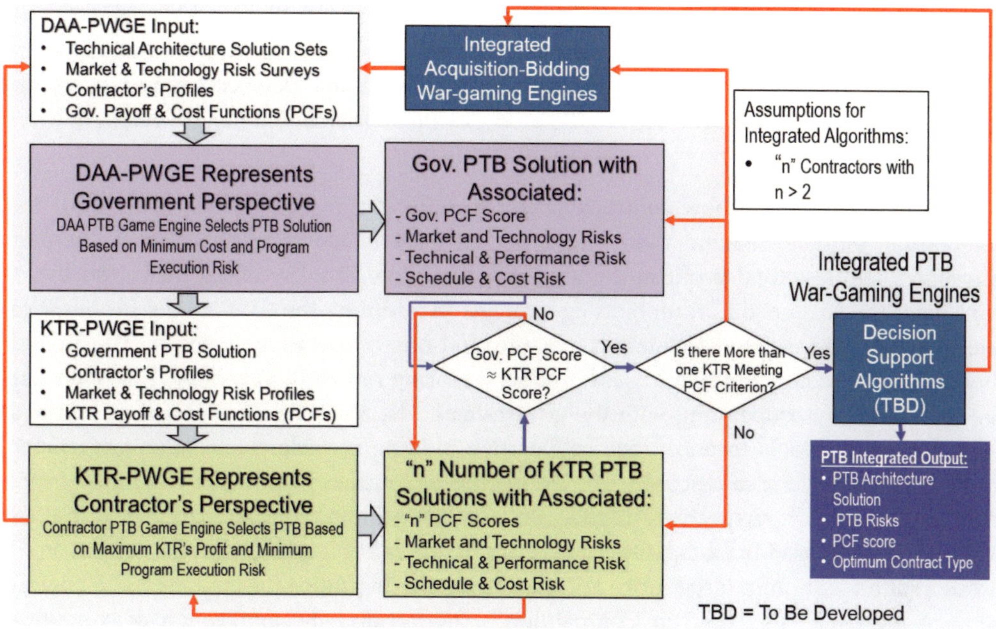

Figure 21. Acquisition-bidding War-Gaming Engines integration algorithm.

forward when the KTR's PCF and "belief" scores converge to DAA's scores. However, when the convergence is not a clear-cut case, a Decision Support Algorithm (DSA) is required to select the optimum PTB solution that can satisfy multiple criteria, including requirements, risks and cost. Our team is currently working on the development of a DSA that leveraged the work done presented in [14–18].

Figures 20 and **21** describe the integration algorithm for integrating DAA-AWGE and KTR-AWGE. The integrated DAA-AWGE and KTR-AWGE algorithm searches for the right "balance" between the DAA's acquisition strategy and KTR's bidding strategy. Our team is currently investigating advanced decision support algorithms that incorporated supervised learning and artificial intelligence to achieve a balance between DAA's and government's perspectives in terms of the government saving and contractor profit, which leads to an estimate the "Expected KTR Profit and Incentives." The "KTR Profit and Incentives" should be compromised with the Government Target Price and associated Target Profit and sharing ratios.

9. Conclusion and way-forward

This chapter provides an overview of the description of PTB optimization games and acquisition-bidding games from both the government and the contractor perspectives. It presents the DAA-PWGE, DAA-AWGE, KTR-PWGE and KTR-AWGE analytical and simulation models. It also provides flow diagrams to show the combination of these models with the

Monte Carlo simulation to generate (i) optimum PTB solutions that can achieve affordability from government perspective, and (ii) optimum FFP and FPIF contract parameters that can achieve affordability from the government's affordability perspective and maximum profit from the contractor perspective. The models were implemented in a collection of MATLAB packages.

Simulation results reveal how contractor behavior affects contractor profit. They show that non-optimal bidders demand more profit per contract which results in a lower winning percentage and less total profit in the long run. Therefore, it is beneficial for contractors to implement the Nash equilibrium bidding strategy. In addition, the CPIF model further separates optimal bidders into cooperative, average, and non-cooperative strategies. The analysis shows that contractors can select a less profitable sharing ratio and in turn increase their long run total profit by cooperating with the government. The resulting information can serve as DAA negotiation tools to encourage cooperative bidding in order to increase government savings. The chapter also discusses the integration of contract parameters from the government and contractor perspectives to generate a set of optimum contract parameters that can achieve the "Increased in Competition." The discussion is at high-level and the subject on the selection of the optimum target price and contractor sharing ratios for the FPIF/CPIF contract types to meet the "Increased in Competition" criterion and the application of supervised learning and artificial intelligence to improve the decision-making process deserve more attention for the future research.

The purpose of the unified framework is to set-up a multi-stakeholder acquisition strategy that encourage cooperative bidding leading to a win-win Nash equilibrium. In such a framework, we seek to change the perspectives of the players from antagonistic to collaborative. Since the simulation results show encouraging evidence that our unified war-gaming framework could help achieve the objective of DII, one of our future research directions is to look into the design of a distributed group decision and negotiation systems that would provide an seamless integration of various acquisition models in such a way that an global optimum solution can be found without negatively affecting local solutions. More importantly, the ultimate goal is to fine-tune our generalized model to help involved parties continuously explore new innovative solutions to meet war fighting needs of the digital age.

Author details

Tien M. Nguyen[1]*, Andy T. Guillen[1], Sumner S. Matsunaga[1], Hien T. Tran[2] and Tung X. Bui[3]

*Address all correspondence to: tien.m.nguyen@aero.org

1 The Aerospace Corporation, El Segundo, California, USA

2 North Carolina State University, Raleigh, North Carolina, USA

3 University of Hawaii at Manoa, Honolulu, USA

References

[1] Hagel HC. Secretary of Defense. Pentagon, 1000 Defense pentagon, Washington D.C.: The Defense Innovation Initiative (DII). p. November 2014

[2] National Defense Authorization Act, § 2446a Requirement for Modular Open System Approach (MOSA) in Major Defense Acquisition Programs. 2017

[3] Air Force Studies Board; Division on Engineering and Physical Sciences. Committee on Owning the Technical Baseline (OTB) in the U.S. Air Force: A Workshop. National Research Council, A Workshop Report. 2015; ISBN: 978-0-309-37431-6

[4] Nguyen TM, Guillen A. Development of an Optimum Technical Baseline for Future Space Systems Using Advanced Game-Based Mathematical Framework—Invited Paper. SIAM—Special Session on Applied Mathematics in Industry, California State University at Fullerton; October 2015

[5] Nguyen TM, Guillen AT, Matsunaga SS. A resilient program technical baseline framework for future space systems. In: Proceedings of SPIE. Vol. 946907-1. 2015

[6] Nguyen TM, Guillen A, Hant J, Kizer JR, Min I, Siedlak DJL, Yoh J. Owning the program technical baseline for future space systems acquisition: Program technical baseline tracking tool. In: Proceedings of SPIE. Vol. 10196. 2017

[7] Nguyen TM, Guillen AT. War-gaming application for future space systems acquisition. In: Proceedings of SPIE. Vol. 983808. 2015

[8] Nguyen TM, Guillen A. War-gaming application for future space systems acquisition: Part 1—Program and technical baseline war-gaming modelling approach. In: Proceedings of SPIE. Vol. 10196. 2017

[9] Nguyen TM, Guillen AT. War-gaming application for future space systems acquisition: Part 2—Acquisition and bidding war-gaming modelling and simulation approaches for FFP and FPIF. In: Proceedings of SPIE. Vol. 10196. 2017

[10] USAF. Report to Congressional Committees: Space Modernization Initiative (SMI) Strategy and Goals. April 2014

[11] Kucsma AI. bidding for contract games—applying game theory to analyze first price sealed bid auctions [master thesis]. Monterey, CA: Naval Postgraduate School; May 1997

[12] Nicolella AJ. Incentive Contracting: Contract Type Overview. Defense Acquisition University.

[13] Vienhage P, Barcomb H, Marshall K, Black WA, Coons A, Tran HT, Nguyen TM, Guillen AT, Yoh J, Kizer J, Rogers BA. War-gaming application for future space systems acquisition: MATLAB implementation of war-gaming acquisition models. In: Proceedings of SPIE. Vol. 10196. 2017

[14] Bui TX. A Group Decision Support System for Cooperative Multiple Criteria Group Decision Making. Berlin, New York: Co-op. Springer Verlag; 1987. p. 1987

[15] Hempsch C, Sebastian H-J, Bui T. Solving the order promising impasse using multi-criteria decision analysis and negotiation. Logistics Research. 2013;**6**(1):24-41

[16] Bui T, Jarke M. A DSS For Cooperative Multiple Criteria Group Decision Making. In: Proceedings of ICIS; 1984;**24**:101-113

[17] Port D, Bui T. Simulating Mixed Agile and Plan-based Requirements Prioritization Strategies: Proof-of-concept and practical implications. EJIS. 2009;**18**(4):317-331

[18] Bui TX, Gachet A, Hans-Jürgen S. Web Services for Negotiation and Bargaining in Electronic Markets: Design Requirements, Proof-of-Concepts, and Potential Applications to e-Procurement. Group Decision and Negotiation. 2006;**15**(5):469-490